Safeguarding Children and Schools

Best Practice in Working with Children Series
*Edited by Brigid Daniel, Professor in Child Care
and Protection, University of Dundee*

The titles in the Best Practice in Working with Children series are written for the multi-agency professionals working to promote children's welfare and protect them from harm. Each book in the series draws on current research into what works best for children, providing practical, realistic suggestions as to how practitioners in social work, health and education can work together to promote the resilience and safety of the children in their care.

also in the series

Child Neglect
Practice Issues for Health and Social Care
Edited by Julie Taylor and Brigid Daniel
Foreword by Olive Stevenson
ISBN 978 1 84310 160 4

of related interest

Supporting Children and Families
Lessons from Sure Start for Evidence-Based Practice in Health, Social Care and Education
Edited by Justine Schneider, Mark Avis and Paul Leighton
ISBN 978 1 84310 506 0

Kids Need...
Parenting Cards for Families and the People who Work With Them
Mark Hamer
ISBN 978 1 84310 524 4 (Card Game)

Understanding School Refusal
A Handbook for Professionals in Education, Health and Social Care
M.S. Thambirajah, Karen J. Grandison and Louise De-Hayes
ISBN 978 1 84310 567 1

Promoting Resilience in the Classroom
A Guide to Developing Pupils' Emotional and Cognitive Skills
Carmel Cefai
Foreword by Paul Cooper
ISBN 978 1 84310 565 7

Safeguarding Children and Schools

Edited by Mary Baginsky

Foreword by Brigid Daniel

Jessica Kingsley Publishers
London and Philadelphia

First published in 2008
by Jessica Kingsley Publishers
116 Pentonville Road
London N1 9JB, UK
and
400 Market Street, Suite 400
Philadelphia, PA 19106, USA

www.jkp.com

Library of Congress Cataloging in Publication Data
Safeguarding children and schools / edited by Mary Baginsky ; foreword by Brigid Daniel.
p. cm.
Includes index.
ISBN 978-1-84310-514-5 (pb : alk. paper) 1. School violence--Prevention. 2.
Schools--Safety measures. I. Baginsky, Mary.
LB3013.3.S262 2008
371.7'82--dc22

2007052108

British Library Cataloguing in Publication Data
A CIP catalogue record for this book is available from the British Library

ISBN 978 1 84310 514 5

Printed and bound in the Great Britain by
Athenaeum Press, Gateshead, Tyne and Wear

Contents

Part 3   Safeguarding and Schools: Training

List of Tables

List of Figures

Foreword

Brigid Daniel

Teachers are among some of the most significant adults that children will encounter. Teachers and other staff encountered in schools have a profound direct and indirect effect on children's social, emotional and cognitive development. Their influence operates on several levels. The staff group contributes to the overall culture and ethos of the school within which children spend a significant proportion of their lives. The way in which children are spoken to, listened to, taught, disciplined and supported helps to shape their understanding of the world in which they live. For some children, a teacher may be one of the most consistent adults in their lives. It is for these reasons that the key role teachers and schools play in safeguarding children is now being properly acknowledged and recognized.

Safeguarding can be exercised via schools as places, teachers as people and education as a process. It encompasses a spectrum of concern, from the promotion of the well-being of all children, to the protection of the smaller number of children whose needs are not being met, including needs for protection. We are increasingly aware of the damaging effects of abuse and neglect upon children's learning. For example, one of the main ways in which neglect is manifested is in the impact on school attendance and performance. Neglected children are often late for school, are evidently tired, hungry and dirty and may show significant emotional and cognitive delay. Too often inter-disciplinary discussions about neglect centre around the problem of establishing the 'right' threshold for action but teachers usually know which children in their classes are neglected and when they need help. Recent policy recognizes that teachers are very adept at recognizing an unhappy child when they see one and aims to provide a legitimate route for teachers to ensure that children get the help they need when they need it.

It would be surprising if the recent policy developments have not raised the anxiety of teachers. There can be a lack of clarity about the limits and extents of their responsibilities for the broad welfare of children. The precise ways in which they are expected to exercise the role of 'safeguarding' has not yet been defined in detail. Teachers may feel that these expectations take them beyond the profession they were trained for and into the realm of other professions such as social workers. It is also the case that, while expecting teachers and other education staff to respond to requests for information, other professionals have not always provided teachers with the information they need to teach effectively. Nor have other professionals always appreciated the challenges that face teachers in balancing the needs of each individual child with the collective need of the whole class.

This book brings together material on policy, theory, research and practice to provide a resource for education staff that will support them in the role of safeguarding. The fundamental premise of the book is that children can only learn properly if they feel safe and nurtured.

Brigid Daniel, Professor of Social Work,
University of Stirling

Part 1

Safeguarding and Schools: Policy

Chapter One

Placing Schools at the Centre of Safeguarding Children

Mary Baginsky

The concept that schools have a role in promoting the health and welfare of children and young people is not a new one. Schools have traditionally offered medical and welfare services of some sort alongside their more traditional educative function. The nature of the services and the extent of the involvement has varied tremendously but since the 1980s it has become more formal. Now following the inquiry into the death of Victoria Climbié by Lord Laming (Laming 2003) the first decade of this century has witnessed a radical reshaping of how services for children are delivered, which has an impact on all agencies that deliver these services, including schools.

While services have been remodelled, the messages that have informed this organization have been around for a long time and have underpinned previous legislation and guidance. The lessons learnt in relation to collaboration and policy implementation will continue to be needed in the future. In order to move forward it is important to learn from the past. Many of these lessons are drawn from the experiences of protecting children, but they are still useful in informing this new era when schools and other agencies are charged with safeguarding and promoting the welfare of children. Over the past 40 years there have been other attempts to develop systematic strategies and programmes to bring agencies together to support families and protect and promote children's welfare. In the 1960s reports such as Central Advisory Council for Education Report (Plowden Report) in 1967 and Committee on Local Authority and Allied Personal Social Services Report (Seebohm Report) in 1968 emphasized the importance of agencies and professionals working together. The next major milestone was the inquiry into the death of Maria Colwell (Department of Health and Social Security (DHSS) 1974a). This identified the greatest failure as being the lack of effective communication and liaison between the agencies involved. There had been a failure both to pass on information and to co-ordinate an appropriate response. As a result a *Memorandum on Non-Accidental Injury to Children* (DHSS 1974b) was issued in 1974 to area health authorities and directors of social services and copied to the schools section of the then Department of Education and Science (DES). The memorandum recommended that the Director of Education was one of the local authority representatives on the area review committee. It also identified the professionals who should attend case conferences and recommended that teachers should be invited as appropriate, along with police surgeons and representatives of the housing department, as well as other agencies that might have information about the child and family. The memorandum also recommended that the area review committees should monitor training and develop a training plan designed to 'increase knowledge, awareness and vigilance' among various groups, including teachers. With a few exceptions it was not applied systematically across authorities – agencies usually continued to operate as they had done before. Too much continued to hinge on individuals' own knowledge and understanding, alongside serendipitous connections across professions. But the continued death of children at the hands of their parents and carers continued to demonstrate the failure of agencies to work together effectively.

The Children Act 1989 was, in part, an attempt to address this failure and at the same time respond to the alarm created by the Cleveland Inquiry (Butler-Sloss 1988) where social workers had been accused of removing children, whom they suspected of having been sexually abused, from their homes with 'over-enthusiasm and zeal' (p.244). The Act introduced the concepts of 'children in need' (s.17) and 'children in need of protection' (s.47). A legal threshold for intervening in a family to protect children was introduced. The concept of 'significant harm' was defined in section 31(2) of the Act as being attributable to the care given or likely to be given to the child by the carer. It became embedded in social work practice but few other professionals really understood (and in some cases had not heard of) it. There are no absolute criteria to support a judgement of what constitutes significant harm, nor was there an operational definition of harm and risk. In addition, and to add to the lack of understanding, different thresholds are used across the country.

The number of child protection cases increased significantly from the early 1990s, a rise that was reflected in a series of studies that the government commissioned to throw light on the very problems that had also spawned the Children Act. These were published in 1995 as *Child Protection: Messages from Research* (Department of Health 1995). The studies clearly showed practice had shifted to the assessment of risk and investigation at the expense of providing services to children in need, with the result that vulnerable children were left to struggle on or go into crisis when they might then get an assessment but sometimes no service. The document *Working Together Under the Children Act 1989: A Guide to Arrangements for Interagency Co-operation for the Protection of Children from Abuse* (Home Office *et al.* 1991) had set out how agencies and professionals should work together to promote children's welfare and protect them from abuse and neglect. However a report by the Audit Commission (1994), as well as the research summarized in *Messages from Research* (Department of Health 1995), indicated that there was still a great deal to be done. So what had gone wrong?

The Children Act 1989 had attempted both to safeguard children and to promote their welfare, providing for both the welfare and protection of children in need. It had been based on a philosophy which recognized that child protection cannot be separated from policies to improve children's lives as a whole. This philosophy was undermined by both a failure to resource its preventive provisions and a failure across departments to address what a 'child in need' was, let alone to arrive at a consistent definition of 'significant harm'. At the same time schools and teachers did not emerge from studies that contributed to the *Messages from Research* as being very engaged in the process. But the research did not reflect a situation that was in transition. Maybe some schools continued to be disengaged. On one level this might be explained, but not excused, in light of the revolution through which schools passed in the late 1980s and early 1990s. But a fairer explanation probably lies in the fact that schools have usually developed their own response to working with families and children on what may be termed 'welfare issues'. The natural role for many schools was not to be linked too closely to the local authority, other than to the education authority. While most teachers have always taken their responsibilities as being *in loco parentis* seriously, they have interpreted their duties in terms of making sure children and young people receive the services they need. In 1988 government guidance recommended that 'a senior member of a school's staff should have responsibility, under the procedures established by the local education authority (LEA), for co-ordinating action and for liaison with other agencies' (DES 1988). Seven years later the Department for Education and Employment (DfEE) issued Circular 10/95 (DfEE 1995), which set out the responsibilities of LEAs, schools and further education colleges for child protection and gave guidance on inter-agency links. In the intervening years between the circulars the amount of training teachers received in relation to child protection had increased, but this was developed significantly by specific funding in the years after Circular 10/95 appeared. This would not have been reflected in the studies that contributed to *Messages from Research*, most of which were concluded by the early 1990s.

However, as welcome as this training was, in hindsight the actual training, usually for designated teachers, was not always fit for purpose. If the intention was to increase the number of referrals of concern to social services the training possibly succeeded. Unfortunately the training usually focused on the recognition and reporting of child protection concerns but failed to address the complexity of the reality and messiness of child protection. For example, it often failed to discuss the definitional and threshold quagmire around 'significant harm' (Baginsky with Davies 2000). But as the number of referrals from various sources increased, social services were forced to raise the threshold of the level at which they responded. In the worst cases schools became disillusioned when they did not get a response, and when social services came across cases where schools had failed to make a referral the lines were drawn for a stand off between the two agencies. The more usual scenario was one where both would become occasionally frustrated with the other but they somehow rubbed along (Baginsky 2000, 2007). But this was not the best scenario for children and young people. Although the legislation was built on an assumption of partnership and inter-agency collaboration, what this was to mean in practice was less than clear. Hendry and Baginsky (Chapter 10) argue that for schools to play their full part in safeguarding and promoting the welfare of children and young people in the future, there is a need for a whole-school approach and a comprehensive safeguarding-training and development strategy. A similar theme emerges from the work of Laskey (Chapter 11), even though her work is based on the Australian experience.

In another arena the plight of looked after children attracted a great deal of attention during the 1990s and a stream of reports including those from Levy and Kahan (1991), Utting (1991 and 1997) and Kent (1997). An increasing amount of evidence emerged to show that the educational achievement of looked after children was low, with most leaving school as soon as they could and with few, if any, qualifications. In the previous decade a number of researchers had looked at the low educational achievement of those leaving care (see, for example, Stein and Carey 1986 and Jackson 1987). Berridge (1985) had found instability and frequent moves impacted on attainment, and little had changed more than ten years later (Berridge et al. 1996). At around the same time, Fletcher-Campbell's (1997) work evidenced inadequate planning and support, while Aldgate et al. (1992) had uncovered the low expectations that professionals had of looked after children. The Social Exclusion Unit (SEU) (1998) found that the permanent exclusion rate among children in care was ten times higher than the average and as many as 30% of children in care were out of mainstream education through exclusion or truancy. Reasons for the high level of exclusion included: the absence of an adult consistently to advocate for them in contacts with education services; difficulties in concentrating at school because of problems at home; possible stigmatization by pupils and teachers; and the level of disruption caused by the movement between care placements. These movements often then involved a change of school. Almost three-fifths of the children in the SEU study changed their place of education during the year of the study and one in ten had three or more changes. There is a great deal of evidence to show links between a history of care and subsequent homelessness, risk of criminality and vulnerability to drugs and prostitution. It is a major contributor to the numbers who have low levels of educational achievement and reduced employment chances. The SEU research pointed to the complex lives of these children which, in turn, demanded a more complex response than the ones that had been tried. Not surprisingly it was based on inter-agency co-operation and responsibility with initiatives and legislation such as the Quality Protects programme,[1] The Children (Leaving Care) Act 2000, *Guidance on the Education of Children and Young People in Public Care* (DoH and DfEE 2000), *Education Protects* (DoH 2001) and now *Care Matters: Transforming the Lives of Children and Young People in Care* (DfES 2007). In Chapter 4 Fletcher-Campbell unpicks the complexities that have developed around this subject and explores the extent and limitations of schools' contribution.

But there are other groups of children with equally significant needs, including disabled children. Miller and Raymond (Chapter 5) describe the role schools should play in safeguarding disabled children. They identify the level of risk of abuse that disabled children face and the reasons for this; they also emphasize the role of the school in empowering and consulting with disabled children, and consider the safeguarding measures that are required.

One of the most difficult situations that schools face involves problematic and abusive sexual behaviours of children and young people. Despite the fact that schools are having to deal with these behaviours there has been no robust research carried out on the incidence, prevalence or how they are being dealt with. In Chapter 6 Hackett and Taylor draw on existing literature to provide information and advice for teachers and other staff in school settings.

While the agenda has now moved from the planning and piloting stage of redesigned children's services into national implementation and operation, many of those working in schools (as is the case with practitioners in other agencies) are still trying to understand how best to make this work. Although the details and organizational arrangements differ across the four countries of the United Kingdom they do share a common vision, which is illustrated in the model adopted in England. The framework for delivering the reforms is set out in *Every Child Matters: Change for Children* (Department for Education and Skills 2004b).

The principal aims are to:

- ensure that no child falls through the net and that all children are helped to achieve their potential
- shift the balance towards prevention through tackling child poverty, improving early-years education and child care, raising school standards and supporting parents
- intervene earlier before children reach crisis point.

---

1   The Quality Protects programme was launched by the Department of Health in September 1998 to support local authorities in transforming the management and delivery of children's social services.

There is an increased emphasis on inter-agency communication and joint working, and on enabling the voice of the child, along with that of their families and carers, to be heard. There is a focus both on safeguarding children and on improving the outcomes of all, supported by the development of integrated structures and collaborative working between agencies.

But as described above this is not entirely new. Throughout the 1990s there had been an increasing emphasis on the need for joined-up government and inter-departmental co-operation, but the literature on the promotion of joint working in the area of social welfare used terms such as 'collaboration', 'co-ordination', 'inter-agency' or 'multi-agency working' both interchangeably as well as in quite distinct ways (for further discussion of this see Leathard 2003). The terms refer to the attempt to achieve government goals by agencies, groups and sectors working together rather than separately. They are generally regarded as highly positive forms of working in that they bring organizations together with beneficial outcomes for service users (Huxham 1996; Huxham and Vangen 1996). However it was hard, if not impossible, to find definitions of what this meant in practice in any government documentation. Despite the fact that the concept of multi-agency working assumed an increased importance throughout the 1990s, there was very little information about how to translate this into practice, and even less about how the expectation of inter-professional co-operation was impacting on education.

Implementation was hampered by the fact that what was to be achieved was ill-defined even in documents such as *Working Together* (Home Office *et al.* 1991) that were intended to provide guidance. In theory the 1989 Children Act provided the solution. In practice central government devolved responsibility for its implementation, without providing sufficient guidance to local authorities whose existence, at that time, was being questioned and undermined. While there appeared to be overall agreement that co-ordination was a necessary and valuable practice, there was less overt recognition of how difficult this would be to achieve. The literature on policy implementation illustrates the tensions that can exist between central and local government (for examples see Challis *et al.* 1988; Clarke and Stewart 1997; Pierre and Peters 2000).

The accepted wisdom over partnership working usually emphasizes structural and process factors without referencing the partnerships between those working in and across agencies on which the development will depend – separating the inter-organizational from the inter-professional. The system was designed on the assumption that agencies would understand and respond to their role, but not all agencies were equipped to do so. There is no doubt that many schools have assumed a greater role in relation to safeguarding children, but there has not always been sufficient clarity about how this should happen. But schools were not alone in facing this challenge. However, the fact that new legislation in the form of the Children Act 2004 together with the *Every Child*

Matters agenda has now been deemed necessary confirms the deficit in what preceded it but does open the way for a fresh start. The old arrangements were challenged by a lack of resources to enable an adequate response to be made to children in need, but of equal importance was a lack of clarity on the part of some professionals about the role they themselves should be playing in supporting children and families and how to harness that support.

The *Every Child Matters* programme establishes five over-arching outcomes for children, which are to:

- be healthy
- stay safe
- enjoy and achieve
- make a positive contribution
- achieve economic well-being.

These are reflected in the outcomes established by all four countries of the UK. Everyone delivering services for children and young people has a role in improving these outcomes, including those working in childcare settings, schools, health services, social care, youth services, the police and criminal justice system, the voluntary and community sector and cultural, sports and play organizations. It is not surprising that better information-sharing is also highlighted as the key to successful early intervention to help children who require additional support to achieve those outcomes. The response to the Laming Inquiry has set in train a series of reforms that are all predicated on a renewed emphasis on the need for agencies to work together and communicate efficiently and effectively. Although little is in fact known about what makes for effective working, it is safe to assume that organizational structures and processes are important for the development of collaborative activity, as are the skills of the individuals who make it all happen.

The largest universal service for children is schools. The role of education has also been given additional weight, reflecting its importance in helping children to have the best possible start in life. Schools, along with other statutory and voluntary agencies, are expected to make a significant contribution to this. Legislative changes mean the criteria for school inspection now cover the contribution schools make to these outcomes, and schools are also expected to incorporate them into their self-evaluations. The school is crucial in meeting the needs of children and in engaging parents, carers, residential workers and foster carers. In addition there is also the wider agenda of providing family and parental learning opportunities, study support, and community use of sports, arts and ICT facilities. But schools also have legal obligations to safeguard and promote pupils' welfare and well-being. In England and Wales Section 175 of the Education Act 2002 has placed schools under a duty not only to safeguard children but to promote their welfare. They are not expected to achieve this alone. An amendment to the Children Act 2004 in the autumn of 2006 extended the duty to co-operate, already placed on other agencies, to schools. This means they are legally required to work with other agencies to develop responses designed around the development and safeguarding needs of the child, and to support families and carers in carrying out their responsibilities.

In moving towards more joined-up and multi-agency working it becomes even more important that a common method of identifying and assessing need exists across different services and provisions. Many schools around the UK are engaged in the processes established to provide a co-ordinated response to need, and provide early intervention to support children, young people and their families. Although there was research conducted for the then DfES (Deakin and Kelly 2006) which showed that school staff felt less engaged in the *Every Child Matters* agenda than any other section of the children's workforce, with almost a third being unaware of the change programme, this is very likely to have moved on as implementation has accelerated and references to it appear in more documents intended for teachers. There are now examples of how they are engaging with the Common Assessment Framework and how staff are taking on the role of lead professionals (Dagley *et al.* 2007; Jones 2007) but it requires greater collaboration between individual workers and agencies at a strategic and practice level. The traditional approach of working in single agency and professional groupings does not fit with this reshaped provision that assumes joint ownership of outcomes and demands a more integrated pattern of service delivery through accessible and non-stigmatizing settings. The intention is to span traditional service boundaries and create responsive, flexible local services with structures that are less hierarchical, less formal and more dynamic, such as those envisaged by Kettunen (1994).

The intention is also to make sure all relevant professionals are working with a common understanding and with common processes. To this end the Common Assessment Framework (www.ecm.gov.uk/caf) has being introduced so that professionals use similar language about children and their needs and reduce the number and duration of assessments to which families are subjected. New information-sharing arrangements are in place to make it easier for professionals across agencies working with children with additional needs to be in contact. New databases and indexes have been introduced to support this, but the success depends on human beings recognizing a concern and then acting appropriately on that concern. The idea is to co-ordinate the support that is given to children with additional needs – whether these are special educational needs, disabilities or social needs – through a lead professional. In some cases the lead professional will be based in a school, in others they will come from a partner agency.

Common sense dictates, although confirmatory research evidence is still required, that inter-agency working will be that much easier where services are co-located. In line with this the government wants schools to become extended facilities where a range of services are offered from one site. No one model has been devised as the intention has been to advocate a response that suits the needs of schools and the communities they serve. It seems likely that many primary schools and integrated children's centres will be co-located, and the hope is that, in time, social and health care will join them. But there will be many schools that do not have such services on their premises and they will need to work in partnership over distances, as will those working on co-located sites with those outside their immediate orbit. In Chapter 3 McCulloch and Tett describe how the community school system has developed in Scotland. The authors set the initiative within its policy context and explore the benefits and challenges of making such a paradigm shift in practice.

Whatever the model that is adopted, school staff are being drawn into new ways of working and while most will welcome this they will require support and training to engage effectively. If the vision for children's services is realized the benefits for children and their families will be immense, but there will also be benefits for professionals, including those working in schools who would always prefer to see support targeted on those in need at an early stage rather than watch a series of crisis interventions or have requests for help ignored because they failed to trigger the required threshold. But this endeavour will also require the support of those with whom schools have traditionally linked. Local authorities are required to lead on integrated delivery and are key to the transition in supporting the development of local capacity. In Chapter 2 John Guest describes the significant role local authorities still have in supporting schools to meet their responsibilities in safeguarding children.

In some cases one of the major barriers is a low awareness of what agencies actually do and how they may be accessed. Despite the close association that existed between education and child guidance in the past the two have drifted apart. According to Booker and Sargeant (2004) the phrase 'mental health difficulties' is viewed by education as health language and not of their concern, while 'mental health' and 'mental health problem' are terms used within health services. Since the Warnock Report (1978), schools have used 'emotional and behavioural difficulties' (EBD) or 'social emotional and behavioural difficulties' (SEBD) to refer to a range of difficulties that can create barriers to children's learning. As Daniels et al. (1999) indicate, these are non-normative constructs and are not consistently employed. They cover a continuum of behaviour and there is often considerable uncertainty about the boundaries between 'normal' misbehaviour, emotional and behavioural difficulties, and mental illness (Atkinson and Hornby 2002). Health may view them as the concern of the school. Yet for most children emotional and behavioural difficulties and mental health difficulties are the same issue. School-based interventions can help to address the emotional well-being of children, which may avoid the need for direct input from mental health professionals or facilitate earlier access.

Schools have long been involved in such work but have not usually viewed it within Tier 1 of the CAMHS model.[2] They will need more support and encouragement if they are to take a larger role, and although not all schools will feel comfortable with this (and that must be recognized) there will be schools that are anxious to work with other agencies and embrace their responsibilities (see Baginsky 2004). Alongside teachers and support workers, educational psychologists, education inclusion officers, education social workers, youth workers in education and behaviour support staff contribute to this work but have not always been linked into the system. But further training and support, alongside specialist staff will be required. At the present time there is neither sufficient capacity nor expertise at Tier 1 to undertake the level of preventative work and identification of further need that are required to shift practice. More primary mental health workers are required to support professionals in schools and other frontline services in refocusing to meet the emotional needs of young people, as well as to allow them to recognize when other services are needed. Music (Chapter 7) explores the benefits of a mental health team based in a school setting, as well as providing a useful explanation of the role of those involved in the team.

As the Nuffield Foundation (2004) recognized, mental health must *also* be seen within the broader field of well-being and the promotion of positive health, as well as measurement of symptoms. There is a real need to address mental health needs earlier and for many this intervention may be at a lower tier than has traditionally been seen to be appropriate. But this requires support for services operating at Tiers 1 and 2[3] in schools and in other settings such as the kind of school-based counselling service described by McGinnis in Chapter 8. While there are examples of excellent services, there is a marked shortage of open access counselling services for this age group, both inside and outside school. More evidence is appearing about the effectiveness of professional counselling in schools, both in terms of ability to function more effectively and achieve academically (see, for example, Cooper 2006; Fox and Butler 2003). Schools have also been identified as having certain advantages over other

---

2   CAMHS stands for Child and Adolescent Mental Health Services. CAMHS at Tier 1 level are provided by practitioners who are not mental health specialists working in universal services; this includes GPs, health visitors, school nurses, teachers, social workers, youth justice workers, voluntary agencies. Practitioners will be able to offer general advice and treatment for less severe problems, contribute toward mental health promotion, identify problems early in their development, and refer to more specialist services.

3   Practitioners at this level tend to be CAMHS specialists working in community and primary care settings in a uni-disciplinary way (although many will also work as part of Tier 3 services). For example, this can include primary mental health workers, psychologists and counsellors working in GP practices, paediatric clinics, schools and youth services. Practitioners offer consultation to families and other practitioners, outreach to identify severe or complex needs that require more specialist interventions, assessment (which may lead to treatment at a different tier), and training to practitioners at Tier 1.

venues for the provision of counselling in terms of providing somewhere that is less stigmatizing and less disruptive. For example, Klinefelter (1994) observed that school is less stigmatizing and less disruptive of studies than would be the case if '[pupils] were sent to specialist mental health services at some distance from school' (p.216). Bor *et al.* (2002) described school as a 'non-pathologising context' (p.16), unlike a health centre.

But schools also have another role to play in supporting the mental health needs of children and young people. There is considerable evidence to suggest that social/emotional competences can be developed in schools (see, for example Weissberg and O'Brien 2004). An EPPI Centre review (Evans, Harden and Thomas 2003) found psychodynamic programmes, aimed at the causes of poor behaviour and seeking to achieve long-term change through personal development, were effective in the short to medium term (over several months). It is important to be realistic about what can be achieved by such initiatives and to recognize that in many instances their development has depended on individuals and their commitment. But in Chapter 9 Coppard explores one such approach through the curriculum that has supplemented an authority's approach to keeping children safe as well as contributing to the empowerment of children and young people.

An important part of this changing scene is to recognize when things did not go right in the past, and understand both why this was and that change is an ongoing process and that any change programme needs long-term goals. One area that has received relatively little attention has been the extent to which the relevant agencies were positioned to work together in the way envisaged. The Children Act 1989 and *Working Together Under the Children Act 1989* (Home Office *et al.* 1991) emphasized a more co-ordinated response that would lead to more effective interventions, the avoidance of failures to communicate and the duplication of services, and the clarification of agency or professional roles. With responsibilities now devolved to areas to shape the services that best meet their needs, they will be required to engage in joint planning, which will require good communication and strong partnerships with local agencies where trust may not have previously existed. It also requires a willingness on the part of all agencies to achieve a better understanding of their potential partners. The following chapters are a contribution towards helping schools do this at the same time as understating the needs of and support available for specific groups of pupils.

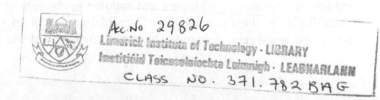

Chapter Two

The Role of the Local Authority in Safeguarding Children

John Guest

The statutory duties referred to in this chapter relate primarily to schools and local authorities in England but the principles that are described apply equally to other parts of the United Kingdom, where they will generally be embraced in equivalent legislation and guidance.

Context

The Children Act 1989 established the principles that remain central to the present systems for supporting children in need and children at risk of significant harm. However, the past two decades have witnessed significant changes in both the governance arrangements for schools and the organization of local authority education services, as successive governments have attempted to reconcile the tensions between the local management of schools, democratic accountability, the school improvement/achievement agendas and ensuring compliance with national guidance.

In 2000, two child deaths highlighted critical gaps in the child protection process and these cases have influenced legislation that has confirmed the strategic and operational importance of local authority education services in safeguarding vulnerable children and young people.

The serious case review into the death of Lauren Wright in Norfolk in May 2000 (see Norfolk Health Authority 2002) noted the failure of staff at her school to report obvious signs of distress that might have alerted social workers to the severity of the mistreatment and neglect that eventually resulted in Lauren's death. This case also exposed weaknesses in the systems for monitoring schools' compliance with local and national guidance, and raised serious questions about the accountability of school leaders and governors for the safety and well-being of pupils. The government shared the frustration of others at the apparent inability of governors to use existing legislation to pursue disciplinary action against members of the school's leadership team. The government amended the Education Act 2002 to place a duty on the governors of maintained schools (and the proprietors of independent schools) to ensure that schools fulfil their functions with due regard to safeguarding and promoting the welfare of all pupils. Section 175 of the Act places a responsibility on the governing bodies of maintained schools to make arrangements for ensuring that their schools operate in such a way as to safeguard and promote the welfare of their pupils. Section 157 of the same Act places the same responsibilities on governors and proprietors of schools in the independent sector. This Section also requires local education authorities to 'make arrangements to ensure that their functions are carried out with a view to safeguarding and promoting the welfare of children', and to 'have regard for guidance issued by the Secretary of State in considering what arrangements they need to make'.

Victoria Climbié spent the final year of her short life in England, having been trafficked into Europe with another child's identity. She had been brought to London to escape the attentions of the social care authorities in Paris. Victoria had been referred by her school because of serious concerns about her school attendance, health and general well-being. Had Victoria been enrolled at a school on arrival in this country, her attendance and welfare would have been monitored on a daily basis by adults who would have placed her needs above those of her carers. It is possible that Victoria would be alive today had she been afforded the protection of a child-centred environment. Lord Laming's (2003) inquiry into the death of Victoria Climbié coincided with the government's consultation on the future of children's services through the *Every Child Matters* agenda (Department for Education and Skills (DfES) 2003). The case influenced the drafting of the Children Act 2004 and, in particular, the requirement that relevant local authorities appoint directors of children's services whose functions would include those of the local education authority (Children Act 2004 – Appendix 1) and the replacement of area child protection committees (ACPCs) with local safeguarding children boards (LSCBs). Subsequently Section 38 of the Education and Inspections Act 2006 enhanced the responsibility of school governors and education services by requiring them to promote the well-being of all pupils and to have regard to any relevant children and young people's plan produced by a local authority. This brought schools and local education authorities into line with other children's and family services by placing them under a duty to co-operate, in order to improve and promote children's physical and mental health and their emotional well-being. The *Every Child Matters* key outcomes for children are interdependent cornerstones of personal development:

- be healthy
- stay safe

- enjoy and achieve
- make a positive contribution
- achieve economic well-being.

Local authority education services play a pivotal role in facilitating these outcomes and helping schools, as direct providers of services, to meet their obligations. It is significant to note that the inspection framework and self-evaluation processes for schools now largely relate to the contribution that the school makes to pupils' development around the key outcomes. Local authority education services are the providers of direct and commissioned services and catalysts in fostering community-based services to support individual pupils, families, schools and learning networks. Critically, the new legal responsibilities require schools and children's services not only to react to individual concerns through effective child protection procedures, but also to contribute towards the development of local partnerships that will promote the welfare and well-being of all children; with particular regard for pupils with additional needs. This brings a number of other pupil welfare issues and partnerships into the broader safeguarding remit, including those connected with pupil health and safety, school security, measures to improve behaviour and combat bullying, supporting children with medical needs, substance misuse, crime reduction, anti-social behaviour and safe recruitment. They also include measures to develop and improve children's physical and mental health and their emotional literacy.

The current Department for Children, Schools and Families (DCSF, formerly DfES) guidance, *Safeguarding Children and Safer Recruitment in Education* (DfES 2006a) describes the role of local authority education services as operating at three levels of responsibility: *strategic, support* and *operational.*

Strategic responsibilities

Allocating resources to support the work of the local safeguarding children board (LSCB)

ACPCs often struggled to agree budgets as local education authority and other agency contributions were invariably determined on the basis of what could be afforded rather than what was needed in order to meet strategic priorities. The evolution of children's services departments should promote greater stability in LSCB funding arrangements and reduce the possibility of disparities of provision, which are a source of particular frustration in those schools and areas that have traditionally been affected by high levels of cross-authority movement. In addition to direct financial contributions, education services also support the work of LSCBs through the allocation of staff time to the work of sub-groups, task-groups and serious case reviews. Other contributions *in kind* may come from opening relevant in-house training opportunities and capacity to professionals from the wider safeguarding partnership.

Allocating resources to enable the authority and maintained schools to discharge their responsibilities for safeguarding children

Education authorities are required to agree funding arrangements for maintained schools within their area, through consultation with the local schools' forum. These discussions should take account of the potential implications of safeguarding responsibilities for allocated schools budgets and for the provision of central services. These will include:

- LSCB funding contributions
- officer participation in meetings of the board, its sub-groups and serious case reviews
- training programmes for school and local authority staff
- the salary and costs of a lead officer/s to provide policy guidance and support to schools
- central human resources functions to support and audit safe recruitment practices and to deal with allegations against school staff
- central support to promote full school attendance, reduce bullying and provide guidance on health and safety requirements.

Senior officer representation to the LSCB and making an effective contribution to planning co-ordinated services to meet the needs of children

A senior officer, who is empowered to make resource and operational decisions on behalf of the chief education officer or the director of children's services, should represent education services at LSCB board and executive levels. It is also important to ensure appropriate representation on the sub-groups or committees of the LSCB, as these are the forums that will influence and determine policy, professional development, standards and performance management across the board's functions. Education representatives will work closely with, but not speak for, schools and other institutions. Commonly, schools will be separately represented through nominees delegated through appropriate head teacher or locality forums.

Local authority education services will routinely be involved in the development and planning of co-ordinated services for children through the local strategic partnership and the authority's children and young people's plan. In addition to the safeguarding boards, education services will participate in a range of strategic forums that are concerned with meeting the welfare needs of vulnerable groups including looked after children, those affected by domestic violence, homelessness and substance misuse, refugees and asylum seekers, travellers, young carers and children with disabilities. They will also be involved in monitoring and steering groups that have oversight of community safety, 'Safer schools' and 'Healthy schools' partnerships.

Liaison with appropriate church authorities

Because of the role that the established church historically played in the development of education as a universal service, most local authorities will have well-established links with diocesan authorities for supporting voluntary aided schools. These are especially important for ensuring that allegations against school staff are properly pursued where the member of staff may be employed by the church authority. Schools that serve non-Christian or non-established faith groups are less likely to fall within the remit of a single church authority or representative body and this will present challenges in establishing working relationships and linking these schools to LSCB structures and services. Many of the newer faith and supplementary schools that serve the newer and emerging ethnic communities have developed outside of the maintained school system but are unlikely to benefit from the structures or the financial security available to the traditional independent sector. While the Working Together (HM Government 2006) guidance expects that independent schools will be offered the same level of support and advice as schools in the maintained sector (Para 2.14) and the current DCSF guidance (*Safeguarding Children and Safer Recruitment in Education*, DfES 2006a, Para 2.2) enables local authority education services to 'provide (and charge for) such support' (Para 2.22), independent schools are not obliged to accept this advice. It is also arguable that the current inspection arrangements for safeguarding within the independent sector are not as comprehensive as those that apply to the maintained sector. Independent schools and pupil referral units can currently obtain provisional registration without having been subject to the same level of scrutiny as maintained schools and units and, in my experience, inspection visits have not always been as regular or as rigorous in this sector in the area of safeguarding.

Area child protection committees commonly struggled to engage fully with the voluntary sector and community groups in child protection processes. In a climate of increasing diversity, it is essential that LSCBs develop processes for involving service users and promoting culturally sensitive child welfare and safeguarding services that ensure consistency of provision across all communities, without compromising basic thresholds for intervention. There can be no latitude to allow lower standards of protection for particular groups of children because of assumptions made by professionals based on heritage, religion, culture or class. LSCBs need to address unequivocally issues such as reasonable chastisement, child trafficking, private fostering, female genital mutilation, forced marriages and domestic violence. The starting point must be that no child is any less entitled to protection, through accident of birth or heritage, than any other child. Links with parents and carers in minority groups, established through faith groups and supplementary schools, can provide positive foundations for community engagement and honest dialogue about safeguarding standards and systems.

Compliance of maintained schools

Local authority education services are required by legislation to ensure that the governing bodies of maintained schools are making appropriate arrangements to safeguard and promote the welfare and well-being of pupils. Many education services have responded to these responsibilities by establishing a system of regular audits to assist self-evaluation processes within individual schools. To be successful, such audits must be seen by schools as being of positive value in fulfilling their statutory obligations and as means for accessing training opportunities, local authority support and escalation mechanisms. Where the local authority is undertaking an audit, there should be verbal and written feedback of findings, with copies being sent to the head teacher and the designated person (where this is not the head teacher). The audit should be considered by governors as part of their annual review of their safeguarding/child protection policy and can be used as a benchmark for future self-evaluation.

Where the audit, or the school's conduct in respect of an individual safeguarding case, raises concerns about the policy or the practice of the school the lead officer will need to bring this to the notice of the school's designated person and, as appropriate, the head teacher and governing body.

Supporting effective partnership working.

Prior to the implementation of the Children Act 2004, local education authorities were increasingly finding themselves in an invidious position as politicians struggled to reconcile the need to promote consistent practice at a local level with the political imperative to delegate resources and responsibility to individual governing bodies. Indeed, in the early drafts of the revised version of *Working Together* (Department of Health, Home Office and Department for Education and Employment 1999), LEAs were not mentioned as having a role to play in the child protection processes for schools and other educational provision. Policy and practice have moved on. The Children Act 2004 confers on directors of children's services (DCS) the functions previously exercised by the chief education officer, and also charges the DCS with responsibility to build and sustain effective partnerships to improve outcomes for children and young people, with a particular emphasis on safeguarding and promoting their welfare and well-being.

This, in turn, requires those managing local authority education services to ensure that there is active participation at an appropriate officer level in multi-agency groups or partnership boards that influence or contribute towards pupil welfare, well-being and safety. Many of these forums will involve or be led by voluntary sector organizations, reflecting the diversity of commissioning and quality assurance arrangements that have been embedded into the fabric of children's services over recent years. In addition to LSCBs, established partnerships that require education services involvement will include:

- children's trusts
- children and young people's strategic partnership boards (and sub-boards)
- community safety partnerships
- drugs action teams
- school governor forums
- safer schools partnerships
- healthy schools partnerships
- youth offending teams
- multi-agency public protection panels
- homelessness forums
- domestic violence forums
- Connexions partnerships
- child and adolescent mental health commissioning groups
- teenage pregnancy steering groups
- local authority emergency planning forums
- voluntary sector umbrella and steering groups.

Resolving inter-agency problems

As universal children's services, schools, early-years settings and education support services will invariably be the largest sources of referrals to the investigating agencies. Even for the most experienced of designated school staff, dealing with individual child protection concerns can pose significant personal and professional challenges. Teaching and other leadership or pastoral responsibilities have to be balanced against meeting the immediate needs of the child, supporting school colleagues and dealing with upset or angry parents. When the response that designated staff receive from the investigating agencies is not perceived to be helpful, or fails to acknowledge that they will already have undertaken an assessment process that has concluded that a referral is appropriate, there is a danger that trust between the school and investigating agency will be compromised. In their worst form, negative referral experiences have been known to undermine confidence in local partnerships and to be used as an excuse by schools not to make future referrals. Equally, if a social worker or police officer has experienced problems in accessing an individual member of staff or in gaining information from a school, there is a risk that this will tarnish the reputation of the school in the wider partnership. Serious case reviews regularly point to poor communications and unfounded assumptions between professionals as areas of weakness in systems that have failed to protect vulnerable children. It is essential to counter attitudes that create this type of negative 'folklore'. The second *Joint Chief Inspectors in 2005* (Commission for Social Care Inspection (CSCI) *et al.* 2005) highlighted continuing concerns about relationships between schools and social services in respect of individual cases where child protection thresholds may not have been reached. Education services can work with schools to negate such risks by:

- ensuring that all designated school staff access training that provides them with the knowledge and skills to make informed and assertive child protection referrals

- providing designated staff with ready access to named senior officers within education and children's social care services, who are able to escalate concerns as part of a quality assurance process encouraging regular opportunities for designated school staff to meet with frontline social workers and their managers in order to promote a mutual understanding of their respective roles and parameters.

Serious case reviews

In many local authorities the lead officer for safeguarding in the education service will be nominated by the director of children's services to oversee, and often undertake, the internal management review (IMR) on behalf of the education services and submit this to the review group established by the LCSB. It is expected that the local authority education service will also examine their procedures and training in light of the IMR and LSCB findings and disseminate learning from reviews to relevant officers within the service and designated staff in schools.

Support responsibilities

Ensuring safeguarding training for all staff in education services

Induction programmes for local authority education service staff and governors in maintained schools should support personnel at all levels to fulfil their responsibilities under national and local child protection procedures. In addition, all school staff who come into direct contact with pupils should undertake refresher training in this area *at least* every three years. Relevant school and local authority staff should also have access to multi-disciplinary training that has been commissioned by or approved through the LSCB.

School staff holding the designated person role are additionally required to undertake training on induction and this should be updated on a two-yearly basis. Although the guidance does not require schools to nominate a deputy for the designated person role, systems that depend on a named individual are inherently flawed and best practice would see the nomination and training of a second or deputy designated person. Most local authorities will additionally support the professional development of designated persons by sponsoring dedicated and multi-disciplinary forums and networks.

Provide model policies and procedures

The local guidance provided to maintained schools should promote consistent identification of, and responses to, safeguarding concerns across the local authority area. Procedures should embrace all aspects of child protection, including safe recruitment and vetting, safe professional practice and responding to allegations made against staff and volunteers. They must concur with national guidance and local protocols and be signed off as compliant by the LSCB. Model policies and procedures can be of value to schools but achieve nothing if they are seen as an end in themselves. The key to successful safeguarding procedures is the leadership and training that reinforces and complements written procedures. A policy describes what adults within the school will do in response to individual child protection or safeguarding concerns. It should be regarded as a 'live' document that has relevance for the whole school community and its effectiveness should ultimately be judged against the level of consistency with which it is applied.

While the government's expectations have concentrated traditionally on local authority roles in respect of maintained schools, many authorities have previously extended their support in this area to independent schools and further education institutions within their areas. The universal safeguarding remit, inherent in the establishment of children's services departments and children's trust arrangements, requires local authorities to consider how safeguarding support and guidance can be extended to both the traditional independent schools and newer faith-based non-maintained schools and education providers. The majority of these institutions are likely to welcome LSCB and children's trust support. However local authorities will need to consider how they will engage with national regulatory authorities where the proprietors of independent schools refuse to co-operate or fail to respond to deficiencies in safeguarding processes that are brought to their notice.

Advice and support for schools and designated school and authority staff

All school and education service staff who have a designated child protection or safeguarding responsibility should be provided with the names and contact details for the education service's lead officer and those who deputize in this role. They should have the authority to instigate the LSCB's escalation protocol where there appear to be unresolved concerns or disputes that might potentially place a child at unnecessary risk. Serious case reviews have commonly highlighted the inability or unwillingness to challenge the opinions or actions of other professionals as a factor in the failure of systems to protect vulnerable children. A robust escalation procedure will both recognize challenge as a healthy quality assurance process and reassure frontline staff who may otherwise feel anxious about questioning the opinion of a more senior professional.

Again, it is vital that back-up systems are in place to avoid reliance on a single named officer. Many authorities will already be operating a duty rota that guarantees schools and partner agencies access to named officers who are able to provide guidance in respect of safeguarding issues and individual child protection cases.

Operational responsibilities

Safe recruitment

Sir Michael Bichard's independent inquiry arising from the Soham murders in 2001 (Bichard 2004) listed a catalogue of failures in the recruitment and vetting procedures that allowed Ian Huntley to be appointed to a position of trust that provided him with unquestioned access to the children who subsequently died. Bichard's findings and recommendations around safe selection and recruitment, at both national and local levels, have influenced the publication of revised statutory guidance, *Safeguarding Children and Safer Recruitment in Education* (DfES 2006a). This consolidates in one document previous statutory responsibilities at government, local authority and school levels and recommends best practice around selection and vetting. This is not only of relevance to local authorities as employers and commissioners of education support services but also as the ultimate employers of staff in community schools, providers of human resources services, facilitators of training for head teachers and governors who appoint staff and as a conduit for Criminal Records Bureau, List 99 (the list containing names, dates of birth and teacher reference numbers of people who are barred under the Education Act 2002 from working with children in the education sector for a variety of reasons including sexual offences) and other vetting arrangements.

Safeguarding children without a school place

Children who are without a school place will require a higher level of vigilance because they will not benefit from the safeguarding systems that are ordinarily available within a school and because of the circumstances that may have led to them being out of school in the first place. Local authorities are required to have in place procedures for identifying, assessing, placing, tracking and monitoring the whereabouts and education arrangements of children missing from the education system. The Education and Inspections Act 2006 imposes a statutory duty on local authorities to keep a database of children in their area who are without appropriate educational provision. These may include excluded pupils, new and mid-year arrivals who may have additional needs, refugees and asylum-seekers, those temporarily relocated because of homelessness or domestic violence and pupils who may have been off-rolled by a school without reference to the home local authority. The local authority will place a number of these children and young people in their own pupil referral units where the safeguarding processes and levels of staff awareness should mirror those found in maintained schools. Some authorities may meet the needs of these children, partly or entirely, through individual tuition or alternative provision that they commission through the private or voluntary sectors. In commissioning such providers, local authorities need to be clear about the safeguarding arrangements within the provision and to ensure that pupil attendance, attainment and welfare are subject to regular reporting and monitoring arrangements.

Local authorities are charged with the responsibility to make enquiries and take appropriate enforcement action where a parent fails to fulfil their responsibilities in respect of school attendance or the child ceases to attend school without explanation. These functions will normally be exercised through the education welfare/social work/attendance service. If children and families cannot be located, local authorities will need to ensure that appropriate information-sharing requirements have been met (see Children Act 2004, Section 12 and DfES 2006b). This is to ensure that vulnerable children who are subsequently presented in another local authority area may be afforded the necessary levels of support and supervision. The DCSF has identified off-site educational provision commissioned by schools and part-time individual timetables as potential routes for pupils to become disengaged and go missing from the education system. The *National School Attendance Codes* (DfES 2006b) require schools to record and monitor the attendance and attainment of pupils who are educated (in whole or in part) at other schools, vocational/further education provision or through work experience as part of an alternative curriculum or provision. While these arrangements are in place, schools retain their duties to safeguard and promote the welfare and well-being of these pupils, and local authorities should satisfy themselves that maintained schools are complying with these expectations. Similarly, part-time timetables that are agreed with parents as a means of integrating or reintegrating vulnerable pupils into full-time attendance should be appropriately recorded, categorized on the attendance register and monitored by the school and, as appropriate, the local authority.

Much as the *Every Child Matters* agenda has promoted increasingly effective partnership working in the area of safeguarding, concerns remain around the consistency of protection that is afforded to children whose parents make home education and other independent arrangements for their education. Although local authorities are currently required to register and monitor home education arrangements, they presently have no authority to see the child or the educational arrangements being made without the agreement of the child's parents, unless there are grounds to suggest that the child might otherwise be at risk of suffering significant harm. Children who have never been educated within the maintained system, particularly those for whom there have been no previous child protection concerns or who attend independent schools in another local authority area, are unlikely to appear in the databases that are currently maintained by local authorities.

Meeting the training needs of local authority staff

In light of the responsibilities conferred on local authority staff by legislation and guidance, the job description/person specifications of those officers working directly or indirectly with children and their families will have been amended, as necessary, to incorporate specific and wider safeguarding and child welfare functions and responsibilities. Individual learning and development plans should reflect these duties and incorporate the need for induction training and continuous professional development, through single agency and multi-disciplinary training. Multi-agency programmes commissioned by the local safeguarding children board have the advantage of fostering local professional networks but tend to be over-subscribed, particularly in those areas of high staff turnover, and should not be relied on as the only training resource. Local authorities (and schools) may also wish to specify minimum safeguarding training requirements in agency staff and services that are commissioned through the independent and voluntary sectors.

The role of the local authority lead officer

Local authorities are required to identify a named senior officer with responsibility for ensuring that the authority fulfils the responsibilities described above. As LEA duties have been subsumed into the broader children's services remit, directors of children's services have to ensure that education support services are appropriately funded and structured to enable the lead officer to support schools and education support services in a number of areas:

Providing advice, guidance and support

The lead officer is there to provide advice, guidance and support in respect of statutory responsibilities and legislative changes and to respond to queries raised about individual pupil support and staffing matters. These may include instances of missing pupils, allegations against staff and the more complex safeguarding issues including domestic violence, child-on-child sexual activity, relationships between pupils, sexual exploitation, female genital mutilation, parental chastisement, forced marriage, domestic violence, fictitious or induced illness, child trafficking, private fostering, substance misuse and parental mental illness.

Developing effective working relationships and partnerships

In addition to membership of the local safeguarding children board, associated sub-groups and designated professionals forums, lead officers will develop extensive professional networks across the statutory, voluntary and independent sectors by virtue of their involvement with the wider children's trust, community safety and partnership arrangements. The lead officer will thereby be able to help schools access services that might otherwise be unknown to them. The development of extended schools has also allowed local authorities to act as the broker or catalyst in fostering child and family focused services within schools as centres of, and for, the community.

In some authorities, lead officers have developed regular forums where designated persons can network and share learning with their counterparts from other schools and where partner agencies can access and consult with key school staff. Newsletters and electronic bulletins may also be used to promote effective communications.

Training and raising awareness

To meet the safeguarding needs of pupils, school staff must have access to good induction processes and ongoing professional development opportunities. Lead officers must make sure that the training needs of maintained schools and pupil referral units can be met through whole-school INSET and by input to relevant induction programmes for senior managers, governors, newly qualified teachers, teaching assistants, other support staff, learning mentors and designated persons. This may be achieved through school or centrally based training that is commissioned from or by the local authority. The lead officer will need to ensure that the local authority agrees the budgets (or a charging policy) that will finance such training, and that the local safeguarding children board's multi-agency training programme reflects the needs of governors and school staff at all levels and must monitor the take-up (and attendance) of school staff at multi-agency training sessions.

The lead officer will also work closely with human resources services to raise awareness of schools' obligations to train head teachers and nominated governors around safe recruitment and selection practices through the DCSF/National College for School Leadership's training programme, in line with one of the Bichard Inquiry's recommendations (number 16). (See www.ncsl.org.uk/managing_your_school/safer-recruitment/index.cfm)

Promoting safe and positive environments

In facilitating or commissioning training and policy guidance for schools, lead officers will be aiming to promote a culture of schools as safe organizations. Central to this process will be the adoption of a clear staff code of personal and professional conduct that supports the well-being of pupils; good training and supervision of staff and volunteers; record-keeping that complies with DCSF standards (including pupil registration and transfer); a transparent complaints/whistle-blowing procedure; and effective support and monitoring of pupils who are the subjects of child protection plans. Lead officers will also link with appropriate local authority advisers, school improvement partners and healthy schools partnerships to encourage schools to access formal and informal curriculum support that will inform pupils' awareness of their rights and responsibilities and help to build children's resilience. Attention must be given to the attendance and attainment of pupils who are known to be at risk and those who are placed in residential provision or otherwise looked after by the local authority.

Development and planning

As child protection procedures have moved into the wider arena of safeguarding, many local authorities have developed the role of lead officer as a *champion* for safeguarding. Children and young people's plans should reflect the importance of safeguarding within education services and acknowledge the strong emphasis placed by the legislation on promoting the welfare and well-being of all children (Education Act 2002, Section 175; Children Act 2004, S11;

Education and Inspections Act 2006). The lead officer will ensure that child protection policy guidance issued to schools and education services complies with, and is signed off by, the local safeguarding children board. In addition, the lead officer should have direct or indirect input to the review and development of local authority policies and guidance in the areas of:

- behaviour management – positive handling/restraint, anti-bullying measures, school exclusions
- health and safety – school journeys, home to school transport, toileting of pupils
- child employment – licensing of child performances and chaperones, work experience, alternative 14–19 curriculum and work-based learning, staff codes of conduct, recruitment, vetting and supervision of volunteers
- pupils with medical needs – first aid and the administration of medicine
- school attendance and follow-up of unauthorized absence
- children at risk of missing education – mid-year arrivals, home education, excluded pupils, monitoring and enforcement of school attendance
- children with additional needs and vulnerable pupils
- emergency planning – supporting schools in the wake of critical incidents involving pupils, parents, staff and communities.

One proven model for co-ordinating and monitoring the safeguarding function is the establishment of a multi-disciplinary education safeguarding forum, where key managers from local authority education services meet on a regular basis to review and scrutinize the authority's statutory functions and ensure that local policies and procedures accord with, and inform, those of the local safeguarding children board.

Monitoring

The lead officer should ensure that arrangements are in place to regularly monitor the application of safeguarding responsibilities within both the local authority's education support services and maintained schools. The local authority must maintain a register of senior designated persons within schools and should undertake a regular audit covering:

- training that has been undertaken by the senior designated person(s), governors and the whole-school INSET deputizing arrangements for designated person

- induction arrangements for new and visiting staff and volunteers

- compliance of the school's policy with national and local guidance and the involvement of pupils and parents in developing the school policy

- frequency and quality of referrals made by the school

- attendance at child protection conferences and core groups and the quality of reports provided

- arrangements for monitoring the attendance, attainment and welfare of looked after children and pupils who are subject to child protection or children in need plans

- record-keeping within the school + arrangements for off-rolling pupils

- monitoring the attendance and attainment of pupils who are educated off-site

- use of premises by external groups and organizations

- use, recording and reporting of reasonable restraint.

The audit model is one that could easily be adapted for use with independent schools and supplementary schools as a means of monitoring compliance and identifying process gaps and training needs on behalf of the local safeguarding children board.

While the development of children's services departments and trust arrangements will undoubtedly prompt debate about the need for a separate lead officer for schools and education services, it is essential that local authority and LSCB quality assurance measures take full account of the unique needs of schools as primary sources of child protection referrals and monitors of children's well-being. The arrangements that are in place must provide high quality advice and guidance for schools and access to sensible and practical support as it is needed.

Managing allegations against those in positions of trust

The role of the local authority in respect of allegations of child abuse made against paid staff or volunteers in positions of trust is described in appendix 5 of *Working Together to Safeguard Children* (HM Government 2006) and detailed guidance concerning teachers and other school staff is contained in *Safeguarding Children and Safer Recruitment in Education* (DfES 2006a). Local authorities are required to nominate a senior officer who will have oversight of the management of individual cases where abuse by an adult in a position of trust is alleged or suspected. They will be the central point of contact for the named or lead officers from LSCB member organizations, including education services, and will co-ordinate strategy discussions/meetings. This officer will generally be located within the quality assurance section of children's social care and is sometimes referred to as the *allegations manager*. The majority of complaints against school staff would not ordinarily trigger external referrals but there is a clear expectation of multi-agency consideration where there is evidence that a member of staff or volunteer:

- has or may have caused harm to a child
- has committed a possible criminal offence
- has behaved in such a way as to indicate that they are unsuitable to work with children or young people.

It is likely that schools will wish to consult with the local authority lead officer when:

- an alleged non-accidental injury to a pupil has required first aid or other medical attention
- a common assault has been independently witnessed
- an allegation is reported to the police as a crime
- a history or pattern of allegations has emerged concerning an individual member of staff or a child/family
- there is evidence of parental collusion or instigation
- there is suspected or alleged sexual abuse
- the complaint concerns a child who is already subject to a child protection plan
- the complaint concerns a child who is vulnerable because they are looked after in public care, a young carer, a child with a disability or significant special educational needs, an unaccompanied minor, or a child affected by homelessness, domestic violence or parental incapacity.

In these circumstances, the lead officer should be consulted by the head teacher (or chair of governors where the allegation concerns the head teacher) and the lead officer will then seek the views of named lead officers in the police and children's social care. This strategy discussion will generally be conducted through telephone or email communications in an attempt to reach a consensus, based on the information available and on the route the investigation should follow. The outcome should be to agree on immediate actions, as appropriate. Where there are considered to be no grounds for a child protection (S47) enquiry or criminal investigation, the school will be advised to commence its own management investigation and this advice will be recorded. Where grounds for external investigation are established, the local authority is required to convene a strategy meeting. At this point, the school would also need to consider possible immediate actions to safeguard children and the adult concerned. The possible options would include a 'cooling-off' period, suspension or temporary transfer of duties. The school also has to consider how and when to inform the child's parents of the incident or allegation. Experience shows that parents and carers are likely to have more faith in the integrity of an investigation process if the school has been open with them from the outset, rather than allowing the pupil to control information about an incident or allegation.

The purpose of the strategy meeting is for professionals to share information about the incident or allegation, and about the child/family and the member of staff; they will also consider witness reports and any medical intervention. Consideration of this information will inform decisions as to the appropriate route and timing of further investigations. The meeting will also need to consider the support needs of the child/ren concerned and personnel issues in terms of suspension and support for the member of staff and to agree strategies to deal with possible wider parental or media interest. The meeting will be chaired by the local authority (most commonly by the allegations managers or an independent chair from the quality assurance unit), with representation from the school leadership team (or chair of governors where the allegation concerns the head teacher), education lead officer, human resources and the police. The member of staff against whom a complaint has been made should not be automatically suspended. This will normally only be recommended where there is an ongoing police investigation or where the nature of the complaint is such that it is untenable for the staff member to continue with their duties.

The possible outcomes of the strategy meeting are:

- a joint investigation between the police and children's social care
- a single-agency criminal or child protection investigation or child in need assessment
- referral back to the school to deal with the incident by means of an internal management investigation.

Police and child protection investigations must take precedence over any internal investigation, but schools would ordinarily be expected to conduct a management investigation under their complaints procedures at the conclusion of any external enquiries. Schools may require guidance and support regarding the reintegration of a member of staff who has been suspended pending the outcome of an investigation. Similarly, consideration has to be given to the support needs of the child/ren involved.

The local authority officer with responsibility for managing allegations (allegations manager) will have oversight of the procedures for dealing with the allegation, for liaising with the head teacher/chair of governors and their counterparts in the education, police and health services and for ensuring that, as far as is practicable, recommended time-scales are followed. Where the allegation is being pursued as a criminal investigation by the police, regular reviews should be undertaken to monitor the progress of their enquiries and the welfare of the pupil and member of staff.

If an internal management investigation leads to disciplinary action that results in the dismissal of the staff member, or if that person resigns during or following the investigation, the school should seek advice from human resources with a view to referring the member of staff to any relevant regulatory body and the Secretary of State for possible inclusion on the list of those considered to be unsuitable to work with children (List 99). From 2008, the Safeguarding Vulnerable Groups Act 2006 empowers an Independent Safeguarding Authority (ISA) to maintain barring lists for adults considered to be unsuitable to work in positions of trust with children or vulnerable adults. *Barred lists* for children and adults will replace List 99 and other existing barring schemes.

Where the adult was not employed by the school, discussions will need to take place with their employer or sponsoring agency to explore the options for disciplinary action and/or notification to the ISA. In those cases where it is not possible to initiate a management investigation, as the adult concerned was self-employed or working in a voluntary capacity, the local authority may interview witnesses involved in the allegation and meet with the alleged perpetrator to seek their response to the complaint. The findings from this investigation can then inform a notification to the ISA by the local authority allegations manager, if this is considered appropriate. If the investigation concludes that the allegation is false or malicious, the local authority will need to consider an assessment of the child as a possible child in need or child at risk of significant harm.

Serious allegations against those in positions of trust are, thankfully, rare but they present significant organizational and emotional challenges for all of those who are involved; both in the incident and in the investigative process. Many allegations that are subsequently judged unfounded are also shown to have been preventable. Allegations always tell us something about the child, the family, the member of staff, the institution or about our systems and we should always be open to this learning (and to learning from the mistakes of others). Through shared learning, local authorities and schools can inform service development around safe organizations and safe professional practice in order to promote ever-safer learning environments.

Overview of a local authority's role

Local authority children's services are coming under increasing scrutiny because successive governments have placed educational attainment, crime reduction, child care and safeguarding at the forefront of the political agenda and given specific duties to local authorities to promote co-operation between agencies. The formative years of this century have seen the introduction of radical changes in the way that services for children and families are configured. Although some of these changes have come about as a result of stark lessons from individual tragedies, the *Every Child Matters* key outcomes are a statement of the community's aspirations for all of our children. These outcomes cannot be achieved in isolation; they are the business of every parent, every school and every professional working in children's services. In delivering these outcomes for children and young people, schools will continue to require access to high quality and well-co-ordinated local authority services.

Chapter Three

Integrated Community Schools and Social Inclusion (Scotland)

Ken McCulloch and Lyn Tett

Introduction

This chapter explores the role of inter-agency partnerships as a key element of the integrated community school (ICS) experiment in Scotland, which had the aim of preventing the exclusion of vulnerable children and young people. The focus is on the school–family–community links designed to protect children, and is explored through a case study of one council. The case illustrates the advantages and difficulties that were experienced by a range of professionals, parents and young people and this analysis of practice is first contextualized in an examination of the shifts in thinking about community schools in Scotland over recent years.

The principle of inter-agency working has been central to many recent developments across the UK in working with young people, both those specifically at risk of exclusion from school and those caught up in wider processes of social exclusion. Joint working between social work, education and other agencies also has a long history in Scotland. The Kilbrandon Report (Scottish Office 1964) proposed that children and young people in difficulty should be dealt with in social education departments, managing both education and social services in an integrated way (Kendrick 1995; Schaffer 1992). While social education departments were never established, collaborative responses have been formalized in youth strategies in Scotland since the early 1980s (Lloyd, Stead and Kendrick 2001; Pickles 1992). More recently a trend has been evident in the merging of local education authorities' education services with those parts of the social work organization concerned with children and families.

The integrated community schools (ICS) programme in the case study council offers insights into the potential of an approach to integrated services using a locality approach. This programme also introduced specialist family support workers as a key element of the ICS approach, and the advantages and limitations of this type of staffing were a central focus of our research. We have also drawn on other research into the role of ICS in work with parents and children to promote social inclusion.

The policy context

Social inclusion initiatives aim to work with children, young people and their families who experience a number of difficulties including poverty, poor housing and health and low educational attainment. The Standards in Scotland's Schools etc. Act states that there is a 'presumption of inclusion' and that 'school education for any child of school age, shall be provided in a school other than a special school' (Scottish Executive 2000a, p.8). It is seen as better for the child to be educated at their local school and within their own community as this may prevent social exclusion later in life. Schools are expected to have a continuum of supports for young people experiencing difficulties. The Scottish Executive have made recommendations such as 'schools having a positive ethos' and 'engagement of parents in their child's learning' (Scottish Executive 2000b, p.10) and 'staged intervention to support children' and 'schools should develop agreed systems for shared responsibility' (Scottish Executive 2001, p.14).

There have been several phases of development in policy and practice in relation to community schools in Scotland. During the 1970s several of the new regional councils deliberately moved in the direction of community schools using models essentially derived from the pioneering work of Henry Morris in Cambridgeshire in the 1930s. Grampian Regional Council built a number of new secondary schools with integral 'community' facilities (Nisbet *et al.* 1980). Lothian Regional Council made similar moves with a number of ambitious new buildings, a revised contract for teachers working in community schools and a programme of 'designating' schools as community schools, with additional resources being allocated, subject to a set of criteria being met. A number of councils also included community facilities in new primary school buildings around this time.

These moves to develop a model of community schools were conceived out of a desire to make schools more accessible to their communities, and to provide a range of educational and community facilities such as swimming pools and libraries on the school site for shared use. Developments at this time were, according to Henry Morris's biographer Harry Rée, directly traceable through a chain of personal contacts and influence to Cambridgeshire in the 1930s (Rée 1973). One of the best known of these Morris-inspired projects was the Sutton Centre in Nottinghamshire (see Fletcher 1983) that was often cited in policy debates at the time as a model to be emulated.

The local authority funding crisis of the mid-1970s and the election, in 1979, of a government determined to reduce the scope and costs of local government put a brake on new developments. Notwithstanding those constraints the community school idea remained alive in several parts of Scotland. Developments in the USA and the notion of 'full service schools' with health and welfare service provision closely integrated into the institutional frameworks were influential in the development of a 'prospectus' for 'new community schools' as part of the pre-devolution government's strategy to promote social inclusion. The prospectus contained a promise of funding totalling £26m over three years for pilot programmes. This was a very different conception of community schools, much more strongly oriented to providing integrated services for pupils and their families. The commitment of the first wave of community schools to a more generalized sense of engagement between schools and their local communities was much weakened although not entirely forgotten.

Several studies of pilot programmes showed that these new community schools were able to provide clear evidence of benefits, and in October 2002 the Scottish Executive announced a commitment to 'roll out' community schools, now called integrated community schools (ICS) in every local authority by 2006, with dedicated funding of more than £47m announced at the same time. This initiative is mirrored under various names across England, Wales and Northern Ireland. However, the climate changed substantially following an equivocal review of the programme by HM Inspectorate of Education (HMIE) who reported that 'the ICS initiative had not been fully successful in its aim of establishing a new over-arching vision and framework for the delivery of education and other children's services, using schools as the hub (HMIE 2004, p.28). So in July 2006 the Scottish Executive announced that it was 'no longer appropriate to think of integrated community schooling as a separate school based initiative'. Some commitment to an integrated approach to children's services is still evident, and we will be exploring this in the rest of the chapter, but community schools as such have once again been erased from the official lexicon.

Developing school–family–community links to prevent social exclusion

The long-term objective of Scottish policy in relation to preventing social exclusion and promoting more inclusive communities is to develop ways of working 'which integrate programmes not just within Government, but at all levels of action right down to local neighbourhoods and communities' (Scottish Office 1999, p.1). Thus schools are expected to work with other agencies both to prevent social exclusion taking place and to help reintegrate those who have been socially excluded into mainstream society. Historically,

targeting resources on the most disadvantaged has been an approach implemented to tackle the effects of economic and social disadvantage, for example,
educational priority areas and community development projects in the UK
(Halsey 1972). More recently, governments in the UK have focused on raising
educational achievement particularly in geographical areas characterized by
severe socio-economic deprivation. This is seen as one way of closing the
opportunity gap for people as the document *Everyone Matters: Delivering Social
Justice in Scotland*, states:

> Social justice is about everyone of us having the chances and opportunities
> that will allow us to use our talents to the full... We want to stamp out
> inequalities – where you live should not determine your health, wellbeing and
> employment chances for your whole life. We want to close the opportunity
> gap between those who succeed in life and those who fall behind.
> (Scottish Executive 2002, www.scotland.gov.uk/Publications/2002/11/
> 15766/13345)

It has long been recognized that agencies must work in close co-operation if
they wish to provide an effective seamless response to the needs of socially
excluded communities (Dyson, Lin and Millward 1998; Tett, Crowther and
O'Hara 2003; Webb and Vulliamy 2001a). Such joined-up thinking lies
behind a number of international educational initiatives such as inclusive
schools, full service schools and education action zones (see Campbell 2002;
Dryfoos 1996; Power 2001). In the UK schools are envisaged as playing a key
role in the current government's policies to promote social inclusion among
children and young people in particular and in tackling social exclusion in
general. Furthermore it is recognized that schools on their own cannot solve
the problems associated with social exclusion. Research has shown (Atkinson *et
al.* 2001; Ball 1998) that multi-agency projects, especially those that are based
outside any one school, have been able to provide a structure where take-up of
services can be addressed and encouraged. Projects that have involved social
and health services, housing, police, community education and non-govern-
mental organizations (NGOs) collaborating together with parents and schools
that focused on providing integrated services at the point of need have been
shown to be the most effective (Semmens 2001; Tett *et al.* 2003). ICS projects
in many areas have developed supportive programmes both within and
out-with school that involve multi-agency working. These include breakfast
clubs, out of school activities and clubs, holiday activities, as well as targeted
support for parents. There is evidence that this type of intervention has led to
the building of local community supports with a whole range of service providers and can lead to professionals developing a more democratic repertoire in
their relationship with local people. This way of working is an asset because it
aims to strengthen local networks and collective self-help, and include the
target community as active participants as a way of building social capital.

A case study

An integrated children's services approach

In the council studied, innovative ways have been found to engage with parents that are positive, purposeful and lead to improved understanding between them and the school community. This council decided not only to provide a range of services but also to develop an integrated children's services approach to ensure service integration at both strategic and local levels through developing common standards of practice, information-sharing and responsiveness in service delivery. Six 'integration managers' were appointed who were each responsible for a specific geographical area. Their remit was to 'co-ordinate and facilitate local groups of service managers that will jointly plan and manage the delivery of integrated services within the locality' and to 'ensure effective communication between schools, service providers and the local community' (Fife Council 2000, p.3). A further 24 'family support workers' were appointed to 'work with families either in their own homes or other appropriate venues, including schools, to provide support and advice on enquiries/issues such as: debt, housing, counselling or more general family/parenting issues'. Staff were mainly drawn from the council's existing personnel and most had backgrounds in social work and community education with a few coming from child care or teaching. We will show how these approaches worked out in practice but first a brief account of our research approach.

The research approach

Interviews were conducted by telephone with 24 key informants using a semi-structured interview framework. A purposive sample of key informants representing a range of organizational and professional perspectives was identified. The sample included all integration managers and one primary and one secondary head teacher, and two or more non-school professionals from each of the six geographical areas. These included staff from social work, health services, the voluntary sector and community education. The informants were identified in partnership with integration managers as people that had already had experience of using the new system. The interviews focused on informants' expectations of the project, their experiences of collaborative work and their vision of outcomes that would represent success.

All interviews were recorded and partial transcriptions made for purposes of analysis. The overall approach followed established procedures for interviewing by telephone (Dicker and Gilbert 1988). Informants were assured that their views would be reported anonymously and invited to indicate where there were parts of the interview that they would specifically not wish to be quoted. The analysis of interviews consisted of two stages. Two analysts working independently reviewed a small representative sample of interviews to identify the main analytic categories that could be used to systematically 'code' the responses of all informants. These two schemes of categorization were then compared and an agreed preliminary framework was developed. This framework was then used as the basis for review and analysis of the whole set of interviews.

In addition to the interviews, examples of effective practice that represented a spread of work across the council area were identified, which covered three broad categories. These categories were:

- working together

- providing particular opportunities for children and families, and

- individually focused, multi-agency interventions with troubled young people.

At least two informants were selected for each example and these included professional staff from both statutory and voluntary sectors, parents and young people, depending on the particular intervention, so that views could be triangulated. In addition the particular practice identified was observed where this would not breach the confidentiality of an individual. These case studies were then summarized and the information was checked by the informants.

Findings

Most key informants cited the role of family workers as central to the success of meeting the objectives of more integrated services. From a school perspective, family workers were seen as performing a useful role, and their actions were frequently spoken of in positive terms when describing the kinds of work that could be done to help families maintain their children in formal mainstream education. One example of an intervention was developing reciprocal links with the educational psychologist, school guidance staff and the social worker in order to support a troubled young man to remain in school. Another was intensive work with parents of an 'out of control' young woman to help the family set appropriate limits for weekend activities. A final example was the family worker's role in supporting the very anxious mother of a child who had been bullied over his transfer to secondary school. The family worker helped both the mother to approach the school in a less confrontational way and also the boy to improve his relations with his peers. This small-scale intervention had a very positive effect on both mother and son and the staff at the transferring and receiving schools who were no longer subject to the rather abusive visits of the mother.

Non-school-based informants were equally positive about this work. In particular a number of informants stressed the link between family worker and social work roles. For example:

We now have additional support for children and families in our area [as well as] the possibility of support being provided at an earlier stage in families we would not have been able to prioritize. Also some additional support for some of the families we are working with. We've got family support workers picking things up, at an earlier stage than we would have been in a position to allocate. (Social work manager)

Some of the most useful interventions were group-based activities designed to work with vulnerable families. One intervention provided a range of school holiday activity programmes for vulnerable parents and their children in collaboration with an NGO, the local further education college and the council's outdoor education team. Another was aimed at preparing and supporting young people in transition from primary to secondary school in order to reduce worries about starting at the big secondary school. As one teacher put it the result was that 'the worry, the anxiety was toned down to the point that they were able to settle down far more quickly'.

The family worker role could also be seen as problematic. This was particularly so when the cases picked up were not always those seen as most urgent and difficult. The focus on early intervention meant that existing 'high-tariff cases' were still understood to be being addressed through more traditional mechanisms, and were not always being referred appropriately. There was also a notable tension between the desire for early intervention and pressure to devote resources to more difficult cases. From a social work perspective child protection takes priority and the family workers tend to be drawn into the more complex and intractable cases leaving less time to devote to more proactive work. Social work services in this council were in a state of flux and were seen by other services and professionals as under-resourced, so family workers were sometimes used inappropriately to intervene in a difficult case instead of an unavailable social worker.

The research also highlighted the need for realistic judgements about what is possible in the most difficult cases. Reducing exclusions is one of the priorities at the policy level but school exclusion is a complex, multi-dimensional process and is used in a wide sense to denote children and young people who are excluded from full participation in school for various reasons such as difficulties in accessing the curriculum, staying away from school or because their families, such as travellers, have traditionally not attended schools (Lloyd, Stead and Kendrick 2003). It was thought that the family workers were able to identify more families at an earlier stage than had been possible before and that meant that exclusions were more likely to be avoided. This, however, led to other dilemmas about the use of the family worker's time. In very high tariff cases they could find themselves sucked into focusing almost exclusively on a particularly troubled young person and their family and consequently neglecting their more proactive interventions with slightly less needy or demanding families.

One of the most striking features of the interviews was the almost universal approval expressed by informants for the idea of working together. This was variously expressed as collaboration, partnership and co-operation and emphasized agencies working together in the interests of young people and families. The increase in joint working facilitated by integration managers was thought to improve clients' access to services (and school access to different funding sources). Informants valued learning more about each others' areas of expertise, and many saw 'blurring the boundaries' between agencies and professional groups as both offering positive potential and presenting new problems and dilemmas.

The integrated community school staff teams were seen as central to this process, in that they could facilitate contacts and network development. Schools liaison groups also played a valuable part in developing increased trust through face-to-face meetings. One aspect of working together mentioned by a number of informants was the potential for, and experience of, joint training. This was seen as a valuable learning process for staff. One particularly useful practice was thought to be cross-professional work shadowing, which among other benefits was thought to have helped to resolve confidentiality issues:

> Social workers say yeah I know what the school nurse does but if they actually came out and shadowed…they would be absolutely stunned to the extent of the work and vice versa. A lot of it has got to be education and training for the actual staff involved to make it a success and to break down barriers to working together. (Integration manager)

One head teacher described the striking benefits of an annual meeting, 'drawing together everyone we worked with as often they didn't know anything about who each other were'. It was clear that most people were realistic about the difficulties presented by different professional perspectives and priorities.

A number of problems existed in relation to collaborative work. There were competing perceptions of where power and control lies. The integration manager referred to the tensions that still existed around different services coming together to work on joint priorities, bringing different perceptions on how these can best be addressed through an integrated approach.

Problems were associated with the physical location of staff, with a widely held view that co-location of specific staff, outside any individual school, would be advantageous. In addition there are a range of more general problems arising from the pressure to work across traditional boundaries. For example one respondent suggested:

There are attitudinal barriers, which are sometimes the hardest to break down. There are organisational barriers, if you are working with schools...you do have to consider how this fits into the school's timetable. There is still a lack of understanding regarding individual services' roles and their responsibilities. (Integration manager)

Working together was framed not only as a matter of collaboration between agencies and professionals, but as something that would involve young people and parents as partners. For example, in response to being asked about their vision of an integrated community school, one respondent offered:

I think that would be a team of people who could work together without having to defend their territory. To get rid of the boundaries, a fluidity, where parents, carers and young people, children, were given equal weighting along with staff, that would be my ideal. To be involved, as an equal partner, not just as a tick the box, we've got them there, but as equal partners. (Public health nurse)

This way of thinking about the relationship between young people, families and the various services was expressed in a large number of interviews. It was characterized in analysis as the idea of 'working with' rather than 'on' clients.

Discussion

A range of research shows the efficacy of using joined-up, inter-agency work in relation to young people in trouble at school or in their neighbourhoods (Lloyd et al. 2003; Parsons 1999; Riddell and Tett 2001). The research suggested that the style and manner of support for young people and their parents/carers was crucial (Cooper et al. 2000; Smith and Tett 2003; Stead, Lloyd and Kendrick 2004). Support offered by professionals was regarded as appropriate when it was perceived as non-judgemental, genuine and equitable. Professionals and families particularly valued the support offered by staff with a specialized focus on vulnerable young people, especially those in voluntary sector projects. This was particularly because they had warm, informal, non-judgemental approaches and considerable expertise in finding alternative ways of working with young people. Professional skills that have been found to be effective for providing support for young people include counselling and group work skills using an informal approach. These are not highly technical skills and are part of the basic repertoire of many professionals such as community educators, social workers and youth workers.

The other main area that research has found to be essential to support for vulnerable young people and their carers is quick and easy access to services and good communication between professionals and the parents/carers. A study of parents of children with a diagnosis of social emotional and behavioural difficulties (SEBD) (Smith and Tett 2003) showed that they had sound knowledge, clear understanding and good insights into their child's difficulties, yet in many cases this was not acted on. Rather they had to wait for professionals to make referrals to support agencies and often had to approach a variety of professionals themselves rather than having just one co-ordinating person to make these connections for them. Semmens (2001) argues that in a crisis situation, which many parents get to before asking for help, 'someone with specialist expertise must step in and take responsibility...however the intervention must be connected with the rest of the client's life' (p.76). One of the key points that emerge from research is that parents want to be involved in supporting their children but professionals can make this a difficult, rather than an easy, process (Kendrick 1995; Stead *et al.* 2004). Clearly, then, a co-ordinated approach to the most vulnerable young people and families is essential if their exclusion is to be tackled. The approach adopted by the case study council described above appears to enable this to happen through having an integrated system of referrals and the ability to respond quite quickly to situations as they arise.

A study by Lloyd and colleagues (2001, 2003) found that it was possible to support the most difficult young people and avoid disciplinary exclusion, but that sometimes the strategies used meant that young people did not actually attend mainstream school. Alternatives to disciplinary exclusion do not always keep young people included in the curriculum or the school and so there must be some questions about how far exclusion was prevented. They found that the key to appropriate support for the young people in their study of three local authorities was 'to take account of the lives, values and choices of young people and to combine imagination and flexibility with a non-judgemental, human style' (2003, p.88). Successful approaches involved young people having their views valued and their responses to the curriculum taken seriously so that all the staff involved in working with them saw them as whole human beings rather than 'problems'. Where this was achieved, however, school staff felt that they had to neglect other things as they were under constant pressure to meet targets for achievement or other pedagogical duties.

In the case study it was evident that family workers could act as a go-between for the school and the agencies working with troubled and troublesome pupils and their families. They also provided both teachers and other agencies, such as those working in drug and alcohol rehabilitation, with information about each other's organizations, working practices, constraints and perspectives. The workers were able to build up an overview of all the factors impacting on particular families and act to improve communications between schools and families and to set up meetings between family members and those involved in providing them with support. Family workers were also proactive and engaged in preventative work and were perceived as independent from other organizations or institutions, whereas families tended to have set views and expectations of interactions with social workers and police.

A major endemic problem in the development of school–community–family links identified by Dyson and Robson (1999) is their fragmented and localized nature. They view the field as 'characterized by a multiplicity of locally-led and locally-developed projects, replicating each other's discoveries and difficulties, but not systematised in any useful way', which they view as 'influenced by the multiplicity of often short-term funding sources' (p.10). As Milbourne (2005) found, in her evaluation of partnership work in primary settings, getting the right people was crucial to success. Personal relationships formed a vital part in developing agency links and inter-agency working. Similarly, Webb and Vulliamy (2004) found in their study of a project designed to reduce school exclusions that 'the amount of co-operation with agencies declined or grew with changes of support worker' (p.66). One of the strengths of this project was that the staff were in permanent posts and so the turnover was low and gave time for relationships to develop.

In addition teachers appreciated that many of the parents of the most challenging pupils were fearful, suspicious or antagonistic towards teachers because of their own unhappy school experiences. Therefore, in such circumstances, the family workers were especially valued for improving home–school communication and for providing 'an indirect bridge to parents' (Teacher) to get teachers and parents working together. Teachers also came to value the skills of the family workers. They recognized the differences in their relationship with young people and found ways to support each other. The family workers also improved communication between specialist agencies, such as those working in the area of sexual health, and schools. They were able to enhance the knowledge of pastoral staff of the services provided, and ways of working, of these agencies. Parents and young people also uniformly valued family workers for their independence, accessibility and availability, skill in developing trusting relationships and sympathetic advice on problems. 'She's always there for our family whatever happens' (Mother with a troubled daughter).

Conclusion

Many services designed to help the most vulnerable families prioritize interventions that focus on acute problems and crisis management rather than preventative work. From our research it appears that the strategy adopted by this council is proving effective in promoting preventative work that addresses both the individual problems of vulnerable families and also some of the institutional factors that contribute to the problems families experience in and out of school. However, the system is at an early stage in its development and there is potential for role conflict ahead. Family workers could spend a great deal of their time intervening in individual cases rather than taking more proactive action that might prevent social exclusion. Although these staff have a clear remit to engage in preventative collaborative work, schools faced with pupils with challenging behaviour can be very demanding of family workers' time. Lloyd and colleagues (2001) suggested that 'effective support was not about a matching of perceived problems with a standard model of support, instead it took account of the wishes and life circumstances of the young people' (p.70). This is quite a hard criterion to meet but family workers, by being based in particular localities and knowing their communities, are in quite a strong position to do this.

Other research shows that 'exclusionary professionalist agendas, often sustained by deficit ideologies' (Hatcher and Leblond 2001, p.55) can operate to marginalize inter-professional collaboration as each partner competes to have their view heard. It appears that the structures established in this project through the integration managers can operate to minimize these effects as their remit gives them development time and they bring the skills and energy to establish and maintain the relationships necessary for collaborative inter-agency work. The council's structure of an integrated children's service also assists in enabling the different parts of the council and NGOs to work together in providing accessible services for families. However, it is too early to say how the key dilemma of early individual intervention versus proactive community development will be resolved.

Acknowledgements

An earlier version of this chapter was given at the 'Service Integration in Scottish Schools: Values, Vision and Vital Voices' Conference in Aberdeen University on 10 June 2005. We are grateful to our audience for their helpful contributions.

Part 2

Safeguarding and Schools: Practice

Chapter Four

Pupils Who Are 'In Care'

What Can Schools Do?

Felicity Fletcher-Campbell

Introduction

It is ironic that those children who most need 'keeping safe' are, in fact, the hardest to keep safe if we mean by 'safeguarding' as being a positive state in which children are able to flourish – rather than the more minimal interpretation of 'freedom from danger'. There are two aspects of 'safeguarding'. One, akin to the more minimal position, focuses on legal responsibilities and is relatively clearly defined. The other is looser, more about a moral responsibility to remove barriers to children's well-being and flourishing where these barriers have been erected by other adults' irresponsibility or lack of care towards them. Arguably, this fuller version is an imperative in situations where other adults have been censured for their (perceived) inadequacies towards their children and where, thus, exemplar or working models may be needed.

The school can, and should, fulfil both aspects of safeguarding: both are necessary and neither is sufficient on its own. Indeed, it is this symbiotic relationship that is so hard to maintain and that brings much of the difficulty in safeguarding: there is cogent evidence that one weak link in the chain is disproportionately detrimental for those children who are the most vulnerable. While some young people in care are remarkably resilient, others have had so many setbacks that any further lack of support will be immensely challenging.

The school can only contribute to pupils' flourishing – it cannot do the whole job itself. Effective work with young people in care depends on, and is characterized by, partnership and collaboration: if a significant difference is made, it is by the interaction of a range of interventions and individuals.

The child protection aspects are addressed in other chapters. This chapter examines the school's role and responsibility in enabling children in need of safeguarding – in particular, those who are in public care – to have a positive educational experience. Not only is this a matter of equity, insofar as there should be some positive action taken to compensate for the disabling conditions in which these children have found themselves – the vast majority through others', not their own, actions and behaviours – but it constitutes effective practice insofar as 'education protects'[1] and a positive educational career can greatly enhance and contribute to a positive experience in care.

What do we need to know about the young people concerned?

When we single out any one group of children at school by virtue of their membership of another group (for example, children from a minority ethnic group, children with a disability, children who have a particular socio-economic background) it is crucial to identify, first, what relevance their group characteristics have on their education and, second, the optimal balance between meeting their needs and enhancing their participation by means of, on the one hand, the general organization and policies of the school and, on the other, by discrete, 'targeted', provision.

There are some contextual facts that need to be remembered. First, the group 'children in care' (of whom there are currently about 60,300 in England)[2] is heterogeneous and covers the whole gamut of ages, abilities, preferences and needs. Indeed, there is considerable evidence that it is when the group is considered to be homogeneous that things go awry as group similarities are wrongly assumed. Second, while these young people formally constitute a 'vulnerable group', they often qualify for other vulnerable groups (so, for example, they may have lived in families in poverty, have disabilities, be economic migrants). Third, children enter and leave care. It is not a static group and individuals move in and out of care, the annual turnover being greater than the snapshot figure (though national data are kept on individual children and not of the numbers of care episodes). Fourth, there are many equally vulnerable children who are not taken into care but who have very similar needs and background characteristics as those who are formally in care.[3] Fifth, taking a child into care is an extreme measure and only happens as a last resort when other support has proved inadequate; thus the young people concerned are usually very vulnerable and have experienced an array of interventions from a variety of sources, many of them with negative outcomes (if an earlier intervention had been successful, the child would probably not be in care).

---

1   The Education Protects programme was instituted in 2000 – see www.dfes.gov.uk/educationprotects

2   See www.dfes.gov.uk/rsgateway/DB/VOL/v000721/index.shtml

3   See www.dfes.gov.uk/rsgateway/DB/VOL/v000647/index.shtml

The parameters of the school's interventions

The implications of these points are that schools must, as far as possible, establish effective support strategies that can be applied to all pupils based on their needs/vulnerability rather than their legal status. The vast majority of young people want to be 'normal' and to do things alongside their peers and they do not want to be singled out. This is often particularly the case for young people who are in care and it should be entirely their decision as to whether they are treated any differently in the normal course of school life. Effective practice depends on, and is identified by, participation on the part of the child. Any positive discrimination, which may be necessary on account of features of the care system (as laid out below) needs to be managed with great sensitivity. This holds for whatever the particular context in which the young person is educated, for example, whether it is a rural primary school, a large inner-city comprehensive school, a faith school, or a sixth form college. However, there are likely difficulties that arise because a young person is in care and, thus, the school must ensure that there are specific strategies in place to address these.

Senior leaders, who know the legal status of pupils on roll, need to consider who else, if anyone, needs to share this information in order for the pupil to flourish. There is research evidence of teachers making inappropriate comments to young people, based on their prejudices about care, and/or making assumptions about those young people's response to school and the curriculum, that are not evidence-based (see, for example, Fletcher-Campbell 1997; Harker *et al.* 2003). Research has shown that the sharing of information about a young person's personal situation needs to be done on a case-by-case basis after discussion with relevant parties (which will normally include the young person) and with clear delineation of the agreed benefits to the young person of the chosen course of action. It should be remembered that a young person in care may not know who else is in care in the school (so specific support groups or targeted activities can be difficult). Some find meeting their peers in care helpful, while others may have a stable network of friends with whom they feel comfortable and may not feel inclined to seek out others in care. Anything that singles out the young person purely for administrative convenience – rather than because it addresses a specific need or is the young person's own preference – should be avoided. For example, a pupil should not be taken out of a lesson in order to attend a meeting with a social worker.

The school that is accustomed to identifying and responding to individual difference will be in a strong position to meet the needs of children in care. This is the case regardless of different legislation, the different policy contexts in the four nations in the UK or different patterns of care in different local authorities. It should be remembered that the distinct group of 'children in care' denotes a legal status and indicates current responsibilities within the family; it says nothing about children's abilities, aptitudes and preferences: there are as many sub-groups within the total 'in care' population as there are in the population at large. However, there are some factors that need to be borne in mind when responding to the pupil as a member of the group of those in care; these factors emerge from the structure of care (which may be different in different countries) and from the fact that the one characteristic that these young people share is fragmentation of their lives: information about them (their personal 'history'), and interventions to support them, are shared among a range of adults including those in health, social care and education. Thus difficulties that present within the classroom and need to be addressed by the school are primarily the manifestations of structural deficiencies in the care system or, in some cases, the inevitabilities of being in this system.

What similarities do these pupils share in relation to their school experience?

Children in care may have had a disrupted educational career, be highly mobile, mostly have moved schools mid-term, missed periods of schooling, and/or have incomplete educational records. Thus an effective identification of their strengths and weaknesses with regard to the curriculum is of importance. Children in care report that they are often automatically put in lower sets or assumed to be poor achievers by virtue of this group membership. It is hardly surprising that they then perform according to teacher expectations, thus perpetuating the myths and activating a downwards spiral. The value of knowing which pupils are in care (as discussed above) is so that assumptions can be challenged and evidence collected to inform progression – rather than for attaching yet more unhelpful labels.

How can we plan for the pupil?

Children in care in England are expected to have a personal education plan (PEP)[4]. The value of a personal education plan is not the piece of paper but, rather, a means of monitoring that arrangements have been put in place, collating vital information, establishing action points, allocating responsibility, determining time-scales and identifying support needs. If the school already has a system of personal tutoring and individual target-setting, the PEP may not be of such importance as in a school where such systems do not operate, but it serves a particular purpose at times of transition (e.g. starting a new school) which often come at non-standard times of year for children in care – mid-year, mid-term or mid-GCSE course. Young people in care can feel aggrieved if, just because they are in care, they have to undertake additional planning that seems

---

4   Statutory in England under the terms of Section 52 of the Children's Act 2004.

to serve no specific purpose or have obvious advantages for them (Fletcher-Campbell, Archer and Tomlinson 2004). The main thing is to achieve the objective of planning and to share that planning with relevant agencies that can support the young person's progression. The means by which it takes place is of less importance, although the system available, if properly administered, has been shown to be helpful.

How can we facilitate routine events?

Another aspect of being in care is that for many of the cohort, regular events, such as transition from primary to secondary school or choice of GCSE, are more traumatic for the child (Fletcher-Campbell 1997). Given the fragmented life that many have led and the consequent lack of security, it is not surprising that anything demanding considerable personal stamina (such as meeting new peers, having to make new friendships, meeting new adults, having to contemplate the future, being under scrutiny with questions being asked about home life and family, etc.) is going to be particularly demanding.

Thus, year six teachers need to identify if a vulnerable child – perhaps with other vulnerable children who may not be in care – needs additional 'taster' days or a longer programme of induction to a new school. Some local authorities arrange special transition days or events for the year six pupils in their care. The pupil may need to be placed strategically with a teacher who is particularly skilled at encouraging a new group of pupils to collaborate and be sensitive to each others' situations. There may be a buddying system in place to support the child or special arrangements may be necessary for a particular young person, for example, if friendship groups are already established. There is evidence that many strategies are not applicable just to this group – as with many inclusive measures, they benefit all pupils. Children in care often change schools at non-standard times. In schools with high mobility, with pupils joining and leaving on a weekly basis, this may pose no difficulties as it is likely that there are well-developed induction programmes and processes in place. However, where there are few such cases the young person is going to be isolated both in terms of not having made friends and in not having become familiar with their peer group, teachers and the school. They will also be regarded with curiosity by peers and will have to talk about a previous school or where they live. This may be an ordeal for which the young person needs to be prepared in advance and supported until they settle.

The end of statutory schooling is another danger point as many young people leave care and go into independent living at this stage. They have to cope with all these challenges at the end of Key Stage 4 – often at a time when they are taking their GCSEs. They may have been disadvantaged in the meantime by a placement move entailing a break in the GCSE course. It is not surprising that many decide to opt out unless support is given. This support might include 'catch-up' classes (alongside other pupils in the school or, perhaps, for all year 11 pupils in care in an area) or individual help. In some cases, it may be appropriate to allow the young person to withdraw from the exam syllabus in the year that, chronologically, they should be taking GCSEs and make arrangements to continue the following year when the young person may be in more control of their life.

What can we do when things go wrong?

Non-completion of homework, poor attendance and challenge to school codes of behaviour can be danger signals for a child in care (and, indeed, for any other child) and usually indicate that something else is going wrong in their lives. Some schools have specific policies that mean action is taken if a pupil in care is absent for a day – while the action may not be so immediate if the pupil is not in care. This is because the indicator at school (the absence, the disengagement from the curriculum) is often a symptom of something else needing attention. While most residential units are far more aware than they were a decade ago of their responsibilities with regard to ensuring that young people have the facilities and opportunities to do homework, and have a responsibility to support children's education under Section 25 of the Care Standards Act 2000, changes of shift and care workers mean that children in residential care can encounter barriers to establishing good study habits out of school. The obvious solutions are regular study support arrangements, but a special attempt needs to be made to ensure that the respective pupils are invited and that they can attend without their feeling that they have been selected for negative reasons.

Positive relationships need to be forged with carers, and this applies whether the child is in residential or foster care. Again, the specifics of the situation need to be recognized. Residential carers will probably work shifts, so the person responsible for getting the pupil to school may not be the same person who is there when the child returns from school and sets about homework. The foster carer, who is also required to support education under the National Minimum Standards for Fostering Services 2002, may be caring for younger children so it may not be easy for them to get along to school or, similarly, to supervise homework. But though these difficulties may be superficially different from the majority of the school roll, in essence they are little different. Many children will come from homes where both parents are working and are not there to ensure that homework is done, or where there is no quiet spot where they can do their homework. Again, there are many children who are not 'in care' but who come from households that are not able, for whatever reason, to support their education. The school has to bear all these in mind and, if it takes inclusion seriously, must ensure that alternative arrangements are offered in school (possibly as part of the extended school offer) and that opportunities are available to pupils to achieve. Thinking specifically about the needs of children in care can heighten sensitivity to the needs of a range of other pupils, just as much as meeting the needs of this cohort can often be done through routine school measures. More specifically, where bureaucratic procedures can obtrude into normal activity, schools need to establish protocols for the young person's participation in school trips and residential activities, and establish to whom school reports need to go (multiple copies may be necessary) so that all the key players are kept involved. Most important is collaboration over objectives, targets and shared expectations. There is research evidence that children in care do best where there is mutual understanding between young people and all supporting adults. While there are successful outcomes for care users despite a fully supportive environment (see, for example, Martin and Jackson 2002), these rely on 'good luck' rather than 'good management'. Unless there is attention to the latter, some care users are going to be failed by the system.

What is the role of the designated teacher?

Schools in England are expected to have a designated teacher for pupils in care. The government has announced that it envisages that the post be strengthened and recommends that resources be available to support it (Cm 6932 2006). As with many other specific posts (for example, the gifted and talented co-ordinator, special educational needs co-ordinator, assessment co-ordinator), the most important thing is that certain responsibilities are fulfilled rather than that one person does them. Individual pupils may be best served if a range of staff fulfil the responsibilities. For example, it may be appropriate for a member of the senior leadership team or the teacher responsible for child protection to have an overview of the legal status of pupils who are in care. But this person may not be the one most appropriate to act as mentor to the relevant pupil. Pupils at schools involved in research carried out by the National Foundation for Educational Research (Fletcher-Campbell *et al.* 2004) were generally able to identify someone to whom they felt they could talk if they had difficulties. In some cases, this was the designated teacher, usually because the designated teacher had been carefully selected as being someone with whom young people in difficulty felt comfortable. In others, it was a teacher with whom the pupil got on particularly well – the teacher of a subject the child particularly liked, for example – or another member of staff to whom the pupil could relate.

All teachers have a responsibility to monitor the progress of pupils. However, because the evidence shows that a small setback can have disproportionate consequences for young people in care, there is an argument for more frequent, albeit unobtrusive, monitoring of the progress of young people in care. When many are having to manage disruption in their personal lives, they may need more frequent, finely tuned targets, for example, and these may need to be compatible with targets in their care plan. While school staff should arrange to talk with the young person's social worker, the best person with whom to discuss compatibility and viability is, of course, the young person, particularly at secondary school age. Young people in care frequently report that they feel that professionals talk around them or at them rather than with them (Commission for Social Care Inspection (CSCI) 2007).

The education system in the UK, and many other countries, assumes that pupils 'fit' a set routine of progress. However, the learning of many children is idiosyncratic in the short term, particularly for socio-cultural reasons. Indeed, we know relatively little about the optimum rates and nature of progress for individuals; we know most about 'norms', many of which are established through top-down pressures. Different sequences may fit different pupils, especially pupils who are subjected to traumatic situations and chaos and extreme challenge in their personal lives. It is for this reason that an education plan is important as it allows a pathway appropriate for the individual to be forged through 'the system'.

How can we encourage participation?

Out-of-school-hours learning

There is considerable evidence that participation in out-of-school-hours learning (OSHL) supports children's learning in the classroom. There is also evidence that, for various reasons, young people in care are often denied access to OSHL (by virtue of the structures of the care system) or do not participate unless encouraged. The designated teacher needs to monitor participation and encourage young people's involvement in relevant activities. Non-participation may be for reasons of transport, for example, or there may be financial difficulties if the young person is in foster care (see ContinYou 2005 for extensive guidance).

What resources do we need? A creative approach

While not denying that professional time involves money, it must be pointed out that many apparent problems can be solved by, first, listening to young people and second, creative thinking and using the resources that are readily available. Young people are often very perspicacious when one of their peers is upset and can often suggest a strategy for helping that child. For example, half an hour with the school caretaker, doing woodwork, at the beginning of the school day when other children were in registration/assembly, meant that one boy who was in care was able to adjust to the routines of the school day after the emotional turmoil of coming to school. Moreover, he had one-to-one attention, learnt new skills that were not shared by his peers, and had tangible evidence of what he had achieved, which could then be displayed and admired by his peers, thus contributing to raising his self-esteem (Fletcher-Campbell *et* al. 2004). This anecdote is important for it reminds us that children are not necessarily helped most by the statutory authorities. They find their own confidants and identify their own sources of support, as we all do.

Nonetheless, the issue of *financial* resources often arises when providing for the needs of children in care is discussed. Bureaucratic arrangements often do not 'fit' individual circumstances and the budgets available for children in care can be inaccessible to those who need to use them, often without a long lead time (for example, if a child wants to take up a musical instrument or go on a sports coaching day or a school trip). As with all allocation for vulnerable groups (see, for example, Fletcher-Campbell *et al.* 2003), there are tensions between longer-term and larger-area planning and the immediate and idiosyncratic needs of individuals. Schools need to consider the use of delegated budgets and decide the balance between discrete allocations (for specific individuals and/or groups) and the way in which the needs of children in care can be accommodated within inclusive approaches and the funding allocations supporting these. Above all, it is essential that bureaucratic arrangements do not inhibit the participation of children in care in education and related activities: other children are not inhibited in this way and it represents a structural barrier that is unacceptable given that it is irrelevant to the situation.

How can we work with carers?

There is a wide range of people who foster children: some may have had positive educational experiences themselves, some may not have; some may be confident in talking to teachers and education professionals, others may not; some may have had their own children through school and others may not. Their needs are, thus, likely to be similar to those of any varied group of parents of school age children. However, given the difficulties that we know that children who are looked after may encounter in their education, the school needs to ensure that there is regular and positive collaboration with the foster carers with whom they are acting in partnership. Foster carers report very different experiences of their child's school, ranging from being patronized or ignored to being treated as an equal and engaged in joint planning and problem-solving around the young person (Fletcher-Campbell 1997). Carers need to know how the child responds to the challenges of the school day, just as school staff need to know when events occur in the child's personal life that will make it hard for them to respond positively to what the school has to offer or the expectations made. Because of the overall vulnerability and fragile nature of their relationships, speedier responses are often needed in the event of problems occurring – thus some schools 'fast track' notification of a child's absence, for example.

Foster carers may need encouragement to join home–school literacy schemes, particularly if they are not confident about their own literacy skills and may need encouragement to identify the particular role that they can take to support the child's strengths and weaknesses in the curriculum. Research has shown that it is this 'moral' support that is more important than any technical support that the parent/carer can give, though carers can be helped to know how to support emerging literacy, for example. As foster parents will be involved in any planned moves, they need to be aware of the child's position with regard to the curriculum, in particular GCSE and examination courses.

How can we work with social care?

All the literature on the education of children in care, from the very early studies, through the most recent government policy documents, stresses the importance of education and social care working together. This should, in principle, be far easier in the light of *Every Child Matters*. But, while it needs a broad policy framework to set the expectations, the realities have to be worked out with respect to the needs and preferences of the individual children in care at a particular school. For one, it may be appropriate for a social worker to attend parents' meetings or options choices; for another, a social worker may hardly visit the school, especially if the child prefers their foster carer to do the things a parent might do in other circumstances. All the evidence suggests it is critical that:

- roles and responsibilities are fulfilled
- it is clear how they are fulfilled
- it is clear who is to fulfil them.

And there is some accountability – even if this is only by way of the social worker taking an interest in what the foster carer is doing (and, of course, enabling support as necessary) or the social care team leader asking questions of the responsible social worker in supervision. Similarly, there need to be decisions about the appropriateness of attendance at 'larger' meetings to review and plan for the young person: and here, the preferences of the young person are important. Again, the critical element is the planning and the ensuring of outcomes – the removal of a child from their classes in order to attend a social care meeting off-site should be something relegated to history, even if there are numerous references to it in the 'older' literature. The particularities around the needs of children in care must, as we move into the second decade of the century, be positioned within a holistic approach to inter-professional working: the point made above about the fact that children in care are not an isolated and static group and individuals move in and out of care while, most probably, remaining 'vulnerable' must not be lost sight of.

Conclusions

Areas for the school to consider in relation to those pupils who are in care have been outlined above. The list may seem formidable and the inevitable question of 'where are the resources?' may be asked. Various points, however, need to be borne in mind.

First, regardless of any legal responsibilities, there is a moral responsibility to do the very best for these children, rather than to let them progress as they would in their own family. They are in care because either 'the state' (local authority/ 'professionals') have deemed their family members unfit to take full responsibility for their children or because the families themselves have asked for help in this role. Making the former judgement brings with it the responsibility of doing the job far better than the original family – otherwise, removal is unjustified.

Second, the school should not be alone in its initiatives: it cannot be uninvolved given that:

- it is responsible for the young person for much of the day during term time

- there is overwhelming evidence about the uneasy position of children who are looked after in the school system.

The school should support, and be supported by, carers on the one side, and professionals and the local authority on the other. It is only when these links are made that the child can be fully supported. The school must have as many expectations of other professional and agencies as they have of schools. Many of the factors outlined above are already in place in many schools: systems may need 'tweaking' and tailoring rather than setting up from scratch.

Third, it is essential to listen to the young people themselves. One of the most striking features of the whole narrative about, and developments in understanding about, the education of children in care is the consensus between policymakers, carers, practitioners, researchers and the young people themselves. There has been none of the opposing or alternative theories and explanations that are so often found in other areas. Thus it is essential to listen to the young people at the centre. But, having listened, it is as essential to take action on what they suggest. Young people have, increasingly, been listened to but there has not been the whole-hearted response that they deserve.

There is a dilemma. It is apparent that many still 'slip through the net'. But we need to ask ourselves if we really want to make such a tight mesh that the net loses its flexibility and tolerance of difference. Inclusion is not about entrapment. It is about ensuring that all are 'acceptable' – that is, able to be accepted. And it is the responsibility of each of us to give this ability, and to ensure that the part of the environment for which we are responsible enables 'the other' to be accepted. Acceptability is not about the other behaving in the way we want – the 'assimilation' model. If we set things up so as to ensure others' participation we may find that our prejudices fall in direct proportion to the heights to which these others soar.

Chapter Five

Safeguarding Disabled Children

David Miller and Ann Raymond

Context

This chapter identifies the level of risk of abuse that disabled children face and the reasons for this. It emphasizes the importance of empowering and consulting with disabled children, and considers the safeguarding measures that are required and the role of education staff within this. It does so having regard to *Safeguarding Children and Safer Recruitment in Education* (DfES 2006a), *Safe and Well* (Scottish Executive 2005), *Safeguarding Children in Education: The Role of Local Authorities and Governing Bodies Under the Education Act 2002* Consultation Document (Welsh Assembly Government 2007a) and *Pastoral Care in Schools: Child Protection* (Department of Education Northern Ireland (DENI) 1999).

For the purposes of this chapter a broad definition of disability has been adopted in order to address the full range of issues and barriers that can exist. This includes children and young people with learning disabilities, autistic spectrum disorders, sensory impairments, physical impairments, mental health needs and emotional or behavioural difficulties. This chapter is applicable to all schools, mainstream and special, day, boarding and residential in both the maintained and independent sectors.

Disabled children and risk

Background

Research, undertaken predominantly in the United States, consistently shows that disabled children are at greater risk of abuse. For example, one large-scale study (Sullivan and Knutson 2000) analysed records of over 40,000 children in an American city and found that disabled children were 3.4 times more likely to be abused or neglected than non-disabled children and more likely to endure multiple episodes of abuse. Overall, in this study, 31% of disabled children had been abused compared to a prevalence rate of 9% among the non-disabled child population. In a retrospective analysis of childhood sexual abuse among deaf adults in Norway (Kvam 2004) a questionnaire, in both written form and on video in sign language, was sent to all adult deaf Norwegians. The research found that 45.8% deaf girls and 42.4% deaf boys had been exposed to unwanted sexual experiences. Deaf girls were more than twice as likely to experience sexual abuse with physical contact as hearing girls and deaf boys more than three times as likely to do so as hearing boys. Nearly half reported the abuser was deaf and half of abusive events took place in connection with a boarding school for deaf children. Forty nine per cent did not tell anyone at the time and 11% did tell someone but were not believed.

Research in the UK has been limited, although key documents from across the four countries recognize that disabled children are more likely to experience abuse than non-disabled children (Department of Health, Social Services and Public Safety 2003; HM Government 2006; Social Work Inspection Agency 2006; Welsh Assembly Government 2007a and 2007b).

Reasons for increased risk

The National Working Group on Child Protection and Disability in England (2003) divides risk factors for the abuse of disabled children into three categories:

1. Attitudes and assumptions that include: not valuing or understanding a disabled child's experiences; lack of awareness or denial of the abuse of disabled children; and a lack of recognition of the impact of abuse on disabled children.

2. Inadequacies in service provision that include: inadequate assessment and planning; failure to communicate effectively with the disabled child; lack of appropriate support services; skills gap between disability and child protection workers; lack of appropriate vocabulary within the child's communication system to communicate abuse; and a lack of effective safety and awareness work.

3. Issues related to impairment, which would, for example, include: a disabled child receiving intimate personal care from a number of carers; having an impaired capacity to resist or avoid abuse; or having communication difficulties that make it difficult to tell others what is happening and to seek help.

These risk factors are compounded by barriers that exist for disabled children at all stages of the child protection process. Education staff may face, or inadvertently contribute to, barriers that can undermine their ability to recognize and act on abuse. These include:

- a reluctance to believe a child may be at risk
- misinterpretation of, and assumptions about, indicators of possible abuse (e.g. mood, behaviour, injuries), assuming they relate to a child's impairment
- a tendency to minimize the harm done by abuse
- over-identification with, or a reluctance to question or challenge, a parent or carer
- unquestioning acceptance of established practices that may be abusive
- absence of therapeutic or other intervention to support the child and enable a fuller assessment of needs when possible concerns exist.

Balancing risk and protection

Schools are sometimes unsure how they should meet their safeguarding obligations to the most vulnerable pupils, and may seek refuge in policies that attempt to eliminate all risk by restricting disabled pupils' opportunities and devising procedures that protect at a superficial level but that can actually disempower pupils and lead to a loss of dignity and control. Examples include denying a disabled pupil a place on a school residential trip because of their medical needs, or requiring the presence of two staff, or an open door, when providing intimate care. Schools must develop secure risk-assessment processes and be mindful of the views of children and young people on the necessary balance between risk and protection. In *Safe From Harm*, a report of children's views commissioned by the Commission for Social Care Inspection in England (Morgan 2004), the children's consultative group called for a recognition that it was not possible to make everything safe. They argued that while many situations carried some risk, trying to make everything safe also removed much of the fun. The group, which included disabled children and children with special educational needs, was clear that everyone has to get the right balance in what they do when trying to protect other people. Getting it right includes creating a culture of empowerment that creates opportunities for growth within a secure structure of risk management, as well as making statutory guidance applicable to disabled children and ensuring that a school's safeguarding policies and practice provide equal protection for all children.

Safeguarding

Responsibility for safeguarding

The Second Joint Chief Inspectors' Report on Arrangements to Safeguard Children (Commission for Social Care Inspection (CSCI) *et al.* 2005) found that agencies other than social services are often unclear about how to recognize the signs of abuse or neglect, are uncertain about the thresholds that apply to child protection or do not know to whom they should refer their concerns. Specifically the report states that more attention needs to be paid to identifying welfare concerns for disabled children. Education staff are particularly well placed to advise on and promote a child's well-being. They are essentially the only professionals who have regular, often daily, contact with children and young people and they have a critical role in both identifying concerns and safeguarding and promoting welfare. All school staff and others connected with the school management and operation, whether in a teaching or non-teaching capacity, potentially have a role to play. This will include governors, teaching and learning support staff, administrative, domestic and maintenance staff as well as all other visiting or peripatetic staff and volunteers. The same principles apply to safeguarding disabled children as to non-disabled children. However, particular considerations may apply and barriers can exist to their implementation. These need to be recognized and addressed by educational establishments within policies, procedures and practice standards.

Schools and other educational establishments do not exist in isolation, and appropriate working relationships should be developed with colleagues in health and social care. The development of effective multi-agency working and information-sharing to promote the safeguarding and well-being of children is particularly important given the number of professionals who may be involved in a disabled child's education and care, the complexity of the child's needs and the barriers that can exist to their safeguarding. Good assessment, planning and co-ordination of service delivery is key to promoting the well-being of disabled children, as is partnership with parents and carers who have a key role in promoting the well-being of disabled children within the school, home and community. A range of documents and programmes across the United Kingdom now recognize the critical role of schools in the multi-agency child protection process, emphasizing their key role in providing advice to or acting as interpreters for the investigating officers (see, for example DfES 2004d; Office of the First Minister and Deputy First Minister 2006; Scottish Executive 2005; Welsh Assembly Government 2002).

The child protection policy

All educational establishments should have a child protection policy and procedures that are in accordance with the children's services authority or their equivalents in Wales, Northern Ireland and Scotland and locally agreed procedures. Many authorities have issued a model policy to schools, such as that which is provided on the teachernet website (www.teachernet.gov.uk). Child protection policies and procedures should recognize the right of all children to be protected from abuse and raise awareness of the risk of disabled children to abuse. They should recognize the barriers and the specific issues that need to be addressed to ensure the effective safeguarding of disabled children. These procedures should acknowledge that disabled children can experience abuse in the same ways as any child but can also experience abuse in ways specifically relating to their impairment. Some of these may not immediately be recognized as abuse. However, if persistent, they may have a cumulative and substantial effect over time and constitute abuse. Others may have a more immediate impact but not be recognized as abuse. For example, physical abuse could include failure to provide treatment or over-use of medication, forcing treatment that is painful or the inappropriate use of physical restraint. Emotional abuse could include the lack of communication or stimulation, teasing, bullying or blaming a child because of their impairment. Sexual abuse could include a young person engaging in sexual activity within an unequal relationship without the level of awareness of the full meaning of that behaviour. Neglect could include failure to support a child's treatment or support needs.

Examples of ways disabled children can specifically experience abuse are set out in Table 5.1.

Table 5.1 Ways disabled children can experience abuse

Physical abuse	• failure to provide treatment • over-use of medication • forcing treatment that is painful • inappropriate use of physical restraint
Emotional abuse	• lack of communication or stimulation • teasing, bullying or blaming a child because of their impairment
Sexual abuse	• young person engaging in sexual activity within an unequal relationship without the level of awareness of the full meaning of that behaviour
Neglect	• failure to support a child's treatment or support needs

The second joint chief inspectors' report on arrangements to safeguard children in England (CSCI *et al.* 2005) found that special schools generally make child protection referrals appropriately. However the inspectors commented on the fact that staff did not always identify and track behaviour patterns and trends, whether the behaviour shows itself as overt challenge or emotional withdrawal.

It notes that these can be indicators of child protection concerns. It is essential that the reasons underlying any presenting behaviours are explored and any needs identified. These may or may not give rise to child protection concerns but may give rise to other needs that should be addressed to promote the child's well-being. The procedures should make clear the responsibility of staff to report concerns or to seek advice from the designated person with safeguarding responsibilities in school or their line manager where they are unsure about the nature of their concerns. The designated person should ensure that appropriate and accessible advice and support systems are in place should they be required.

Empowering disabled children and promoting well-being

The primary responsibility for safeguarding and promoting the well-being of children lies with adults, as does the responsibility to empower children. Cultures and practices that empower disabled children will give them more control over their lives and strengthen their ability to protect themselves from harm. Recognition of the rights of disabled children to safety, to communication and to express and have feelings taken into account is key to the safeguarding of disabled children (National Working Group on Child Protection and Disability 2003; Scottish Executive 2006). In schools this will be translated through effective communication and consultation, including complaints procedures, anti-bullying policies, and effective education on personal, social and health issues. It also means ensuring that there are routes by which children and young people can seek help.

Communication

Communication is fundamental to empowering disabled children. However, it should be acknowledged that many children do not have sufficient opportunities to express their views or concerns and that insufficient account is taken of the complexities of communicating with children with language and communication difficulties. Clearly, a child in these circumstances will be at greater risk of abuse that goes unrecognized. Barriers to communication are risk factors for abuse and active steps should be taken to overcome these. Disabled children need an understanding, and repertoire, of words, signs or symbols to communicate their opinions and concerns. Some children with communication impairments are effectively prevented from raising such matters in school because their communication boards or other communication aids do not include the necessary words and concepts. Children who use alternative or augmentative communication methods will need a vocabulary that enables them to talk about sensitive issues, including bullying, anxiety, their bodies, feelings, family and relationship problems and matters of a sexual nature. *Safeguarding Disabled Children: A Resource for Local Safeguarding Children Boards* (Morris 2006) includes information on a range of resources that support the communication process with disabled children.

Consultation

At the beginning of this decade *Pastoral Care in Schools: Promoting Positive Behaviour* (Department of Education Northern Ireland (DENI) 2001) recognized the importance of schools developing a culture in which pupils are confident about expressing their views and in which they know that their views are listened to, respected and acted on. Where pupils are used to being consulted about aspects of school life they will feel more secure, individually, about raising any particular worries or concerns. Both the NWGCPD (2003) and Morris (2006) stress the importance of consulting with disabled children to reach a better understanding of the risks they face and the safeguards that can be put in place. We know that children and young people who feel secure and valued, and who are routinely involved in decisions that affect them, are more likely to seek support when they are anxious as they will have an expectation that they will be believed and that their concerns will be acted on. Newman (2002) explains in detail the benefits of building resilience in enabling children to develop self-esteem and exert control over their lives. For example, children who require intimate care need to know that they have a right to comment on the support they receive. They should be involved in drawing up their care plan and receive explicit information about what is and is not appropriate (see later section on intimate care). This is reinforced by Featherstone and Evans (2004) who, in their review of the helping strategies children employ when they are experiencing maltreatment, conclude that a societal context is needed that listens to children and young people, respects them as active participants in society and in decisions that affect their lives, and responds to them appropriately.

A whole-school ethos of listening, consulting and valuing pupils' opinions is therefore crucial to the provision of effective safeguarding. Children should be enabled to participate at an appropriate level and in their preferred language. Processes for consultation might include circle time, representation on school councils, group discussions, questionnaires and work with individual children. As way of illustration, the importance of school councils reflecting diversity is recognized in the National Assembly for Wales *Guidance for Governing Bodies on the Establishment and Operation of Schools Councils* (Welsh Assembly Government 2006), which makes clear the need to ensure that these bodies are inclusive of ethnicity and disability. Similarly the views of all pupils, including those with special educational needs and specific health conditions, should be sought and appropriately reflected in curriculum planning, teaching and learning, and in all aspects of the school's life. The Education (Disability Strategies and Pupils'

Educational Records) (Scotland) Act 2002 requires schools' accessibility strategies to demonstrate how they increase disabled pupils' access to the curriculum and improve their access to information that is normally provided in writing.

Complaints procedures

Complaints procedures are not yet widely developed in the education sector but they provide a mechanism for children to raise concerns about a range of matters. Effective procedures will also contribute a culture where concerns are identified and can be dealt with at an early stage. Their usefulness will depend on the child's awareness and understanding of the procedure, the processes in place to facilitate communication and the child's trust in the process. Children need information about the procedure that they can understand and an accessible addition to a complaints procedure could be a simple poster showing in words, symbols and photographs the message that 'If you are worried, angry or upset you can speak to...'. The complaints procedure should also be readily available to parents. Advocates play a potentially important role in assisting a disabled child who may need support, find difficulty expressing their views directly or fear consequences to their actions because of their particular circumstances. Peer supporters and disabled advocates have a potentially valuable role to play in supporting a disabled child and may also act as role models.

Anti-bullying

Bullying is a major risk factor for children and young people. This is reflected in the statistics within ChildLine's Annual Review (ChildLine 2005), which identifies bullying as the single most common reason for all children and young people to call, with 70% saying the bullying took place in school.

Mencap (2005) talked to children and their parents and found that children with learning disabilities or communication difficulties are especially vulnerable to bullying. A child or young person with a learning disability is seen as being different; which may make them an easy target for bullying and even exploitation. They can be more easily hurt or upset. They may not realize that it is acceptable to say 'no'. They may take threats more seriously and it may be easier for them to get into trouble. They may not be able to give clear and detailed accounts of what has happened and changes in behaviour may not be recognized as being the result of bullying.

Anti-bullying policies are not always adapted to the needs of disabled children. They need to address specific issues, concerns and experiences that many disabled children face, alongside a whole-school approach that raises awareness of disability issues within a broader context of respect for diversity and provides disabled children with ways of seeking advice and support.

Someone to turn to

Disabled children can face a range of barriers when seeking help. They may not know how or where to go. There may be a range of communication barriers that limit their options to communicate. Helplines may not be familiar with deaf or disability issues or other methods of communication and some disabled children may lack the awareness or vocabulary to describe their concerns and may not have private and independent access to a telephone or computer. All these factors place constraints on their social network and options for seeking help and advice. This emphasizes the part schools must play in bridging the gap. Children recognize the importance of having a real choice of people to go to with worries and problems – including people inside and outside the home, school, college or fostering or adoption service. Disabled children need these choices as well. They may feel more able, for example, to seek help from a particular member of staff, someone outside the school, a disabled person or a disability organization.

Education providers are well placed to address many of the barriers that disabled children can face in trying to seek help. They are able to:

- ensure the child has a vocabulary to communicate concerns and to seek help

- provide the child with accessible information about sources of information and advice

- provide opportunities for children to contact sources of help in private

- develop links with outside disability or advocacy organizations that may enable some children to seek help in circumstances where they might otherwise feel unsafe to do so

- develop independent visitor schemes

- provide opportunities and options for children to speak to a range of staff and the necessary time and support to listen and to respond.

It is crucial that staff respond to approaches by children for help. Effective responses to abuse, bullying, complaints and other concerns or worries will help build trust and empower children to raise concerns and seek help when they need to do so.

Key care issues

In recent years there has been a steady growth in safeguarding legislation and guidance that has helped to offer clarity and ensure compliance across the education sector. Unfortunately, the specific safeguarding needs of disabled children have not been addressed in detail, and schools will need to think creatively and develop innovative policies and procedures to translate the plethora of advice into effective action for disabled pupils.

Maintained schools will normally be able to access support and advice on child protection and safeguarding issues from the local authority lead officer. Non-maintained special schools and independent schools should put together a list of possible avenues of support and advice, which may include child protection specialists from a local authority, an umbrella body, a voluntary agency or an independent consultancy.

The following key issues have particular relevance for the safeguarding of disabled children.

Training

It is imperative that appropriate child protection training, regularly updated, is available to all staff and volunteers. Staff working with disabled children will need to ensure that the training they receive not only addresses the additional risks faced by disabled children, but also equips them with practical and effective strategies that will provide equal protection for these pupils. Standard or basic awareness training will rarely provide the necessary detail and schools should ensure that key staff attend specialist courses, which may be offered by a local authority or voluntary agency.

Learning support

The importance of trained and experienced learning support staff is recognized across the United Kingdom (see, for example, DfES 2006a and Scottish Executive 2006). The importance of this group of staff should not be underestimated. They often work in a one-to-one situation with the most disabled, disadvantaged and disaffected pupils in the school. They are often the first to notice changes in a child's demeanour or behaviour, and the less formal nature of their relationships with pupils may mean that children will choose these staff to talk to about their concerns and worries. For these reasons learning support and other similar support staff should receive the same child protection training and support as the teaching staff.

Out of school and extended school activities

Pupils and students may spend part of their week in other environments, including further education colleges, work experience placements and in breakfast and after school clubs. The extended school provision may also lead to an increase in the number of staff and volunteers on site who are not directly employed by the school. The school should take various steps to ensure the safety of disabled pupils as they access different environments from the school. The child protection policies and procedures of the college, work placement or other provider should be checked to satisfy the school that they are adequate. Special school staff and special needs co-ordinators (or equivalent staff) in mainstream schools will be able to provide advice on any additional arrangements necessary for disabled pupils. Providers who do not have their own child protection arrangements should be asked to read and endorse those of the school, and appropriate police and professional checks should be undertaken for anyone who will be acting in the role of individual keyworker/supporter/carer or trainer. Schools should offer disabled children and young people the same extended school opportunities as their fellow pupils, ensuring that any additional risk factors are identified and managed. Guidance on additional safeguards for work experience placements is included in *Safeguarding Children and Safer Recruitment in Education* (DfES 2006a). When additional services or activities are provided under the umbrella of an extended or community oriented school, whether during or outside school hours, the school's child protection policies and procedures will normally apply, unless the school has agreed to transfer control to another body. The school will need to ensure that all providers using the school site are aware of the procedures, and this will include any additional arrangements for disabled pupils.

Box 5.1 Publications offering best practice guidance

- *Guidance on the Use of Physical Interventions* (children with learning disabilities and/or autistic spectrum disorders) (DfES and DoH 2002)
- *Guidance on the Use of Physical Interventions for Pupils with Severe Behavioural Difficulties* (DfES 2002)
- *Pastoral Care in Schools: Promoting Positive Behaviour* (DENI 2001)
- *Framework for Restrictive Physical Intervention Policy and Practice* (Welsh Assembly Government 2005)

Staff in England should also refer to Circular 10/98 on the use of force to control or restrain pupils (DfEE 1998).

Physical contact

For some disabled children physical support will be necessary to enable mobility, meet their welfare needs, support learning or manage behaviour. The inherent possibilities for abuse of disabled children are magnified, as are the possibilities for misunderstandings around professional standards. There are many situations where both pupils and staff may feel vulnerable, and clarity about appropriate interventions is vital. Physical intervention and restraint is a particularly difficult issue and schools should develop policies and procedures that provide protection for children and support for staff. It is also imperative that such procedures comply with the relevant legislation. Several publications offering best practice guidance are contained in Box 5.1.

Intimate and personal care

The provision of personal or intimate care is probably the most sensitive practice undertaken in schools. All such situations in schools should serve to enable and empower disabled children, to help them to differentiate between appropriate and inappropriate touch and develop in them the confidence to speak out if anyone touches them in a way they find uncomfortable. The intimate care policy should seek to minimize risk without compromising the pupil's right to privacy and dignity. The views of the child or young person should be sought and incorporated in their personal care plan and staff should use the process of personal care to help children value their own bodies and the right to safe care. Personal care is also seen as a process whereby children can learn about appropriate touch, and those involved in providing care are required to ensure that communication by touch is clear, consistent and safe. A sample intimate care policy is available on the teachernet website and is a good starting point for schools wishing to develop their own policy (www.teachernet.gov.uk).

Staffing issues

Recruitment

Schools have specific responsibilities in relation to procedures for the recruitment of staff and volunteers. In England, for example, the requirements are clearly set out in *Safeguarding Children and Safer Recruitment in Education* (DfES 2006a) and in 2008 a new vetting and barring scheme was introduced under the Safeguarding Vulnerable Groups Act 2006. Effective safeguards for their disabled pupils can be met by checking that in all stages of the recruitment process a commitment to equal safeguarding for disabled children is apparent. This should include a statement of the school's commitment to safeguarding disabled children in any advertisement, clear information about the specifics of the role in the job description, and the requirement of either direct experience of, or commitment to, safeguarding and promoting the welfare of disabled children in the person specification. A member of the interviewing panel should be aware of the increased vulnerability of disabled children and should be able to ask questions that will assess the applicant's attitude towards disabled children. The request for references should ask the referee to comment on the applicant's suitability to work with disabled children. Disabled children should be involved in the selection process, enabling them to contribute their opinion of each candidate and also to allow the interviewers to observe the candidate's interaction with the children.

Most schools and local authority human resources departments will have developed a recruitment checklist to help those responsible for recruitment to progress logically through each stage and to record when each stage has been completed. The checklist also provides evidence that the correct procedure has been followed. *Safeguarding Children and Safer Recruitment in Education* (DfES 2006a) contains useful flowcharts to aid the recruitment of staff and volunteers. It would be useful if every school took disability issues into account at every stage of the recruitment process to ensure that the safety of disabled children is a constant consideration.

Managing allegations against staff

Effective recruitment processes should filter out the most unsuitable candidates, but it is a sad fact that there is always the possibility that someone unsuitable, who is determined to find a role in a school, will slip through the net. For this reason schools must ensure they have procedures to manage allegations made against their staff or volunteers.

Malicious allegations by children that are entirely without foundation are rare. Misunderstandings are more common, but schools should not pre-judge the truth or possibility of the allegation. Clear procedures are necessary both to safeguard children and to offer staff an unambiguous and standardized process in a very difficult situation. Staff who work with disabled children do sometimes feel that they are more vulnerable than most to allegations of abuse because of the nature of their role. Schools can reduce the possibility of misunderstandings leading to allegations by ensuring that they have clear policies and procedures, high quality staff training, good staff supervision and management, a staff code of conduct and an ethos that promotes the open discussion of professional standards. Schools must also accept that disabled children are more likely to become targets of abuse and they must empower children to feel confident in disclosing matters of concern.

Whistle-blowing

Staff may be reticent to raise concerns about the behaviour of a colleague, so it is important that schools develop a whistle-blowing procedure that supports staff to approach the head teacher with any concerns. School staff and other professionals may sometimes be inclined to accept a standard of behaviour towards disabled children that they would question for other children. Would they, for example, feel the trousers of a non-disabled child in public to check if they were wet? Or would they tie a child to a chair? The latter is the equivalent of turning off the power or applying the brakes of a wheelchair without consent. Occasional lapses in conduct by staff, such as an over-zealous physical intervention or a failure to respond to a child for long periods, are also sometimes justified on the basis that a particular child is difficult or the job is stressful. Poor professional practice must never go unchallenged. The thresholds for intervention to safeguard children must be equal for all children and the management of allegations a fair process for all staff.

Children and young people: emotional and sexual issues

PSHE and sex education

The curriculum can also be used to raise children's awareness about themselves, relationships, rights, responsibilities and risks, as well as promoting a positive identity, self-esteem and general well-being. It can also be used to show them how to seek help and advice if they are worried or have concerns will enable them to take steps to prevent or stop abuse. Disability-specific personal, social, health and sex education is particularly important in promoting the safeguarding of disabled children and can help disabled children and children with special educational needs to develop the skills to reduce the risks of being abused and exploited and to learn what sorts of behaviour are, or are not, acceptable. Effective and creative ways of delivering personal, social and health education (PSHE) and sex education need to be found for disabled children and this may include the need for more explicit language and images to ensure the material is both accessible and meaningful. Blake and Muttock (2004) have, however, found that PSHE and citizenship for children with special needs was not always given the required level of importance within schools and that some children in mainstream schools were removed from PSHE for other activities such as extra tutoring or therapy. Given the increased risk of disabled children to abuse it is even more important that they should access PSHE and that the learning is reinforced throughout the school environment. *The Safe and Well* guidance produced by the Scottish Executive (2005) makes the important point that children with additional needs should not be regularly withdrawn from personal and social development lessons for additional lessons or other support needs. Unfortunately, Blake and Muttock (2004) also found that despite developments over recent years in working with children and young people with learning disabilities, many teachers and support staff remain unskilled in both the content and methodology of personal, social, health and sex education. They identify the need for resources that encourage creativity and stimulation and are explicit and straightforward.

In partnership with the National Deaf Children's Society (NDCS), the National Society for the Prevention of Cruelty to Children (NSPCC) has been piloting and developing a safety and awareness pack for deaf children (Kovic, Lucas-Hancock and Miller forthcoming). This recognizes the gaps in awareness that often exist for deaf children and the importance of a range of materials to support the learning process. The pack includes illustrations that convey feelings, relationships and differences; animations that illustrate growing up, role plays and group exercises. The materials also use deaf young people to present information in British Sign Language (BSL), audio and sub-titles. Clearly, staff training and materials of this sort are needed to ensure all staff have the relevant skills to work with and support disabled children as is a recognition of the importance of this work and commitment to ensure its delivery.

Children and young people with harmful sexual behaviours

This issue is dealt with in more detail in Chapter 6, but it is also worth considering the issue here. It must be acknowledged that some disabled children may themselves display concerning behaviour. Disabled children are capable of becoming bullies, or may threaten or use violence towards their peers. In addition, research has suggested that around 25% of all sexual offences are committed by juveniles, and studies show that 'a significant proportion of these young people have suffered some form of abuse or trauma and many have severe emotional or learning difficulties' (Lovell 2002, p.7; see Lovell 2002 for a more detailed discussion of these studies, alongside Hackett and Taylor's chapter in this book).

This is an area where guidance is sadly lacking, resulting in wildly differing responses and inconsistent support. Some young people may find themselves plunged into the criminal justice system and placed on the sex offenders register, while others will be dealt with as a child in need of services and protection. Whittle, Bailey and Kurtz (2006) comment that local and national guidance currently offers very little information about interventions following initial assessments, and recommend the development of effective regional strategies for assessment and treatment. Schools faced with a disabled pupil who is displaying sexually harmful behaviour will need to balance the rights and needs of that young person with the responsibility to keep all pupils in the school safe. Disabled children may engage in this behaviour through a lack of understanding of social norms, an imbalance between their sexual and cognitive maturity, poor impulse control, deliberate malice or even as a result of their own abuse. Knee-jerk reactions, based on panic, distaste, preconception or disbelief, are rarely effective and the school should always involve other relevant professionals at the earliest opportunity. An assessment of the child's needs should be initiated along with a risk assessment to determine the interventions necessary to keep the young person and the other pupils safe. Sexually harmful behaviour in a disabled young person is a highly complex issue, requiring a multi-agency response and a commitment to involving the young person and their parents or carers at every stage.

Residential and boarding schools

In addition to all the functions and requirements already considered, residential and boarding schools will be subject to additional standards in relation to accommodation and 24-hour care. Utting (1997) concluded that disabled children living away from home are extremely vulnerable to abuse of all kinds, including peer abuse, and that a high priority needs to be given to protecting them and ensuring that safeguards are rigorously applied. NSPCC research (Paul, Cawson and Paton 2004) conducted in eight special residential schools identified considerable variation between their child protection procedures and practice that, in turn, had significant implications for their ability to safeguard the children and young people in their care. These included child protection awareness and procedures, training, communication with children, the management of children and adolescents' sexuality and behaviour management.

Clearly, providers of residential education need to ensure that effective policies and procedures are in place that address all aspects of the school's 24-hour operation and children's experience. These should include guidance on situations specific to residential care, for example sleeping arrangements, family visits, missing children and independent advocates. All staff and volunteers should be aware of their responsibilities and have the relevant knowledge and expertise in both recognizing and responding to concerns and have a way of seeking advice when they are unsure how to proceed. Child protection advice and expertise must be available to both day and residential staff. Children should have the awareness, communication and opportunities for seeking help and advice from a range of potential sources when they need this.

NWGCPD (2003) identifies the need for the outcomes of residential placements to be agreed by all concerned, including parents and the children themselves, with a key aim being the inclusion and participation of children in their local communities. Robust reviewing systems should be in place and children should have well-supported family contact plans and have access to independent visitors.

Conclusion

This chapter has identified the risks of abuse that disabled children face and the role of education staff in safeguarding and promoting well-being. It has emphasized the importance of effective communication and consultation with disabled children and confirmed the rights of disabled children and young people to equal protection. The need for general school policy, procedure and practice to apply to the particular circumstances of disabled children has been highlighted. All staff must play a crucial role in safeguarding disabled children and all children have an equal right to protection from abuse.

Further reading

Department of Education Northern Ireland (DENI) (2001) *Relationships and Sexuality Education (RSE).* Northern Ireland: DENI.

Department of Education Northern Ireland (2006) *Child Protection: Recruitment of People to Work with Children and Young People in Educational Settings. Guidance for Employers on Pre-employment Checking and Safer Recruitment Practices.* Northern Ireland: DEN. www.deni.gov.uk/circular_2006_06.pdf

Scottish Executive (2001) *Better Behaviour – Better Learning: The Report of the Discipline Task Group.* Edinburgh: Scottish Executive. www.scotland.gov.uk/library3/education/rdtg-00.asp

Scottish Executive (2002) *'It's Everyone's Job to Make Sure I'm Alright'. Report of the Child Protection Audit and Review.* Edinburgh: The Stationery Office. www.scotland.gov.uk/library5/education/iaar-00.asp

Scottish Executive (2004) *Protecting Children and Young People: Framework for Standards for Professionals in Child Protection.* Edinburgh: The Stationery Office. www.scotland.gov.uk/library5/education/pcypfs-00.asp

Scottish Executive (2006) *Changing Childhoods? The Same as You? National Implementation Group: Report of the Children's Sub Group.* Edinburgh: Scottish Executive. www.scotland.gov.uk/Publications/2006/04/24104745/1

Scottish Parliament (1995) *Children (Scotland) Act 1995.* Edinburgh: Office for Public Sector Information. www.opsi.gov.uk/acts/acts1995/Ukpga_19950036_en_1.htm

Scottish Parliament (2000) *Standards in Scotland Schools etc. Act.* Edinburgh: Office for Public Sector Information. www.opsi.gov.uk/legislation/scotland/acts2000/20000006.htm Cardiff: Welsh Assembly Gorvernment.

Scottish Parliament (2003) *Protection of Children (Scotland) Act.* Edinburgh: Office for Public Sector Information. www.opsi.gov.uk/legislation/scotland/acts2003/20030005.htm

Welsh Assembly Government (2002) *Child Protection: Preventing Unsuitable People from Working with Children and Young Persons in the Education Service.* Cardiff: Welsh Assembly Gorvernment.

Welsh Assembly Government (2002) *Sex and Relationships Education in Schools.* Cardiff: Welsh Assembly Gorvernment.

Welsh Assembly Government (2003) *National Standards for the Provision of Children's Advocacy Services.* Cardiff: Welsh Assembly Gorvernment.

Welsh Assembly Government (2003) *National Minimum Standards or Boarding Schools.* Cardiff: Welsh Assembly Gorvernment.

Welsh Assembly Government (2003) *Personal and Social Education (PSE) and Work-Related Education (WRE) in the Basic Curriculum.* Cardiff: Welsh Assembly Gorvernment.

Welsh Assembly Government (2003) *Respecting Others: Anti-Bullying Guidance.* Cardiff: Welsh Assembly Gorvernment.

Welsh Assembly Government (2005) *National Service Framework for Children, Young People and Maternity Services.* Cardiff: Welsh Assembly Gorvernment.

Welsh Assembly Government (2006) *Guidance for School Governing Bodies on Complaints Involving Pupils.* Cardiff: Welsh Assembly Goverment.

Welsh Assembly Government (2007) *Consultation on a New Service Model for Delivering Advocacy Services for Children and Young People.* Cardiff: Welsh Assembly Gorvernment.

Chapter Six

School Responses to Children with Harmful Sexual Behaviours

Simon Hackett and Abi Taylor[1]

Introduction

This chapter is concerned with problematic and abusive sexual behaviours perpetrated by children and young people and their implications for schools. Despite a growing international literature base exploring treatment issues in respect of children and young people who have sexually abused others, there is a lamentable lack of research into either the educational needs of children with such behaviours or the needs of schools in managing such children. A systematic review of the literature into the issue of children and young people with harmful sexual behaviours in schools conducted by the authors revealed virtually no empirical research on this specific issue. Despite this, many schools are dealing with the expressions of inappropriate, problematic and abusive sexual behaviours by pupils on a very frequent basis. There appears to be an enormous void on this issue in terms of both research and practical support, which leaves schools, in many cases, unsupported. How should schools manage situations of inappropriate sexual behaviour safely? Should young people with a history of abusive sexual behaviours be educated in a group setting? If the sexual behaviours occur within the school environment, what are the implications for the institution? The whole issue often brings with it an enormous level of fear, anxiety and uncertainty for schools. Our aim here is therefore to provide a clear and concise analysis of the existing literature so that teachers and other staff in school settings who are on the frontline of professional responses to this issue

1   The authors are grateful to the NSPCC who provided a small grant to fund a critical review of the literature relating to school and young people with harmful sexual behaviours. The results of this review, in part, form the basis of this chapter.

can feel empowered to act in the best interests of the children they are educating.

The scale and nature of the problem

Researchers have acknowledged the difficulty of accurately estimating the numbers of children and young people with harmful sexual behaviours, because of under-reporting and a general level of fear and intolerance about the existence of young perpetrators of sexual abuse in UK society (Hackett 2004; Masson 2001). Official statistics suggest that harmful sexual behaviours perpetrated by children and young people account for a significant minority, somewhere between a quarter and a third, of all sexual abuse coming to the attention of the professional system in the UK (Erooga and Masson 2006). There is little hard evidence of the scale of the problem in school settings, though our discussions with head teachers, designated teachers and local authority child protection officers about this issue suggest that the majority of schools experience examples of inappropriate sexual behaviour in pupils over time and many schools experience dilemmas about how to deal with such behaviours. It is hard to conclude anything other than that the problem of harmful sexual behaviours in children and young people is far more common than the relatively small number of official convictions or cautions would suggest, and that schools are often on the front line in dealing with such children and young people.

Identification of harmful sexual behaviours in children and young people can be a fraught experience for education and social care professionals alike. Understandably, many professionals are anxious about the stigmatizing impact of labelling a child or young person as an 'abuser'. Coupled with this, the broader social context of almost total hostility and negativity towards 'sex offenders' makes this a contentious area, where the stakes for schools, as well as for individual children and families, are very high.

What are 'problematic' and 'abusive' sexual behaviours in children?

One of the most difficult tasks for professionals in this area is defining harmful or abusive sexual behaviours in children and young people (Hackett 2004). At the same time, it is important for professionals to have some shared language and concepts that can be used to effectively communicate concerns about children. A wide variety of labels such as 'young abuser' or 'young sexual abuser' (Vizard 2002), 'young people who sexually harm' (NOTA 2003) and 'sexually aggressive children' (Araji 1997) have been suggested previously. There has been a general move away from describing children and young people as 'sex offenders' or 'paedophiles' as these are both inaccurate for most children and are also highly stigmatizing terms.

A range of terms, rather than one catch-all label, is needed as the issues that professionals face when responding to children and young people with sexual behaviour problems are diverse. A helpful definitional distinction can be drawn between sexual behaviours that are 'abusive' and those that are 'problematic'. The term 'sexually *abusive* behaviour' is mainly used to indicate sexual behaviours that are initiated by a child or young person where there is an element of manipulation or coercion (Burton *et al.* 1998) or where the subject of the behaviour is unable to give informed consent. By contrast, the term 'sexually *problematic* behaviour' refers to activities that do not include an element of victimization, but that may interfere with the development of the child demonstrating the behaviour or might provoke rejection, cause distress or increase the risk of victimization of the child. For instance, it would clearly be wrong to label a young child's masturbation in a nursery class as 'abusive' as this behaviour (although potentially distressing) is unlikely to *victimize* other people. However, as the behaviour might provoke rejection of the child among its peer group and could therefore inhibit the child's social development, it is clearly problematic. The important distinction here is that while abusive behaviour is, by association, also problematic, problematic behaviours may not be abusive. As both 'abusive' and 'problematic' sexual behaviours are developmentally inappropriate and may cause developmental damage, a useful umbrella term is 'harmful sexual behaviours'.

A framework for distinguishing 'normal' and 'harmful' sexual behaviours in children and young people

Another major problem often identified by professionals is uncertainty about whether a child's sexual behaviours should be the subject of concern and professional response, or whether they are part of normal developmental processes in childhood. Sexual behaviours presented by children and young people exist on a continuum that ranges on the one hand from normal and developmentally appropriate to highly abnormal and abusive on the other. Making distinctions in individual cases about where on this continuum any given behaviour fits is a complex process. At the same time, without a clear sense of what is 'appropriate' childhood sexual behaviour, we run the risk of incorrectly labelling children whose sexual behaviours come to the attention of schools as deviant and subjecting them to unnecessary and even potentially damaging interventions.

A number of authors have sought to describe frameworks to help in the identification of types of behaviour across this notion of a continuum (for example, Cunningham and MacFarlane 1991; Ryan 2000; Ryan *et al* 1993). Ryan's (2000) framework is perhaps the most clear and provides a helpful guide for teachers and other professionals about levels of sexual behaviour in relation to both pre-pubescent children and adolescents, as represented in Tables 6.1 and 6.2. The distinction between pre-pubescent and pubescent children is a vital one to make when considering and assessing sexual behaviours. This is not only because of the differing status of children within the education and criminal justice systems, but it is also clear that sexual behaviour often has very different meanings and motivations across these two developmental stages. As Ryan (2000) points out, some behaviours are normal if they are demonstrated in primary school aged children, but concerning if they continue into adolescence. Others, by contrast, are considered a normal part of the development of secondary school aged children, but would be highly unusual in pre-adolescent children, thereby warranting referral for specialist help.

Sexual harassment and sexual bullying

Sexual harassment and sexual bullying represent types of harmful sexual behaviour hardly covered in the orthodox sexual aggression literature but that, we believe, have enormous significance for schools. In a large North American survey in one school district (cited by Steineger 2001) a third of 14-year-olds reported that they had been the targets of offensive sexual comments at school or on the way to and from school. The incidence for girls was twice as high as for boys. Sexual harassment is defined by Shoop and Edwards (1994) as 'unwelcome behavior of a sexual nature that interferes with [the life of the victim/s] and is unsolicited and nonreciprocal' (p.17). Such behaviours have the potential to be both problematic to the person engaging in them and also harmful to those on the receiving end. However, in contrast to many other manifestations of sexual abuse where the perpetrator abuses the victim in a 'secret', one-to-one context, sexual harassment is a behaviour that is more likely to occur in the context of peer group interaction.

Lipson (2001) investigated school sexual harassment in over two thousand North American pupils aged 14 to 17. She found that sexual harassment was widespread in school life, mostly involved pupils harassing other pupils, and had a negative effect on victims' educational and emotional functioning. Boys were significantly more likely to harass than girls and a substantial minority of both boys and girls admitted to using the following means of sexually harassing others in school:

- making sexual comments, gestures or looks (48% of boys v. 29% of girls)
- calling someone gay or lesbian (38% v. 29%)

Table 6.1 Range of observable sexual behaviours of pre-pubescent children

Normal/ developmentally expected	• Genital or reproduction conversations with peers or similar age siblings • Show me yours/I'll show you mine with peers • Playing 'doctor' • Occasional masturbation without penetration • Imitating seduction (i.e. kissing, flirting) • Dirty words or jokes within cultural or peer group norm
Requiring adult response	• Preoccupation with sexual themes (especially sexually aggressive) • Attempting to expose others' genitals (i.e. pulling other's skirt up or pants down) • Sexually explicit conversations with peers • Sexual graffiti (esp. chronic or impacting individuals) • Sexual innuendo/teasing/embarrassment of others • Precocious sexual knowledge • Single occurrences of peeping/exposing/obscenities/ pornographic interest/frottage • Preoccupation with masturbation • *Mutual masturbation/group masturbation • Simulating foreplay with dolls or peers with clothing on (i.e. petting, French kissing)
Requiring correction	• Sexually explicit conversations with significant age difference • Touching genitals of others without permission • Degradation/humiliation of self or others with sexual themes • Inducing fear/threats of force • Sexually explicit proposals/threats including written notes • Repeated or chronic peeping/exposing/obscenities/ pornographic interests/frottage • Compulsive masturbation/task interruption to masturbate • Masturbation that includes vaginal or anal penetration • Simulating intercourse with dolls, peers, animals, with clothing on
Always problematic; requiring intervention	• Oral, vaginal, anal penetration of dolls,** children, animals • ***Forced exposure of others' genitals • Simulating intercourse with peers' clothing off • Any genital injury or bleeding not explained by accidental cause

* Although mutual or group masturbation is not uncommon among children, the interaction must be evaluated.

** Concern about behaviour with dolls that may be rehearsals for behaviour with peers or more vulnerable children.

*** Although restraining an individual in order to pull down pants or expose breasts may occur in the context of hazing among peers, it is clearly abusive.

Table 6.2 Range of sexual behaviours of adolescent children

Normal	• Sexually explicit conversations with peers • Obscenities and jokes within cultural norm • Sexual innuendo, flirting and courtship • Interest in erotica • Solitary masturbation • Hugging, kissing, holding hands • *Foreplay (petting, making out, fondling) • *Mutual masturbation • *Monogamist intercourse (stable or serial**)
Requiring Adult Response	• Sexual preoccupation/anxiety (interfering in daily functioning) • Pornographic interest • Polygamist sexual intercourse (promiscuity***) • Sexually aggressive themes/obscenities • Sexual graffiti (especially chronic or impacting individuals) • Embarrassment of others with sexual themes • Violation of other's body space; pulling skirts up/pants down • Single occurrences of peeping, exposing, frottage with known agemates • ****Mooning and obscene gestures
Requiring correction	• Compulsive masturbation (especially chronic or public) • Degradation/humiliation of self or others with sexual themes • Attempting to expose others' genitals • Chronic preoccupation with sexually aggressive pornography • Sexually explicit conversation with significantly younger children • Touching genitals without permission (i.e. grabbing, goosing) • Sexually explicit threats (verbal or written)
Illegal behaviours defined by law; requiring immediate intervention	• Obscene phone calls, voyeurism, exhibitionism, frottage, sexual harassment • Sexual contact with significant age difference (child sexual abuse) • Forced sexual contact (sexual assault) • Forced penetration (rape) • Sexual contact with animals (bestiality) • Genital injury to others

* Moral, social or familial rules may restrict, but these behaviours are not abnormal, developmentally harmful, or illegal when private, consensual, equal and non-coercive.

** Stable monogamy is defined as a single sexual partner throughout adolescence. Serial monogamy indicates long-term (several months or years) involvement with a single partner which ends and then others follow.

*** Polygamist intercourse is defined as indiscriminate sexual contact with more than one partner during the same period of time.

**** Although these are not necessarily outside the range of behaviour exhibited by teen peer groups, some evaluation and response is desirable in order to support healthy and responsible attitudes and behaviour.

Source: Ryan, G. (2000) 'Childhood sexuality: a decade of study. Part 1 - Research and Curriculum development.' *Child Abuse and Neglect 24*, 1, pp.42 and 44. Reprinted with kind permission of Elsevier, copyright © Elsevier 2000.

- touching, grabbing or pinching someone in a sexual way (28% v. 22%)

- intentionally brushing up against someone in a sexual way (26% v. 18%)

- flashing or mooning at someone (22% v. 15%)

- spreading sexual rumours about someone (19% v. 14%)

- showing, giving or leaving someone sexual pictures (19% v. 10%)

- pulling at someone's clothing in a sexual way (17% v 10%)

- blocking someone's way or cornering someone in a sexual way (13% v 7%).

Assessment of instances of sexual harassment in schools calls for careful attention to the following factors (adapted from Steineger 2001, p.9):

- the nature of the behaviour

- how often it occurred

- how long it continued

- the age of the victims and the perpetrator/s and the nature of their relationship

- the extent of the power differential between those involved

- whether the behaviour adversely affected one or more pupils' education

- where in the school setting it occurred; and

- other incidents at school involving the same or different students.

Therefore, it can be concluded that sexual harassment type behaviours occur relatively frequently in school, often in a peer group contexts. Although these behaviours are distressing to those who are the subjects, they are unlikely in themselves (and in the absence of other risk factors) to be predictive of more serious sexual assaults. In many cases, such behaviours should be dealt with through the school anti-bullying or behaviour policies.

Research findings regarding pre-adolescent children with sexual behaviour problems

Prevalence and context

In a context of little research evidence and policy guidance, it would be easy to assume that primary school aged children are simply mini versions of adolescent sexual abusers, but this would be incorrect:

> It has become crystal clear that children with sexual behavior problems are not just miniature versions of adult and adolescent sexual offenders. In the first place, the variation in the severity of the problems is much greater… The majority of children with sexual behavior problems are not coercing other children into sexual behaviors. (Johnson and Doonan 2005, p.53)

According to Johnson and Doonan (2005), only a small sub-group of children demonstrating *problematic* sexual behaviours are engaging in sexually *abusive* behaviour. To reduce confusion about the criteria used to define a child who is sexually abusive, they suggest that for a child aged 11 and under to be defined as sexually abusive, all of the following criteria should be met:

1. The child has intentionally touched the sexual organs or other intimate parts of another person, or orchestrates other children into sexual behaviours.

2. The child's problematic sexual behaviours have occurred across time and in different situations.

3. The child has demonstrated a continuing unwillingness to accept 'no' when pressing another person to engage in sexual activity.

4. The child's motivation for engaging in the sexual behaviour is to act out negative emotions toward the person with whom they engage in the sexual behaviour, to upset a third person (such as parent of a sibling), or to act out generalized negative emotions using sex as the vehicle.

5. The child uses force, fear, physical or emotional intimidation, manipulation, bribery, and/or trickery to coerce another person into sexual behaviour.

6. The child's problematic sexual behaviour is unresponsive to consistent adult intervention and supervision.

Gray and colleagues (1999) report data on the demographics, psychological adjustment, victimization and perpetration histories of 127 children aged 6 to 12 years who had engaged in what they termed 'developmentally unexpected' sexual behaviours. The average age of the children concerned was 8.8 years and just over two-thirds of the children (65%) were boys. Most of the children had engaged in sexual behaviour involving some element of implicit or explicit coercion. The vast majority of these children (84% overall) had extensive sexual abuse histories, with a higher proportion of girls having been sexually abused (93%) than boys (78%). Gray and colleagues also found that physical abuse had been experienced by just under half (48%) of children displaying the problematic sexual behaviours and over half (56%) had experienced multiple forms of abuse. Many of the children had a conduct disorder (76% overall), with boys more frequently diagnosed (83%) than girls (62%). Attention deficit hyperactivity disorder (ADHD) was also common. Most frequently these children's sexual behaviours were directed at siblings (35%) and friends (34%). Most of the behaviours took place in the child's own home, however the second most common location – in 19% of cases – was school.

Most research in respect of children who have demonstrated inappropriate sexual behaviours has focused on children aged six or above. However, descriptions of programmes working with pre-adolescents such as those described by Araji (1997) have suggested that, at times, children as young as three or four years of age are referred as a result of concerns about problematic sexual behaviours. Little empirical work has yet been done on the sub-group of children identified very early in their childhood with problematic sexual behaviours. However, Silovsky and Niec (2002) investigated the history, sexual behaviours and social environment of 37 young children aged between three and seven years of age who had been referred to an assessment and treatment programme for children with sexual behaviour problems. The average age of the children was just under five years of age. In contrast to other research on children with sexual behaviour problems described above, more of these children were girls (65%) than boys (35%). All but one of the total sample of children had prior involvement from the child protection system, with over three-quarters (76%) having been investigated as victims of sexual abuse. Only four of the thirty-seven children had no known history of sexual abuse, physical abuse or domestic violence.

Although the problematic sexual behaviours of younger children are sometimes viewed as trivial by professionals, Silovsky and Niec found that the children who had been referred had engaged in frequent and severe problematic sexual behaviours, with over half (54%) touching other children's genitals after having been told not to, over a third (38%) attempting to have sexual intercourse with another child or adult, and one-fifth (20%) putting their mouth on another person's sexual body parts.

The risk of continuing inappropriate sexual behaviour in pre-adolescent children

There has been little research into the likelihood that children's problematic sexual behaviours will persist and escalate through childhood and into adolescence. However, two randomized control studies (Bonner, Walker and Berliner 1999; Pithers and Gray 1993) have found that short-term therapeutic intervention with children and their parents can greatly reduce, if not eliminate, inappropriate sexual behaviours in most pre-adolescent children. In these studies, only about 15% of the children continued to demonstrate inappropriate sexual behaviours after 12 weeks of group sessions. When followed up one and two years after the intervention, change had been sustained in most cases. In both of these studies, more general play approaches were just as effective as more focused 'sexual abuse specific' work. The important message here is that with short-term intervention and with ongoing support, it is unlikely that such behaviours will continue. Indeed, as young children demonstrating sexual behaviour problems are generally trying to solve feelings of confusion, anxiety, shame, or anger about sex and sexuality through these behaviours, they need responses that are supportive, understanding and promote their integration into their peer group, rather than more punitive responses that simply serve to add to their problems (Johnson and Doonan 2005).

Research findings regarding adolescents with harmful sexual behaviours

Importance of context

As adolescence is a developmental stage characterized by a significant increase in the importance of sexual arousal and sexual expression, it is more difficult than with pre-adolescents to define problematic and abusive sexual behaviours on the basis of aspects of the behaviours themselves. Often, it is the context of an adolescent's sexual behaviour, rather than the behaviour itself that raises the concern.

Although it is sometimes assumed that young people's problematic sexual behaviours are experimental or of a minor nature, this is not borne out in the literature. In Taylor's (2003) UK study of all 227 young people referred for sexually abusive behaviours in one city over a six-year period, 93% were referred for behaviours involving physical contact with the victim's genitals, with only 7% referred for non-contact behaviours. 31% of young people had actually penetrated their victims and a further 15% had attempted penetration.

The vast majority of adolescents engaging in sexually abusive behaviours are male, even taking into account under-reporting of young women and the lack of available specialist treatment programmes for young women. For example, in Ryan et al.'s (1996) study of a large sample of 1600 adolescent sexual abusers, males represented 97.4% of the total sample. Most victims of young people who have sexually abused appear to be children known to the young person. In Taylor's (2003) study, out of a total of 402 alleged incidents, only 3% involved strangers. The average age of victims was just over eight years old, but Taylor found two peak ages for victims of 5 and 12 years old. It could be that this finding reflects differences in sub-groups of young people; in other words some adolescents target vulnerable young children, while others pose little risk to children but target vulnerable peers. It is also of interest that the peak ages of victims in Taylor's study represent periods of transition for children in terms of schooling.

Similarly, while research typically suggests that females are abused by young people at approximately twice the rate of males, most young people appear to select either male or female victims. For example, Dolan and colleagues (1996) found that only 7% of young people had abused victims of both sexes and Manocha and Mezey (1998) found only 6%. We can conclude that most young people who have abused pose risks to particular groups of children, but in most cases not to all children in all contexts. This emphasizes the importance of careful assessment of risk in each individual case to help inform decisions about risk management. This is an important message for schools. If a 15-year-old young man is known to have abused a child of five years of age, but is assessed as posing little risk to peer aged children, it may be very possible to maintain this young person in the school environment with an appropriate level of monitoring.

Young women with harmful sexual behaviours

Although there is increasing recognition of the small proportion of young women who sexually abuse others, empirical research into this population is thin on the ground. Of 227 young people in Taylor's (2003) sample, only 19 were female. None of these young women had been cautioned or convicted as a result of their behaviours. The vast majority (74%) were the subject of one complaint only. All victims were known to the young women concerned and the overwhelming majority of victims (80%) were younger children. In contrast to findings on gender of victim in the whole sample, 58% of the young women had victimized only males, as opposed to 32% whose victims were exclusively female. Only two of the young women had victims of both genders.

Young people with learning disabilities
with harmful sexual behaviours

Recent evidence suggests that a significant minority of young people being referred to sexual aggression service providers in the UK have learning disabilities (Masson and Hackett 2003). Anecdotal evidence derived from interviews with teachers and one local authority child protection officer in education services, obtained in the course of an exploratory study conducted by the authors into school professionals' experiences of this issue, supports a view that sexually inappropriate behaviours are commonplace in special school settings.

In a review of the available literature on adolescents with learning disabilities, O'Callaghan (1998) warns against concluding that learning disabled young people have a greater propensity to sexually abuse than non-learning disabled young people. He points out that learning disabled young people are much more 'visible' than other young people to professionals and thereby are subject to a higher level of scrutiny in terms of their sexual behaviour. At the same time, young people with learning disability are often afforded fewer opportunities to develop intimate relationships with their peers and may be given limited sex education. Timms and Goreczny (2002) suggest that young people with learning disabilities are often indifferent to social taboos existing around sexual behaviours. As a result, it is important that we do not portray exploratory behaviours as 'abusive' or pathologize young people with learning disabilities as 'abusers' when the behaviours being demonstrated would be seen as normal in non-disabled teenagers.

There is also some evidence that the sexually abusive behaviours of young people with learning disabilities are often less sophisticated, use fewer grooming strategies and are more opportunistic when compared to non-learning disabled groups (Timms and Goreczny 2002). O'Callaghan (1998) suggests that some young people with learning disabilities may relate on a psychosocial level to children whose chronological age is much lower, but whose functional age is similar to theirs. He suggests the concept of 'abuse without abuser' to describe sexual behaviours in which the person initiating the sexually abusive interaction does not understand the nature of consent or the impact of the behaviour on others. O'Callaghan (1998) stresses that the responses that are made to these abusive sexual behaviours should not be the same as those directed to non-disabled young people. He advocates a balanced approach, which both understands their differential life opportunities and developmental processes, but also takes the abusive behaviours seriously.

School histories of young people who have sexually abused

One of the most significant findings in samples of young people who are identified as having sexually abused is the frequency with which they are reported to have had school problems, as well as involvement with other professional services, prior to the emergence of their sexually abusive behaviours. In Dolan et al.'s (1996) UK study, the majority of young people referred for sexually abusive behaviours (57%) had been assessed by educational psychologists and had been educated in special schools (56.2%). A significant minority (44%) had a history of non-school attendance. In Manocha and Mezey's (1998) UK study, a third of young sexual abusers were described as poor academic achievers. Nearly a third (31.4%) of the sample had a statement of special educational need, mostly for a combination of learning and behavioural difficulties, and a significant minority (15.7%) had attended special school. There were frequent reports of school exclusions (21.6%), chronic non-attendance (13.7%) and of being bullied at school (17.6%). Taylor (2003) also found strikingly high levels of school problems in his UK sample. Seventy per cent of the children and young people had at least one marked school problem, 36% had a statement of special educational need and 44% had been referred for professional help before they were ten years old.

Thus, as well as extensive histories of multiple adversity, loss and discontinuity of care, a staggeringly high proportion of young people with harmful sexual behaviours appear to have experienced long-standing school difficulties. Despite this, traditional models of adolescent sex offender treatment have tended to focus primarily on offence-specific work and:

> have had relatively little to say about the role of educational disadvantage or about the process of re-engaging young people into education systems. This is despite evidence from outside the sexual aggression field that educational achievement can serve as a vitally important protective factor in the life of high-risk youth. (Hackett 2004, p.27)

These findings lend support to a view that schools are not only in a good position to identify behaviours at the earliest stages in their development, but also that in many cases maintaining young people in schools can contribute significantly to decreasing the overall risk that they will re-offend. By contrast, young people who drift through the system without appropriate placement and educational opportunities are likely to remain isolated, low in self-esteem and without opportunities to build normative and fulfilling peer group relationships.

Risk factors and the likelihood that adolescents with harmful sexual behaviours will re-offend

Although it is commonly assumed that young people demonstrating sexually abusive behaviours are highly likely to re-offend and also to develop into adult sex offenders, this is not supported in the research. The average sexual recidivism rates for young people who have sexually abused are between 3 and 14%, according to Prentky *et al.* (2000). There is a suggestion that practitioners persistently over-estimate the level of risk presented by young people (Chaffin, Letourneau and Silovsky 2002).

Worling and Curwen (2000) collected recidivism data on 148 adolescent sex offenders assessed at a specialized community programme in Canada. The follow-up period averaged six years and the mean age of the young people at follow-up was just over 21 years. The authors compared young people who had been offered 'treatment' as a result of their sexual behaviours as against those who had not, and they found that 5% of treatment completers and 18% of the comparison group were reconvicted of a sexual offence, though the figures for non-sexual recidivism were higher for both groups. Importantly, Worling and Curwen also looked at what was different about those young people who re-offended sexually as opposed to those who did not. They found that the two factors that best characterized sexual recidivists were reports of past and present sexual fantasies about children and more ongoing child-victim grooming behaviours.

Even taking into account under-reporting and the difficulties associated with conviction rates, recidivism studies do indeed suggest that a significant number of young people committing sexual abuse do not continue to sexually offend into adulthood. Indeed, the risk for non-sexual offending appears to be higher than that for future sex offences. At the same time, there appears to be a sub-group of young sexual offenders who are at higher risk for recidivism. While we need more research on this issue, factors such as general delinquency and anti-social behaviours, violence, psychopathy, impulsivity and conduct disorder appear to be the most significant risk markers for this group (Prentky *et al.* 2000; Rasmussen 1999) and should therefore serve as the key high risk factors for professionals when assessing the risk of sexual re-offence in either a school or a community context.

Supporting children and young people with harmful sexual behaviours in schools

The potential role of schools as part of a systemic response

Righthand and Welch (2001) state that interventions offered to children and young people with harmful sexual behaviours have traditionally focused overtly on the offending behaviour. Emerging research about effective interventions in this area suggests that while an abuse-specific element to the work is required, there is also a need for a systemic approach that seeks to address need within all dimensions of the child's life, including their school context and their educational needs (Hackett 2004). Providing children and young people with the opportunity to form secure attachments to counteract the adverse experiences of inappropriate or impaired family attachments is a significant role for schools (Miner and Crimmins 1995 cited in Righthand and Welch 2001). Schools can help to foster 'the capacity of a person to develop positively and in a socially acceptable way in spite of adversity' (Little, Axford and Morpeth 2004, p.109). Gilligan (2000) delineates three dimensions of resilience – a secure base, self-esteem and self-efficacy – and goes on to demonstrate how schools can be effective in encouraging growth in all of these areas.

Assessment

Whether a child or young person has abused outside of the school environment or in it, schools should play a part in assessment. Calder (2001) states that although core assessments will be undertaken by colleagues in other agencies, schools can play a vital role in contributing to a wider picture of a young person by providing information relating to the young person's:

- overall functioning, as witnessed in the school context
- school performance, which can inform an assessment of the young person's goal-setting abilities, self-control skills and self-esteem
- peer relationships and ability to relate to authority figures in a productive manner; and
- ability to take responsibility for their own behaviours.

Developing Calder's work, we identify the following school-related areas to which explicit attention should be given in an assessment:

- the child's observed classroom behaviour
- attendance history
- isolation or degree of involvement in the school environment
- behavioural or disciplinary history at school
- any periods of suspension or exclusion
- any experiences of bullying or being bullied
- the child's interests, aptitudes, strengths and abilities in school
- special educational need
- any school changes, including their reasons; and
- the level of the child's academic attainment in school.

Interventions

Recognition has grown significantly in the UK for a more consistent approach to young people presenting with abusive sexual behaviours that identifies a range of responses commensurate with risk and need in individual cases. For example, in England and Wales, although its specific guidance on children and young people who sexually abuse amounts only to one short paragraph, the DfES document *Safeguarding Children and Safer Recruitment in Education* (DfES 2006a) states that a 'distinction needs to be drawn between behaviours best dealt with by anti-bullying policies and more complex behaviour which can be particularly sexually harmful and where both the perpetrator and the victim may need specialist help' (p.74).

This statement reinforces the notion of a tiered response, such as that described by Print, Morrison and Henniker (2001). Conceptualizing harmful sexual behaviours in this way is a helpful development that can ensure that children presenting with low-risk inappropriate sexual behaviours receive a level of support and information that is commensurate with their needs, but are not subjected to long-term, highly intrusive and potentially damaging programmes of intervention. Conversely, a tiered approach would ensure that young people with more extensive and chronic problems receive intensive and specialist support. Building on, and adapting specifically for school contexts, the work of Print *et al.* (2001), we propose the model below to assist schools in decision-making about different levels of inappropriate and abusive sexual behaviour they encounter (see Figure 6.1).

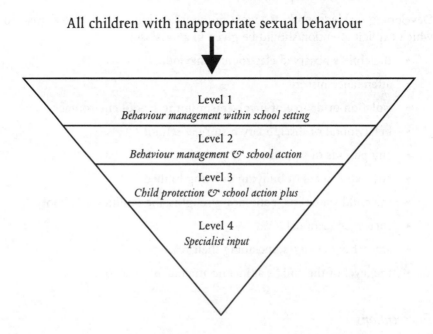

All children with inappropriate sexual behaviour

Level 1
Behaviour management within school setting

Level 2
Behaviour management & school action

Level 3
Child protection & school action plus

Level 4
Specialist input

Figure 6.1: Levels of response in schools

Level 1: Single instances of sexually inappropriate behaviour within the school setting that are reflective of either age-appropriate behaviours in the wrong context or behaviours indicative of sexual harassment. If there are no elements of aggression or coercion and no concerns about the child's wider school or home functioning, the response should be low key. It is likely that many of these incidents can be dealt with appropriately through the school's anti-bullying or behaviour policy. The child should be made aware of the inappropriateness of the behaviour and given guidance and information.

Level 2:   Multiple instances of low-level inappropriate sexual behaviours/sexual harassment despite prior guidance and warnings, or single instances of unwanted sexual behaviours involving an element of coercion. If the young person's sexual behaviours are having an effect on the child's own learning or that of others in school, it will be appropriate to place a young person at school action, following the guidance in the DfES (2001) *Code of Practice*. It would be necessary to consult with parents and implement an individual education plan (IEP).

Level 3:   More concerning sexual behaviours (as indicated on Ryan's framework, see Tables 6.1 and 6.2) or more compulsive expressions of lower-level behaviours. Referral of the young person and parents to social services and a community-based treatment programme is likely to be appropriate. However, in many cases, it will be possible to maintain young people within mainstream education, placed at school action plus.

Level 4:   For the most intrusive and abusive behaviours (on the Ryan framework) where child protection, specialist assessment and/or possible criminal justice involvement are likely. Referral to a specialist service for detailed assessment and intervention is warranted to offer advice on risk management. Assessment will determine the feasibility of maintaining the young person safely in the school context. High levels of supervision are likely to be required. It is likely at this level that the school would consider making an application for statutory assessment.

When children and young people (at levels 3 or 4) are offered external therapeutic intervention as a result of their harmful sexual behaviour, schools can and should be involved in the treatment process. This is important because, as Green and Masson (2002) stress, inadequate management of such behaviour in a young person's broader social context may compound the individual's difficulties. Griffin et al. (1997) highlight how young people who have sexually abused need a consistent response in all settings so that the messages from individual treatment are not undermined by inappropriate or conflicting responses in other settings.

Inclusion and the importance of a whole school approach

Inclusion is clearly a central plank of current UK government education policy. In England *Safeguarding Children and Safer Recruitment in Education* (DfES 2006a) supports the notion of inclusive education for children and young people with harmful sexual behaviours, irrespective of the level of their abusive behaviours 'even when sexualised behaviour is identified and a pupil is on a treatment programme, they still have to be educated and managed in a school setting' (p.74).

However, at the same time as encouraging greater inclusion, teachers are being asked to raise academic standards for all children. Gray and Noakes (1998) suggest that this has resulted in a dichotomy for teachers. They believe that as a result of the introduction of league tables and the pressure to drive up standards, children with emotional, behavioural and social difficulties (EBSD) are being increasingly neglected in favour of those who appear more likely to achieve academically within mainstream education. The difficulty associated with including children with EBSD in mainstream education was recognized in the governmental strategy for Special Education Needs (SEN) *Removing Barriers to Achievement* (DfES 2004c), which recognized that some children are more difficult to include than others – typically because they exhibit challenging behaviour.

Both Chazan (1994) and Norwich and Poulou (2000) cite the results of studies in which inappropriate sexual behaviour was classified as among the most difficult behaviours to deal with in the school setting. Indeed, the results of research examining the views of young people with harmful sexual behaviours found that one of the biggest problems that they faced was exclusion from school alongside the subsequent difficulties of obtaining a place within another school (Hackett and Masson 2006). This suggests that for some young people, once their behaviour has come to light, exclusion from school can further compound their problems.

Successful inclusion of pupils with EBSD can be said to depend on the attitudes of a school and its staff. More specifically, research points to those aspects of in-school practice that characterize highly inclusive schools. Cole, Visser and Upton (1998) found that the following 11 factors were characteristic in schools that managed pupils with EBSD without resorting to exclusion:

- effective, consultative style of leadership of head teacher and senior management team that takes into account pupil and parent opinion
- clear school-wide policies on education and behaviour management that are meaningful to pupils and consistently and humanely enforced
- differentiated curricula
- high but not unreasonable academic expectations
- positive attitude to pupil behaviour with more rewards than sanctions

- high professional standards (efficient planning, setting, marking, punctuality)
- skilful teaching that arouses pupil interest and motivates
- preventative rather than reactive strategies to classroom disruption
- supportive and respectful relationships between all adults and pupils in the school system
- involvement of pupils in school's life; giving pupils responsibility
- an effective system of pastoral care.

Conclusions

The characteristics of children and young people with harmful sexual behaviours point to the need for a holistic approach, which considers all areas of the child's life. Schools have the potential to play an important role in supporting children and young people both in preventing the onset of the behaviour, and in supporting them after the behaviour comes to light. The evidence suggests that schools do not always feel confident or able to fulfil this role. In the majority of cases, children and young people displaying harmful sexual behaviours can be maintained safely in the school environment. However, at higher levels of concern a careful multi-agency assessment should be undertaken in order to inform decisions about risk management in schools. In all cases where a pupil is being offered work by an external agency as a result of sexually abusive behaviours, the school should be made aware of this work and its possible impact on the pupil concerned. For too long, schools have been seen to be marginal to the process of such work. Without an awareness of the process and content of this work, schools are unable to support a pupil or reinforce key messages.

Chapter Seven

Child and Adolescent Mental Health Services (CAMHS) in Schools

Graham Music

Background

In recent years there has been an increasing awareness of mental health issues in children. The Office for National Statistics has estimated that one in ten children has a diagnosable mental disorder (ONS 2005). There is also evidence that the situation is getting worse. For example research by Collishaw *et al.* (2004) has shown that in Britain in recent years mental health problems in adolescents have increased at a higher rate than in other European nations. As worrying as this might be, one can nonetheless reasonably ask what such issues have to do with school life, and what schools should do when they are already over-burdened. But there is evidence that Child and Adolescent Mental Health Services (CAMHS) can decrease the burden on school staff by sharing concerns that schools have been carrying for far too long, and which take attention and energy away from their core tasks.

This chapter attempts to give some concrete examples of how CAMHS has worked in schools and community settings in recent years, and some of the gains that have resulted. It also tries to tease out and differentiate what is specific to CAMHS as opposed to other professional input, such as that of educational psychologists or pastoral support services, personal, social and health education (PSHE) programmes that support emotional literacy, or schools' counsellors. Before that the chapter explains the nature of CAMHS, its place in public sector services for children as part of the NHS, and the hopes for its new role within a reformed children's services agenda.

CAMHS: What is it? Then and now

Specialist services offering help to children and families where there are psychological or emotional issues have been part of the broad spectrum of public service provision for many years, although it is only in recent years that such services have come under the umbrella title of CAMHS, and have been seen as having a central place in the provision of services for children and families. Until the last few decades of the twentieth century such services were often known by the slightly quaint title of child guidance clinics. These began to appear in the 1920s under the auspices of the Child Guidance Council and such services existed in most geographical areas, although the number of staff, quality of training and access to the services varied considerably. Traditionally clinics were staffed by health professionals such as child psychiatrists and child psychotherapists, as well as social workers funded by the local authority, and they were outpatient clinics that offered appointments, rather like other clinics and hospitals. In more recent years such services have tended to be called by newer, slightly less paternalistic names such as child and family consultation centres, but have continued to exist as before, often with increasingly long waiting lists.

CAMH services have traditionally been situated within the health service and for this reason have often been viewed as somewhat alien, incomprehensible and hard to access by professionals working in schools or elsewhere in the local authority. Ironically child guidance clinics were one of the first models of genuinely joined-up services for children. Often these clinics had within them not only child mental health professionals, but also educational psychologists and psychiatric social workers. The result was a joined-up provision that proved extremely helpful in linking schools and child mental health services. Psychotherapists and others in the clinic were closely linked with local schools through their daily contact with educational psychologists and so work with pupils and families was usually co-ordinated. Unfortunately these original multi-agency systems were slowly dismantled. Now much government policy is aiming to re-invent this particular 'joined-up services' wheel. In recent years there has been both an expansion of CAMHS and a change in thinking on how it should be delivered. Community-based services, such as in schools and GP practices, have become more central, while clinic-based CAMHS remain central to all CAMHS provision, forming the lynchpin and central pillar of delivery, and supporting the functioning of community-based provision.

Government policy and expansion of CAMHS

With increased understanding of the long-term impact and cost of poor mental health of children and adults for society as a whole, government policymakers have become more aware of the paucity of current provision and its uneven spread across the country. Policies have evolved to ensure that something is done to change this, with radical plans being made to improve CAMH services. In England the *National Service Framework for Children, Young People and Maternity Services* (NSF) (Department of Health 2004) and the *Every Child Matters* (ECM) agenda (see Department for Education and Skills (DfES) 2004b) were born in separate government departments but share similar aims. The children's NSF has a section devoted entirely to CAMHS and sets out very clear standards for what should happen in terms of CAMHS delivery in forthcoming years, and indeed is a ten-year plan. One of the *Every Child Matters* outcomes is to improve the health of children and young people, with indicators being set across the country that reflect much-needed improvements in their mental health. The success of both initiatives is intimately connected.

The delivery of CAMHS has been organized according to 'tiers' that denote the locus of interventions. Tier 4 refers to specialist services such as inpatient units, whereas Tier 3 services are the traditional outpatient clinics described above. The NSF has particularly argued that CAMHS needs now to be delivered in Tier 2 settings such as GP practices and schools, working alongside other professionals in a multi-agency way. Tier 1 services are those provided by other professionals, such as teachers and GPs, who are generally the first point of contact with professionals. The aim is for the service to cover the period from birth until 18 years old, encompassing all children, including those with disabilities and with particular reference to groups who can miss out on services, such as those from black and minority ethnic (BME) groups (see Pugh and Meier 2006). The NSF is a big initiative that was to be supported by a large increase in funding, with spending on CAMHS in England nearly doubling between 2003 and 2006, although the total national spend remains small compared to other areas in health. It has given professionals in the field hope that at last this often neglected and 'Cinderella' area of service delivery might at last be taken seriously and make more of an impact.

CAMHS staff

CAMHS professionals come from different professions and have tended traditionally to work in multi-disciplinary teams, relying hugely on the very specialist skills and knowledge of their colleagues. The main child mental health professionals in CAMH services tend to be child psychiatrists, clinical psychologists, child and adolescent psychotherapists, and systemic family therapists. Many CAMHS clinics also have social workers, often trained in systemic family or adult psychotherapy. Some clinics may employ nurses with specialist mental health trainings, as well as art, music or occupational therapists.

A child psychiatrist is a central professional in a CAMHS team who might be involved in assessing the risk of suicide or serious self-harm in adolescents, assessing for psychotic symptoms or the precursors of these, and where necessary making referrals to inpatient units. A psychiatrist would screen for serious depression, be involved in carefully monitoring young people with serious eating disorders and, where necessary, prescribe drugs. In relation to younger children, psychiatrists are increasingly involved alongside their paediatric colleagues in assessing children for attention deficit hyperactivity disorder (ADHD) and those who might be on the autistic spectrum, as well as screening for other potential medical or organic issues in children who present with mental health concerns. Their services are often similarly required in making recommendations to the courts. Many psychiatrists have also undertaken further therapeutic training, such as systemic family therapy, psychoanalysis, cognitive behaviour therapy or others.

Other CAMHS professions offer other skills and interventions that make up CAMHS. The child psychotherapist is trained to work in depth with children of all ages for a substantial period of time, as well as working with parents and families. The in-depth understanding of children can then be applied in different settings where briefer and more applied work is appropriate, such as with parents, professionals and families. Within a CAMHS team child psychotherapists might be asked both to offer a unique and clear perspective on what might be going on at the deepest levels of a child's mind, and also to work with children with particularly complex needs when others have not been successful.

As important as the 'depth' that the child psychotherapist aims at, is the attention to 'breadth' and the wider system with which the systemic family therapist is trained to work. They are trained to take account of the wider context surrounding a child; the child who is referred for psychotherapy because they are 'angry' might well be reacting appropriately to an abusive situation at home, or might be responding to a parent's serious illness. Teachers and other professionals will often want to locate the problem in the child and try to resolve it through an individual intervention, but often this will not be the most effective form of help. Systemic therapists work with the whole family, often across generations, and with the wider system, such as other professionals, to ensure that the child gets the help at the level that is required.

Clinical psychologists are trained in a variety of other forms of assessment, as well as in a very broad array of therapeutic interventions, such as cognitive behavioural therapy and other brief therapies. Many will also go on to specialize and develop expertise in specific areas of interest, such as learning disabilities or eating disorders. In many areas CAMHS also employ psychiatric nurses, usually trained in a specific therapeutic modality, such as systemic therapy, as well as in areas such as psychiatric risk. All the professionals that make up a CAMHS team will generally have been trained in the NHS and have experience of day-to-day direct clinical work in a multi-disciplinary context alongside colleagues, and all will have very specific skills that, when combined, mean that the most complex cases can be worked with in a coherent and professional way, using appropriate diagnostic and treatment frameworks. These core skills can be transplanted to community contexts such as schools where a range of ways of working can be applied.

Applications in schools

Given the focus on the community delivery of CAMHS, it is legitimate to ask what can or should CAMHS add to the life of a school. There are various ways CAMHS professionals can be deployed in schools. This depends on a number of factors, not least the culture of the school, the degree of interest in emotional matters, what other professionals are working or linking with a school and, of course, what the specific needs of the school are. Working in a high achieving girls' comprehensive might well lead to many young people being referred for issues such as self-harm, eating disorders, anxiety disorders or suicidal thoughts. In a neighbouring school for pupils with emotional and behavioural difficulties (EBD) the issues are likely be very different, and focus on managing acting out behaviours, working with the aftermath of trauma and abuse, linking with statutory agencies such as social services and the courts, and very often, helping staff to manage and process the often overwhelming experience of trying to help children who are aggressive, abusive, cynical and denigratory. Entirely separate issues are present in a primary school where the majority of the children do not have English as a first language, as opposed to a school in a predominantly middle-class area. Nevertheless CAMHS can offer a range of interventions, supportive activities and linkages in most school contexts.

The range of interventions

Work with families

Family work is maybe not an obvious intervention in the minds of school staff who might tend to focus more on individual children and their strengths and weaknesses. If a child is not learning, or misbehaves, or is unhappy, or aggressive, then not surprisingly the view is often that the child needs help as the problem is 'in the child'. Even when it is clear that a child's issues link to what is happening at home, schools often baulk at the idea that we should work with the family or parents, rather than the child. Yet all too often a child can be sent for individual help such as counselling in schools, when what might be most effective is to offer some help to the family or parents. Box 7.1 is a typical example of skilled work with parents. Very often a child's state of mind is profoundly affected by what is happening in their home life, even as they move into early or late adolescence.

Box 7.1 Work with families

Shirley was in her second year at a girl's comprehensive and had been a model pupil, but recently had begun not to do her homework. When a teacher asked about this she had at first been non-committal and then become insolent. She was referred to the counsellor but she did not want to engage. After consultation with the CAMHS worker the parents were contacted and offered a meeting in school. A tearful mother explained that her own mother, to whom she was very close, had had a stroke and suddenly needed constant care. This had meant that Shirley's mother had been away from home a lot, and had returned quite stressed and with little to offer Shirley and her younger brother, who was still in primary school. Shirley's father had also been affected by his wife's absences, and in a second session was bravely able to admit that he felt both neglected and abandoned by his wife, a little jealous of her preoccupation with her own mother, and also a little awkward taking on the primary caretaking role for his adolescent daughter. Furthermore, he and his wife had both been somewhat taken aback at Shirley's increasing independence in Year 8. She had started seeing more friends, going out on her own, and being less overtly affectionate. This left both parents feeling rejected and not needed. Couple sessions were offered for several weeks, during which much thinking was done about the different tasks facing parents of fledging adolescents, how to allow independence but remain 'there to be left' by teenagers who still needed more of their parents' time, attention and worry than they were prepared to admit. Alternative arrangements were put in place to allow mother to be at home much more, the couple seemed to feel closer again, and arrangements were made for the family to have some special time as a unit, something that Shirley protested about a little, but seemed in fact to be relieved by. Shirley joined some of the later meetings, but by then was doing better, seemed to have settled down again, and her year tutor was no longer concerned. Around the time of Shirley's referral the local CAMHS clinic received a referral concerning her brother, who was also playing up a little in primary school, yet by the time the clinic contacted the family things had settled down. The work with the parents in Shirley's school seemed to have a 'knock-on' effect on her brother's behaviour in his primary school.

A child might be struggling because all manner of things are happening at home, from bereavement, loss, divorce, to parents trying to bring up severely disabled children, as well as more chronic issues such as adopted or fostered children whose carers need help in making sense of the very particular ways of interacting and behaving that one often sees in children who have been traumatized. Working directly with children and families in a school setting, or using a school-based meeting with a family as a conduit for a referral to an outside agency, can make a huge difference to the lives of children, and hence also to their teachers and other staff. Similarly, feeding back to school staff one's understanding of the home situation can be a huge relief, and can alter a teacher's perception of a child from 'bad', 'aggressive' or 'nasty' to 'sad', 'upset' or 'struggling'. This in turn can allow a teacher to soften in their interactions with a child, which can then stop a vicious cycle of hostile interaction. Working with parents, and allowing them into the consciousness of school staff, as well as into school life, is one way in which CAMHS workers can help to make life in school more manageable and bearable.

Work with networks

Often the CAMHS worker might be asked to get involved with a case where the referral clearly needs very particular input from the wider professional system (see Box 7.2).

Box 7.2 Work with networks

In one school, ten-year-old Martin was continuously acting out in class to such an extent that he was disrupting his classmates and seemed to be learning nothing. He would fly into temper tantrums, and yet at other moments appear very near despair, often before lashing out again. Staff were rightly concerned and thought a referral for individual therapy might be appropriate. Yet when the CAMHS worker explored a little further they found a far from straightforward situation. Martin was living with his grandparents following a period on the child protection register, and his father had been violent and his mother a heavy user of alcohol. The courts had stated that there could be monthly supervised contact with his mother. The CAMHS worker met with the grandparents and discovered that grandfather had been recently diagnosed with a terminal illness. The grandmother was distraught in the meeting and admitted to being at the end of her tether, and that her doctor had prescribed her anti-depressants. Martin was

---

getting very little attention at home and was roaming the streets and mixing with unsuitable people. Furthermore, his grandmother had felt unable to withstand the demands of her daughter and contact between mother and Martin had been occurring in inappropriate circumstances in which he had witnessed his mother drunk and out of control. Although these matters soon became a matter for child protection and social services, the CAMHS input was vital, particularly in ensuring that when the network of professionals met they reflected on the real issues, in advising social services about issues to do with contact, as well as helping all those involved to consider what might be going on inside an overwhelmed young mind. Martin was offered play psycho-therapy sessions in which he explored his relationship with adults. Following several professionals' meetings, help was offered to the grandmother in the local CAMHS clinic, better controls were put in place to do with contact, some respite care was offered with a more stable aunt nearby, and Martin calmed down in class.

Such work needs to take account of both the internal and wider world of children. Often children are referred for individual therapy, particularly children in the care system, and a little investigation of the network reveals a system in disarray. What often is most helpful to the child is to work with the wider system; this might include advising a social worker that it might be best for the child to have less contact with an abusive carer, offering support to foster carers, and linking closely with the school staff to help them understand what might be going on for a child that leads to disturbing behaviour.

Individual therapeutic work with pupils

A pupil who is struggling with emotional matters can often benefit from speaking with a trained therapist. This is probably the most obvious and least controversial of all CAMHS interventions, and is often the one schools who refer to CAMHS want most. Children and young people often need the help of someone who can bear what they are going through, who can listen in a way that they maybe have not been listened to before, and can help them see the world from a different perspective. Examples might include the child whose parent devotes too much time to their disabled sibling, a boy who cannot admit fears in his peer group, an adolescent overwhelmed by hormonally inspired infatuations, children who are worried about exams or young people who are suicidal or self-harming. There is ample evidence from the literature (e.g. Kennedy 2004) of the usefulness and importance of such help. Sometimes this can be offered by a well-trained school counsellor and at other times maybe more specialist help is necessary, such as from a CAMHS trained child psycho-therapist, or even a clinic-based service. Very often a child is preoccupied with emotional matters and so cannot concentrate or learn, and their school work suffers, and the support of one-to-one therapy helps them process and manage their worries so that they can once again make use of the learning environment.

While one-to-one therapy is an essential element of any mental health service, a skilled psychotherapist will often see beyond the individual to issues in the family or the system that might be affecting a child. The recently pub-lished government guidelines about childhood depression from the National Institute for Clinical Evidence (NICE) suggest, for example, that an array of supportive interventions, such as counselling, might be attempted initially, before referral to more specialist modalities such as long-term psychotherapy. There is good reason for individual psychotherapy for pupils to remain a central and essential intervention by CAMHS professionals in schools, but skilled and experienced therapists will also show some caution about assuming that children who evidence distress or other symptoms are always best helped by one-to-one attention.

Group work

Seeing children in groups is often seen as something of a panacea. Often teachers are aware that there are several children who seem to have similar problems, such as aggressive behaviour, and there is an understandable wish that they can all be taken out of class and placed in a group where such matters are addressed. Teachers often want work on 'anger management' although unfortunately it rarely provides the solution that is craved. Groups obviously have a lot going for them, not least economies of scale as several pupils can be seen at once. There are many types of groups based on an almost infinite number of theoretical assumptions, but one thing they all have in common is that children can and do learn both good and bad things from each other. One of the perpetual difficulties about running groups, such as for anger manage-ment, is that a group of children are together in a room who may then demon-strate and learn behaviour patterns that most professionals would not approve of. In fact some researchers (such as Kazdin 1987) have suggested that one of the most proven outcomes is that placing a group of highly acting out boys together actually is likely to make their behaviour worse.

There are also other factors to consider. First, the perceived economic advantage of seeing many children at once often turns out to be a myth. The process of setting up a group can be complex and laborious. It is often helpful to talk to staff about the pupils first; ideally parents are met at various stages to inform them and gain their perspective on the child. One would aim to meet each child before the group as well, to try to convey what might happen in a group and why they are being suggested for it. For groups to function well a lot of time and effort needs to go into their planning and organization, and a lot of work must take place alongside, before and after the time actually spent in a room with children. Groups rarely work well if careful thought is not given to the selection process, to the numbers in the group, the mix or composition and the format, and time needs to be set aside to think beforehand and to process the group afterwards. Careful preparation is then necessary to reintegrate children back into classrooms after groups, to avoid manic acting out or other states of mind that leave children less amenable to learning. Inevitably issues arise during a group that might require further work. A child may disclose abuse, or another might urgently need a psychiatric assessment, and time must be taken to link with other professionals.

Nonetheless, groups, when run by skilled practitioners with specific training, can be a very powerful resource and intervention. What they then have in common is that children are helped by each other as well as the facilitators; they are able to model behaviour, reflectiveness and understanding, and they can share experiences which otherwise can leave them feeling isolated and ashamed.

Box 7.3 Work in groups

A group for girls who had been sexually abused provided the context where the girls could share their experiences, and allowed them to feel less alone; it also allowed them to process and make sense of what had happened to them, so they were less haunted by what they had experienced. They also learnt from the facilitators and each other how to ensure that they had the best chances of avoiding potentially abusive situations in the future, and they received feedback about which of their actions might be placing them in possible danger. These groups were proven to be effective (Trowell and Bower 1995), but they were not quick, and required substantial amounts of work with parents, social workers, teachers, other professionals and even with the courts and the police. Yet there is something particularly touching about being able to receive support and encouragement and empathic understanding from others who have undergone similar trials and who might have felt that no one understands them.

Similar groups to the one described in Box 7.3 can be successfully run for young people in other situations and also for parents facing particular challenges. CAMHS professionals will often have experience of a range of group-work modalities, some of which will be more directive and structured, and others which provide a more informal and reflective space.

As well as groups of children who have issues in common, it is also extremely effective to work with children who have very different issues and concerns (see Reid 1999). Although such groups require skilled therapists to ensure that ganging up and scape-goating does not occur, often children develop from learning from the strengths of others. A shy year 6 boy might find he is the oldest in the group and, with encouragement, take on a newly found assertiveness that might be exported to other contexts, such as the playground. The shy child may have their empathy and sensitive attunement praised and be encouraged to use this elsewhere, while a bully might learn to manage the feelings that give rise to the tendency to attack and bully, as well as using their strength at times to support weaker children. Groups can also be an effective way of working closely with and alongside core members of the school staff, and there have been numerous successful examples of groups that have been co-run by a CAMHS worker and a member of staff, which can in time allow these members of staff to run groups themselves. Overall groups can be rich and exciting places of emotional learning and growth, but are also time-consuming and not the quick-fix panaceas they are often thought to be.

Work with school staff

CAMHS professionals can have a role in supporting staff in a number of ways, although the idea of an expert coming in is not always well received. Classroom teaching is a solitary activity and the staffroom is not always a place where fear of failure or stress can be admitted. Teachers often feel that they need to put on a brave face and a coping 'front' while struggling to manage and contain some of the most disturbed and complicated children that society throws up, and with little training in child development or behaviour management. On top of this, their primary task is to help large numbers of children to learn and understand the curriculum. It seems to be asking too much to expect that they can be specialist counsellors and behaviour experts while meeting the needs of high achieving children as well as these others who seem to be on a trajectory leading to much more worrying outcomes. There are a number of ways in which a CAMHS worker can offer support.

Space for school staff to think about the arduous nature of their work, as well as gain greater understanding of the emotional life of children, can have a huge impact on a school's culture by providing a way of responding to serious emotional and psychological issues. This has been written about eloquently elsewhere by Jackson (2002). This may take various forms, and may involve group or one-to-one work. Sometimes a teacher can be driven to tears and desperation by a child taunting them and making it impossible to teach. Often the obvious reaction is to retaliate in return, or to want to blame someone, maybe the parents or the social worker, or possibly the head teacher for not excluding the child; or worst of all, the teacher may blame themselves. Yet often sharing these experiences, and making sense of why the child is behaving as they are, can help (see Box 7.4).

Box 7.4 Work discussion groups for staff

In one school a support group was set up for learning support staff. These are staff who often have to manage the most worrying children, but usually have little training for the work; they also do not have the status (or financial reward) of teachers. They were encouraged to talk about the children they worked with, and the kind of issues that arise in their practice. One child, Frank, was flagged up as a worry. He was described as being a 'spoilt brat' and 'annoying'. It became apparent both that the assistant formally assigned to Frank knew little about his background and that the teaching staff tended to keep such information to themselves. Other assistants in the group were glad to share the bits of information they had about him, and with each nugget of information one could see a softening of how he was viewed. He had been placed on the child protection register for neglect by social services, and was living with his mother at his grandparents' home. His grandmother had been awarded parental responsibility. It soon became clear that support staff can feel rather like the children they care for; they are often told what to do with no warning and they were unaware of educational or behavioural plans. In some instances they might not be told of school trips that meant children would not be there. This led to discussions with school management on how best to facilitate class teachers and pastoral support staff sharing information about the children and jointly planning work.

In the group described in Box 7.4 the members began to digest ideas on how children like Frank see the adult world and how when they communicate their feelings it can make workers like themselves feel inadequate and angry. It allowed staff members to share many of their own difficult experiences, both in and out of the classroom. The feeling of mutual trust, coupled with a renewed interest and excitement about the work, had a noticeable impact on how they went about their daily tasks. This was less about learning new techniques and more about the impact of a change in state of mind. Such meetings can be more or less formal, and more or less regular (see Dowling and Osborne 1985). They have been successful with very different groups of staff, including heads of year and senior management teams, as well as with a group of head teachers from across an authority.

Sometimes the CAMHS worker will realize that some form of consultation and support is needed, even when it is not asked for, and this can be more complicated. For example, in one school with two parallel classes for children of the same age, several children in the same class were flagged up as needing therapy yet none were referred in the parallel class. On the surface these referrals seemed appropriate; the referred children were evidencing signs of disturbance and were clearly struggling in many aspects of their lives. Yet when a therapist observed the two classes in action there was a sharp contrast between a well-boundaried and experienced teacher in the class where no children had been referred, and the rather inexperienced teacher struggling to impose her personality on the other class. Maybe the experienced teacher was more 'out of touch' with the emotional worlds of her children, maybe she deflected her anxiety or was slightly thick-skinned; however therapy for the referred children was not the answer to problems bound up with teaching techniques and anxiety arising from working with such children. In this instance the teacher received support from both the CAMHS worker and the special educational needs co-ordinator (SENCO), but such a consultative approach is most effective when the teachers themselves request it. Such work also requires a leap of faith by staff, and particularly by heads, who are being asked to invest staff time and allow an outside professional to scrutinize roles and practice.

CAMHS staff may also deliver training on aspects of child development, on the challenges of becoming an adolescent, on the signs of depression, and much else. While these formal trainings are often useful, CAMHS workers then need to be available to support staff who are likely to have many questions after such training. CAMHS can also inform discussions around children flagged up in pastoral support or inclusion forums by helping the responsible staff members decide on the most appropriate referral. The intention should be to support the school in thinking about psychological matters so it becomes part of the school's culture, including the preoccupations facing teachers and other school staff. Overall the consultative aspect of a CAMHS worker in school should be to help staff manage some of the pressures and anxieties that inevitably arise in their work, and both to take some of this burden off them (for example through direct work with pupils or specialist referrals elsewhere), but also to give staff the confidence that they can manage these complex children without being overwhelmed. Jackson (2002) has noted that the CAMHS work in a school often begins by receiving many referrals for individual children to be seen. However through supporting, staff referrals can actually decrease over time as staff experience their concerns and anxieties being contained and processed, and they come to feel that they can manage these children themselves, without recourse to an expert.

Joined-up work with clinic-based CAMHS

There are innumerable routes whereby direct work in and with schools can be linked up efficiently to the traditional 'Tier 3' clinic-based CAMH services. A typical example might be situations where there is an urgent psychiatric risk of some kind (see Box 7.5).

Box 7.5 Linking with clinic-based CAMHS

In one local school a learning mentor had been asked to work with a 14-year-old girl, Janine, who had been falling behind in her school work. Various teachers had begun to get frustrated with what they saw as her withdrawn and uncommunicative manner, which had been dismissed in the staffroom as typical adolescent rebellion. Janine seemed wary of the mentor, and the mentor, a sensitive and thoughtful worker, felt inadequate and without much to offer to Janine. The mentor then received a piece of work from Janine that unsettled her. This was a story filled with themes about death, and with characters who felt hopeless and who died young and unfulfilled. The mentor took this piece of work to her English teacher who, at first, noticed only the spelling mistakes and poor punctuation. But the mentor trusted her feelings of unease and took advice from the CAMHS worker who visited the school. The CAMHS worker was concerned and suggested that the mentor should gently explore with Janine how she might be feeling. Janine was, at first, untrusting but soon began to open up, relieved that her rather faint and subtle communications had been received. A session with the CAMHS worker was arranged, which showed up a worrying picture. Janine's mother had a history of drug use and had left the family home a few years previously, leaving Janine with her loving and committed but rather weak father. He had also in recent months begun a new relationship. Janine had in fact taken a small overdose some months previously but her father had not spoken to anyone about this. The CAMHS worker did a full risk assessment and discovered that Janine had recently attempted to renew contact with her mother, which had come to nothing. Janine had also had an early and emotionally painful first sexual encounter. It was also clear that she continued to have suicidal thoughts. The CAMHS worker decided to refer the family to the local Tier 3 clinic, where a psychiatrist and a family therapy colleague met with Janine and her father. The father was very relieved to be offered some help in the complex task of parenting his adolescent daughter. The psychiatrist offered to meet Janine occasionally to monitor progress and Janine accepted the offer to see a counsellor at school. With Janine's permission the CAMHS worker was able to offer sensitive and confidential feedback to her form tutor and mentor. Within a few months Janine was doing better at school and, although she remained a fragile girl, she seemed genuinely perkier and back 'on track'.

The CAMHS worker can get involved in similar psychiatric issues that might either go unnoticed in a school, or else leave teachers and pastoral support staff feeling out of their depth (see Box 7.6).

Box 7.6 Further psychiatric issues

Sharon had seemed a little out of sorts, was rocking herself, mumbled quite a lot, and although some teachers saw her as just 'odd', and others as shirking, she was referred to the CAMHS worker. On closer examination it became clear that she was seeing imaginary things, hearing voices, and showing many disturbed states of mind. More worrying, her 'new age' mother seemed to think that this was relatively normal, as she too saw things, and regarded it as a 'gift'. The father, an erstwhile musician, was a heavy user of whisky and skunk. The mother had in the past been hospitalized following psychotic episodes. Sharon's problems were complex, and included some psychotic and paranoid thinking, and she too was referred to the local Tier 3 clinic when the issues were seen to be too challenging for the school counsellor. She was referred to a psychiatrist and then to a specialist psychotherapist. Meanwhile the school child protection officer had also contacted social services to check out the rather chaotic family situation. The CAMHS worker was on hand to work with staff as needed.

However, links with the local clinic might concern a whole host of issues other than psychiatric risk (see Box 7.7).

Box 7.7 Making sense of children.
A case of Asperger's syndrome

George was six years old when he was flagged up by his class teacher in primary school. He had been in nursery and the staff there had seen him as a rather unusual boy, who in many ways was extremely precocious and able. He could do jigsaw puzzles that were far too difficult for his peers, and seemed to know a great deal about the mechanics of cars. He kept himself to himself in nursery and reception, and was accepted but not sought out by his peers. His new teacher had found that she struggled to warm to George; she felt that he did not take her seriously, and that he was rather cold and obsessional. She would get frustrated with the stubbornness shown when he was asked to do something he did not want to do. The primary school valued CAMHS and had been prepared to invest in mental health work, and the teacher had conveyed her feelings in a staff 'work discussion group' led by the CAMHS worker. The CAMHS worker decided to observe George in various contexts, and then to meet with his parents. This provided sufficient information to refer him to a paediatrician, the result of which was a diagnosis of Asperger's syndrome. Extra educational support was sought and the parents were also referred to the local CAMH service where they received specialist help in making sense of the very different task of parenting a child with this kind of disability. Six months or so later George was offered a form of child psychotherapy that would allow him to develop the more flexible aspects of his personality and understand his own condition. Although labels are not always helpful, in this instance there was relief all round. The parents had been struggling to understand why George was so different from his brother and sister, and they were able to access help for themselves. The teacher was able to make sense of her own feelings and was helped to devise strategies both to help George manage in the classroom as well as helping other children be sensitive to his needs. This understanding informed the wider staff group, many of whom were struggling with children with similar issues.

CAMHS usually consists of an array of services in different locations, and an essential contribution to school life should be to ensure that good links and pathways are established so that pupils and parents can access the resources they need. This often means, as in the examples above, referral into a clinic-based CAMHS team, usually with work continuing in the school context and good communication between the professionals. The pathway may, of course, be reversed. A young woman may be coming out of an inpatient unit after an overdose and will require support in school. Other children and families will not manage to attend a clinic regularly and are more likely to access resources within a trusted community context such as the school. Overall, the aim must be to ensure that CAMHS delivered in community settings is carefully linked up with other tiers of CAMHS so that there are good lines of communication and effective referral pathways.

Conclusions

CAMHS has been around for a long time in various guises and incarnations, and yet recently with the NSF and with more government awareness of child mental health, there has been increased acknowledgement of its importance and of the need for the delivery of CAMHS in community locations such as schools. Although there have been some important examples of CAMHS work in school contexts (Dowling and Osborne 1985; Salzberger-Wittenberg, Williams and Osborne 1999), much of this service initiative is relatively new and under development. This is a time of great change, and also of great opportunity for schools and for children's services generally. The higher profile of CAMHS in recent years and the expectation that CAMHS professionals deliver their specialist services in settings such as schools, means there are huge possibilities for establishing innovative ways of joined-up working, and for children's mental health issues to be placed firmly in the mainstream of service delivery. Of course, change and innovation can be unsettling, and can lead to unhelpful outcomes, such as professional rivalries and huge anxiety. However, it is to be hoped that greater understanding will develop about the importance of children's mental health, of how psychological stress and mental pain can affect learning and indeed disrupt the life of not only the pupils concerned, but also their peers and teachers. CAMHS staff do not hold the monopoly for working with mental health issues in children, but by working alongside professional colleagues in schools they can make an effective contribution to ensuring that schools become healthier, happier and more rewarding places.

Chapter Eight

Counselling in Schools

Susan McGinnis

Background and context

Why do schools have counsellors? There are no doubt as many individual answers as there are schools and school counsellors, but among those responses would probably be these three: the growing recognition of the importance of young people's mental health to their overall development and well-being; an acknowledgement of the particular skills and professional expertise of counsellors; and the statutory responsibilities now incumbent on schools to provide support for pupils.

There has been a change in education ethos since the 1980s when the more simplistic view was taken that schools were primarily for achievement-oriented learning. The steady rise in the percentage of young people experiencing some degree of emotional distress and the knock-on effect of this for schools have prompted many to add a school counsellor to the staff or seek the services of external counselling agencies. This phenomenon also suggests that schools have been finding that troubled young people do not perform as well academically as their peers. A research report by the University of Strathclyde supports this with findings that indicate a 60% increase in concentration and motivation in clients who have attended counselling at school (Cooper 2006).

Even those teachers whose remit is pastoral care will say that they wish they had more time or better skills to offer to pupils who are struggling or unhappy; it can be a source of frustration to know that more individual and focused attention could make the difference between a child who is argumentative, withdrawn or failing academically and one who is happy and functioning well. Counsellors who are integrated into schools contribute to an ethos that demonstrates care for both pupils and staff, and bring a range of additional expertise to the school environment and its internal and external support systems, including those designed to safeguard children. The safe and confidential context of the counselling room and the nature of the relationship that can arise between a young person and a school counsellor mean that it is often the counsellor who is first aware of any risks to a pupil's well-being.

While most schools already recognize the importance of supporting pupils in all aspects of their development, there is a growing body of legislation and government guidance that looks increasingly to schools as providers of both preventative measures and remedial support for the emotional well-being of pupils under their duty of care. Throughout the United Kingdom government guidance on early years and school settings recognizes the importance of promoting positive mental health. Within the last five years, additional legislation has been passed to ensure that children and young people with special educational needs have access to mainstream education. These special educational needs may include emotional and behavioural difficulties and counselling is identified as an appropriate support. For instance, section 7.60 of the *Special Educational Needs Code of Practice* (DfES 2001) states:

> Children and young people who demonstrate features of emotional and behavioural difficulties, who are withdrawn or isolated, disruptive and disturbing, hyperactive and lack concentration; those with immature social skills; and those presenting challenging behaviours arising from other complex special needs may require help or counselling for some or all of the following:
>
> - flexible teaching arrangements
> - help with development of social competence and emotional maturity
> - help in adjusting to school expectations and routines
> - help in acquiring the skills of positive interaction with peers and adults
> - specialised behavioural and cognitive approaches
> - re-channelling or re-focusing to diminish repetitive and self-injurious behaviours
> - provision of class and school systems which control or censure negative or difficult behaviours and encourage positive behaviour
> - provision of a safe supportive environment.

Counselling not only supports special needs but also offers to less troubled young people an opportunity for the personal growth and development that is at the core of the curriculum guidelines in England, Wales, Scotland and Northern Ireland.

Compliance with these statutory obligations will be one of the criteria to be considered when schools are subject to government inspection. School pastoral care systems will be judged on the range of responses they can provide, given their key role in both supporting and safeguarding pupils.

School counselling: meeting the objectives of legislation and guidance

'Safeguarding children' is most commonly understood to apply primarily to child protection concerns but it covers a broader remit, including health and safety, bullying, substance misuse and attending to children with special medical requirements. Government guidance on safeguarding children is based on similar principles in England, Wales, Scotland and Northern Ireland.

School counselling meets many of the stated objectives and recommended arrangements for protecting children from significant harm. The DfES document *Safeguarding Children in Education* (DfES 2004a) reiterates the direction given by the Children Act 1989, which puts a duty on local authorities to provide 'a range and level of services' appropriate to children in need and has as one of its shared objectives: 'Identifying children and young people who are suffering or likely to suffer significant harm, and taking appropriate action with the aim of making sure they are kept safe both at home and at school' (p.6).

It also recognizes that: 'Experience, and consultation with children, shows that they will talk about their concerns and problems to people they feel they can trust and feel comfortable with. This will not necessarily be a teacher' (p.25), and stipulates that 'all education establishments should seek to demonstrate to children that they provide them with a safe environment where it is okay to talk' (p.25).

The Scottish government guidance on protecting children and young people, *Safe and Well* (Scottish Executive 2005), is specific in its mention of counselling as an option for vulnerable children: 'Every child has individual coping mechanisms and support needs. Additional support for learning may involve...counselling or mental health support' (Section A, p.3).

Perhaps most important are the words of children and young people, expressed in the Children's Charter adopted in Scotland in 2004. Developed by Save the Children after consultation with children and young people who have experienced harm, it sets out what they need to help protect them when they are in danger of being, or already have been, harmed by another person. They expect adults to:

Get to know us

Speak with us

Listen to us

Take us seriously

Involve us

Respect our privacy

Be responsible to us

Think about our lives as a whole

Think carefully about how you use information about us

Put us in touch with the right people

Use your power to help

Make things happen when they should

Help us be safe.

This is followed by a pledge to children that includes promises that children will:

- get the help they need

- be seen by a professional such as a teacher, doctor or social worker to make sure children are all right and not put at more risk

- be listened to seriously, and that professionals will use their power to help children

- be able to discuss issues in private, if and when children want to.

Although the charter is stated with a view to child protection, many of its principles are also consistent with the values of counselling.

How does counselling support safeguarding children in school?

While children and young people who wish to share a trouble will very often seek out a teacher or member of staff that they know and feel comfortable with, some find this very closeness, and the fact that they will need to encounter that person on a daily basis, a hindrance rather than a help. This is especially true where they feel embarrassed or ashamed about what is happening to them. In these cases, a counsellor – who may be seen as someone slightly separate from other school staff – could be the person to whom a pupil might wish to speak. Children and young people in schools where there is a counselling service will know that the counselling room is a safe place to talk. They may come for any number of reasons but it is often through building a relationship with the counsellor that they reveal that they are being bullied or that they have been experimenting with drugs. All of the research on school counselling indicates that family problems top the list of issues that young people bring to counselling. It is not unusual for a child protection concern involving a family member or friend to arise from the starting point of simply talking about how things are at home.

The school counsellor also has a uniquely privileged overview of the emotional life and well-being of the whole school in a way that even a head teacher might not. When the counsellor hears the same issue being raised by several clients, such as a slight increase in bullying in a third year class or a cluster of self-harming among fifth year girls, there is an opportunity for it to be considered on a whole-school level as well as being worked on individually with clients. Very occasionally it might be a certain teacher's name that comes up repeatedly as someone whose manner of discipline is experienced by pupils as extreme or humiliating. In all of these cases, a discreet, non-judgemental and problem-solving approach to feedback from the counsellor to the head teacher can support the school's remit to safeguard its pupils.

School counselling in practice

Professional counselling is distinct from the use of counselling skills that are employed to enhance the performance of other jobs such as teaching and social work. Its focus is to attend fully and respectfully to a young person's inner world, enabling them to express thoughts and feelings that may be new or worrying, reflecting on those thoughts and feelings in a way that can bring clarity and understanding, facilitating them to identify ways in which they might manage differently and, if appropriate, explore options for changing those things that can be changed. Children and young people can often do little more than respond to the situations that affect them and counsellors working with this age group find that young clients will experience counselling as an opportunity to 'get things off their chests'.

Counselling in schools, especially when considered from a perspective of safeguarding children, works best when it is integrated into the school's pastoral care system. Even if the counsellor's presence in the school is minimal it is important that links with school staff are established and maintained not only for instances in which there might be a child protection concern, but also to facilitate the general flow of communication that is necessary for making referrals and providing feedback.

Counsellors working in schools should be trained on an accredited diploma course, hold membership of a recognized professional organization and be either accredited or working towards accreditation. Additional training or experience is recommended for those who work with children and young people; at the very least they should be familiar with the legislation that applies to this client group and have an understanding of the professional challenges involved in child protection cases. They may work in a variety of ways that can include individual counselling, group work and creative therapies and will usually practise within one of several theoretical approaches, or use a combination of approaches. Some school counsellors may also counsel staff, provide training and consultation, contribute to the personal and social education curriculum and support pastoral care staff in their work with pupils with emotional and behavioural difficulties. Any counsellor working with children and young people should pass the same level of criminal records check as other school staff.

School counsellors will have arrived there through one of several possible routes. Some schools will employ a counsellor directly; this might be a teacher or former teacher known to the school who has completed counselling training. A counselling service may be provided by the local education authority, with counsellors either employed by, or self-employed and contracted to, the authority. These counsellors may be peripatetic, travelling between schools as needed, or they may have set days they are available in a school. A local education authority may also have an agreement with an external counselling agency to provide counselling in schools or as a referral resource for counselling outside school hours. Each of these models, and the contracting involved, may affect the ways in which a counsellor responds to child protection situations and can offer the school counsellor some thought-provoking dilemmas.

Confidentiality and safeguarding – are they incompatible?

Confidentiality, especially with regard to children and young people, is one of those issues that perpetually demands thought and dialogue and about which there is little that is universally agreed, other than that it evokes strong feelings and, where there is any hint of a child protection concern, some anxiety. There will be differing views from all parties – young people, counsellors, teachers, parents, social workers, religious leaders – and most will feel that they are right. The laws that help us to understand confidentiality are, like all good laws, open to interpretation to some extent and present schools, and school counsellors, with some challenging paradoxes.

The UN Convention on the Rights of Children, adopted by the United Kingdom in 1991, says that children have a right to be protected; it could be argued that measures taken to ensure their safety take precedence over confidentiality. The Convention also, however, recognizes a child's right to privacy. Case law in England such as Gillick v. West Norfolk and Wisbech Area Health Authority, Axon v. Secretary of State for Health [2006] EWCH37, and, in Scotland, the Age of Legal Capacity (Scotland) Act 1991 enshrine the rights of children to make certain choices if they have the capacity to do so. One of these rights is to seek help without their parents' knowledge or consent and to have certain relationships and contracts they enter into, and their content, kept confidential. This is considered by child law experts to include counselling and is true regardless of whether the counselling takes place within or outside a school, and regardless of a child's age. The law does not stop at the school gates, despite the sentiments of one head teacher overheard exclaiming, 'I don't care about the law. It's my school and I will do what I want!'

Some schools will accept that parents may not have to give consent but will erroneously require that someone – either the head teacher or a member of senior management – provide consent for counselling. While teachers and others employed in schools do have what the law calls a 'duty of care' that requires them to 'do whatever is reasonable in all circumstances of the case for the purpose of safeguarding or promoting the child's welfare' (Children Act 1989, Sections 3.1, 3.5), there is a lingering misconception that this entitles them to take parental responsibility for children while they are in school. In fact the position is that they do have a duty of care to behave as a reasonable parent would do to ensure the child's safety. This is sometimes called 'in loco parentis'. In an emergency they can take reasonable steps to promote the child's welfare. School staff have a legal duty of care towards pupils in their care. This is interpreted in case law as the duty to act as a careful parent would. Scottish law is even more explicit; the Children (Scotland) Act 1995 states, in the section on parental rights and responsibilities, 'Nothing in this section shall apply to a person in so far as he has care or control of a child in school' (Children (Scotland) Act 1995).

In the normal course of events, where there is trust, goodwill, clear protocols and good communication, respecting young people's right to confidentiality is not a problem. When it comes to concerns over a child or young person at risk of harm, however, what is a straightforward matter of reporting for a teacher or other member of staff will not be so for a school counsellor. Unlike anyone else in the school, the counsellor owes what is known as a 'duty of confidentiality' to clients. This is recognized in law as an obligation, in cases where a counsellor has contracted either explicitly or implicitly with a client in a relationship where there is an expectation of confidentiality, to keep any information shared confidential. Should a counsellor breach this confidentiality, a client is entitled to have their case considered by a court and counsellors may be prosecuted. Given that a child who is deemed to have legal capacity can instruct a solicitor, a school counsellor must take their duty of confidentiality seriously. Additionally, while schools should always ensure that the counsellors they employ are fully trained and belong to a recognized professional body, they may not be aware that such organizations require counsellors to practise according to a code of ethics that has confidentiality as one of its core principles. It is recognised by the British Association for Counselling and Psychotherapy in *Confidentiality: Counselling: Psychotherapy and the Law* (2003) that practitioners are under an ethical obligation to regard what their clients tell them in complete confidence.

If a counsellor has signed a contract with a school or local education authority that expects automatic disclosure, they are already presented with a dilemma. Where a counsellor is employed directly by a school or the local education authority, it is most often a condition of employment that authority employees abide by child protection management circulars. These will describe in detail what is meant by child protection, what behaviours and incidents are considered necessary to report and the procedures for reporting and will have the authority's duty to safeguard children as their primary aim. Some have been in place for years and have not been updated to accommodate changes in law and government guidance. Balancing a contractual obligation to report with a professional obligation to maintain confidentiality is a challenging process for counsellors; the principle that joins the two is that of the welfare of the child or young person. It is interesting to note that, more recently, the newly updated child protection management circulars tend to be more child-centred and take into account a young person's right to confidentiality as well as the authority's responsibilities.

Counsellors not employed directly by the education authority are usually expected, often automatically without there being any discussion, to agree to work within the authority's guidelines, regardless of the fact that there is no legal obligation for counsellors to report anything other than cases of terrorist activity, traffic offences or money laundering.

Finally, counsellors might argue that if they are not able to offer confidentiality to their clients, it is unlikely that pupils would use the counselling service. The very fact that a young person can speak privately to someone whose sole purpose is to enable them to explore their thoughts and feelings without judgement or agenda is exactly what makes school counselling such a vital, and unique, part of a school's support systems. To undermine that is to lose sight perhaps of the original reason for engaging a counsellor.

How, then, can a counsellor balance their legal, ethical and professional obligations with the demands and expectations of working within a school environment where one person's definition of 'safeguarding' may be quite distinct from another's?

Facilitators, not disclosers

Schools are naturally information-sharing environments; most pride themselves on the fact that they work in partnership with parents and statutory agencies. 'Joined-up' and 'multi-agency' working are favoured phrases, especially with regard to children and young people, and it is considered best practice for those involved in services for children to communicate with each other. On a day-to-day level, teachers routinely discuss pupils informally in staffrooms or in more structured circumstances such as meetings. In schools where a counselling service has been newly introduced, it is not unusual for a teacher to ask the counsellor how a young person is doing and expect to be kept informed of the content of counselling sessions, with the best of intentions.

The word 'disclose' is an uncomfortable one for counsellors; it implies difficult legal and ethical decisions and the possible loss of relationship with a client. Perhaps a better way of framing it is for counsellors to see themselves as *facilitators* of information instead. It is entirely possible to share information in a way that is sensitive and respectful and does not violate confidentiality.

The concept that underpins this process is transparency and it must take place at all levels of interaction between the counsellor and the school. As soon as a counsellor – or a counselling service – is approached to work in a school, their first step should be to consider all of the legal and ethical challenges involved and give careful thought to the position the individual or organization will take with regard to them; it is best to be proactive rather than reactive in the initial discussions with schools or education authorities. Counsellors should be able to present their legal and ethical responsibilities clearly so that others will appreciate the complexities involved and not perceive the counsellor's views on issues such as confidentiality as precious, naïve or secretive. Equally, the counselling service provider should understand and be fully informed about the authority's legal duty to safeguard the children and young people in its care. It is important to remember that everyone is on the same side when it comes to protecting children from harm and it may be necessary to revisit this common ground occasionally.

Once agreement on the fundamental ground has been established, and bearing in mind that this will – and should – inevitably be an ongoing dialogue as the service develops, the next step is to develop protocols for all aspects of the service including referral, record-keeping and, perhaps most importantly, child protection procedures. There is nothing worse for a counsellor than having to make a child protection disclosure and not knowing what to do or what will happen once the disclosure is made; the nature of the situation means that feelings will be running high and, for the young person's sake, the process must be as calm and reassuring as possible.

One of the thornier issues to be decided is what constitutes grounds for disclosure. Counsellors and others who work with young people may take a different view from schools on self-harming behaviour, for instance. Where the self-harm is occasional and not life-threatening, those in the helping professions often will not see it as an issue requiring a significant intervention, whereas those less accustomed to dealing with the problem may feel it justifies an immediate psychiatric referral and social services involvement. *Safe and Well* (Scottish Executive 2005) takes a moderate and practical view on self-harm in school settings:

> Schools may offer support to the child or young person in the same way as their response to any other sign of distress or need for help. Occasionally, staff may consider that the harm is more serious and presents a higher risk to the child or young person's health and wellbeing. Staff should contact their school's Child Protection Coordinator and may consider if emergency intervention is required... (Section M, p.4)

Another complex issue is that of consensual underage sexual activity. The law is clear that this is illegal and it should, therefore, initiate a child protection investigation. Until very recently, some local authority child protection guidelines included normal exploratory sexual behaviour such as kissing and touching as grounds for child protection action. Again, *Safe and Well* takes a pragmatic view while also recommending action that is appropriate to the level and type of activity:

> Young people's involvement in sexual activity may vary widely from the possibility of willing participation in intercourse and exploratory childish activity to rape or inappropriate adult pressure to participate in sexual activity... These different situations will ultimately result in different responses to children's needs. (Section T, p.1)

When protocols have been agreed between the counsellor or counselling service providers and the school or local authority for these and any other potential child protection concerns, the protocols should be written down and made available to everyone who might need them. Should any questions arise about actions taken to protect young people in school, being able to show that protocols have been followed will be helpful in reviewing the situation.

The next step should be the production of young person-friendly information on the counselling service that describes what counselling is and how to make an appointment, and makes clear the limits of the confidentiality that is offered. An information leaflet should be given to every pupil who asks to speak to the counsellor or is referred by someone else. Parents may also be informed about the service through the school newsletter or by letter. When a counsellor sees a young client for the first time, they will talk through the boundaries of confidentiality and ensure that the client understands them. Pupils may be asked to sign a simple statement that they have understood that the confidentiality offered to them cannot be absolute in situations where the counsellor is concerned for their safety.

Establishing this foundation for a school counselling service is essential and, once it is in place, the counsellor can assume their role of facilitator of information, the person through whom information flows when necessary or appropriate. In practice it works as shown in Box 8.1.

Box 8.1 Good practice for sharing information

Stephen is 13 years old and both his behaviour and his school work have deteriorated recently. One of his teachers is concerned about him and wonders if there is something worrying him. She approaches the school counsellor, Joan, and asks for an appointment to be made for Stephen. Joan is able to see Stephen that week and discusses with the teacher the protocol for giving feedback to her about her pupil. Stephen is then asked if he might like to speak to the counsellor and is given a leaflet and the opportunity to ask any questions he might have. He agrees to meet with the counsellor and see how things go.

In the first session, Joan starts by telling Stephen that what he says to her is confidential and that she will not tell anyone what they talk about without his permission unless she is very concerned about him. She will explain that if she feels that he is at risk to himself or from others, she will let him know and they will need to tell someone. Stephen is reassured that he will be made aware of, and be part of, that process. Joan also tells him that, should he not give his permission, she would still need to inform someone if she felt he was at risk and would let him know what she would say, and to whom. Stephen says that he understands and agrees to this contract by signing a brief statement. Joan also tells Stephen that she does not actively seek any information about him but occasionally a teacher or other member of staff may mention something about him. If this happens, Joan will tell Stephen so he doesn't feel that he is being spoken about without his knowledge. At the end of the first session, she says to him that the teacher who referred him for counselling may ask how they are getting on. Joan and Stephen agree what Joan might say in case that happens and Stephen decides to return the following week. Joan does, in fact, see the teacher and is able to tell her what she and Stephen have agreed.

It emerges over the next few sessions that Stephen's parents are splitting up and that he is having trouble coping with this. He feels angry and upset all the time and cannot concentrate on his school work. This worries him and he finds it hard to sleep, making him tired and irritable at school. Joan explores with Stephen what he might find helpful to make things easier at school and Stephen says he wishes his teachers would ease off. Encouraged by Joan to consider how he could make this happen, Stephen chooses the option of delegating Joan to speak to someone on his behalf since he does not feel that he can tell his teachers what is happening at home himself. Stephen decides which teacher he wants Joan to speak to and together they agree what Joan will say. Joan then makes an appointment to speak with the teacher in a confidential place and explains that she is speaking on behalf of Stephen and gives the information Stephen wishes to convey. The teacher is grateful to have an explanation for Stephen's recent behaviour. She then discusses with Joan how the school might support Stephen, and when Joan next sees Stephen she tells him how the meeting went and what was said.

The example in Box 8.1 demonstrates how information can 'flow' through the counsellor while respecting everyone's boundaries. Each step is transparent and, by working in this way, young people feel included and empowered while still getting the help they need. The school is reassured that the counsellor will keep them informed about situations affecting pupils so that they can take steps to support them and are comfortable with the level of feedback they receive. While Stephen's story is not one in which there was a child protection concern, the same principles apply in more extreme cases as well.

Assessing risk

Because counselling is confidential and takes place behind closed doors, it can give rise to some anxiety on the part of schools over whether the counsellor is disclosing everything they should. How do counsellors assess risk? Where they are not governed by contractual child protection procedures provided by the local authority, they will rely on government guidance and their own experience and expertise, supported by their professional and personal ethics. They may also employ a standardized risk assessment inventory such as the Children's Depression Inventory, Beck Depression Inventory or Goodman's Strengths and Difficulties Questionnaire.

When there is perhaps some cause for concern about a pupil but not to the degree where it would require a full-scale child protection intervention, the counsellor might consult their clinical supervisor, take general advice – maintaining the confidentiality of their client – from a local child protection committee or social work office or confer with the area child and adolescent mental health services (CAMHS) team with a view to deciding what action to take. With permission from the client, they would also speak to the teacher responsible for the pupil's pastoral care, who frequently has more extensive knowledge of the child's family circumstances or other related information that can help the counsellor and the school to identify the best way to support the young person.

In cases where there is a need to report significant risk or harm, this will frequently be straightforward and immediately clear to the counsellor from listening to a young client. Sometimes, however, counsellors will respond to less obvious clues – their own sense of unease, a word or a phrase a child uses, the mood or body language of their client – and skilfully work to understand more about the child's situation.

Supporting children and young people
through the disclosure process

Disclosure of significant harm means a cascade of interventions that may have a huge impact on a young person's life. The first instinct of a counsellor faced with a young person who is struggling to talk for the first time about something harmful will be to work with what it is like for the young person to reveal their experience, listen to what the client has to tell, prepare them for what might happen when others intervene and discuss how they, as the client, can be involved in that process. These aims are not at odds with a school's child protection procedures but there may need to be some discussion when protocols are being developed about how quickly disclosures are made and the degree to which the young person is involved, especially if reporting is contrary to their wishes. In more complex cases it is considered good practice for a counsellor to consult their clinical supervisor before deciding to make a disclosure. Counsellors will also refer to their professional code of ethics and perhaps seek legal guidance.

When a counsellor has to make a child protection disclosure without the co-operation and consent of the child or young person involved, a significant concern will be the damage this might cause to the relationship they have built with their client. Vulnerable children can find it hard to make relationships and, when they do, the trust that is implicit in that relationship is precious to both the young person and their counsellor. Regardless of the careful contracting about confidentiality in an initial session with pupils, at that stage it may not feel relevant or the young person may forget that they have agreed the limits of confidentiality. When the counsellor expresses concern and says that someone else needs to be told, it can feel like a betrayal. This moment can be equally distressing for counsellors. The young person may feel angry, hurt and frightened and not hesitate to express these feelings. Experienced counsellors will acknowledge the effect this might have on their relationship. Offering another appointment with the option to attend or not can be a way of maintaining some stability and continuity, as well as providing them with an opportunity to retain control of the relationship after an apparent loss of power and equality.

If the young person has not stormed out of the counselling room, or if they have agreed to the disclosure – many are actually relieved when it happens – the counsellor will talk through exactly what will be disclosed. If a young person does not wish for information that is not relevant to the disclosure itself to be shared, this should be respected; disclosure is not a blanket invitation to reveal everything about a client. When the information to be shared is agreed, the young person should be invited to be present when it is disclosed and should be able to decide where that will take place. Since the counselling room is usually a quiet and discreet place, the child protection co-ordinator could be asked to join the client and counsellor there. The pupil should then be told what will happen next and asked whom they wish to have support them during the process. This could be their counsellor, a teacher, a social worker or anyone else with whom they feel safe.

Onward referrals

In cases where there is concern about a pupil, but not to the degree that it would necessitate an investigation, one option is to involve other agencies such as a drugs and alcohol support team or CAMHS. The counsellor may work in tandem with these outside supports and continue to see the client, or may refer the young person to other agencies and counselling will be suspended. Making contact and building a relationship with other services is one of the first things a counsellor should do when invited to work in a school so that there is goodwill and mutual respect already in place when any concerns about a pupil arise. The school counsellor can not only be a link between the school and these outside agencies but can also have the security of knowing that backup is available when it is needed.

The school counsellor and child protection investigations

If a school child protection co-ordinator decides to report a case to the police and social work services, the counsellor may be drawn into any investigation that takes place. The expectation may be that the counsellor no longer has a duty of confidentiality to their client in cases where a child is at risk and, in fact, the law supports this to some extent when it acknowledges that a duty of confidentiality can be limited where there is an overriding public interest in disclosure. The DfES document *What To Do If You're Worried A Child Is Being Abused* (DfES 2006c) addresses sensitively the fact that some practitioners who work with children and young people will be required to respect their confidentiality, and offers guidance on how to share information appropriately.

Counsellors who continue to work with clients when a child protection case is to be tried in court need to be aware of how this might affect the counselling sessions. Both England/Wales and Scotland have published information packs for therapists detailing what must be avoided in order not to contaminate evidence provided by the young person who is the subject of the court case. Additionally, school counsellors involved in court cases may have their case notes subpoenaed, including notes for their personal use. This is another complex issue for counsellors, especially school counsellors, since some keep limited notes – or no notes – in order to avoid confidential material being considered part of the school record. Good practice guidance for school counsellors on record-keeping recommends that practitioners shred any notes that they use for clinical supervision.

Conclusion

For all of the challenges, inherent dissonances and delicate negotiations involved in counselling in schools, most of those who do the job would not dream of doing anything else. Equally, both anecdotal and research evidence indicate that schools value the added element that counselling brings to their commitment to safeguarding pupils. Finally, and perhaps most importantly, the growth of school counselling, and the increasing body of research evidence of its effectiveness, is also good news for young people, especially those who are vulnerable and for whom school is the safest place to be.

Chapter Nine

The Curriculum and Safeguarding

Yvonne Coppard

Safety and the curriculum

It is easy to view the curriculum as a collection of discrete subjects, each with its own objectives and targets – the latter usually related to test or examination scores. Personal, social and health education, going by a number of titles, is often the subject mentioned as the one where safeguarding and personal safety 'fits'. It is here that the school exemplifies its commitment to a set of values and ambitions for the whole child, healthy in body and mind. David Finkelhor (1984) refers to the 'front of invulnerability' that a child needs to be safer from the attentions of a would-be sexual attacker.

It is not enough to tell children to stay away from strangers or to say no to unwanted touch or to report someone who tries to hurt or humiliate them. These are all actions that require a sense of self and of being a valuable person who deserves to be protected. It requires the confidence to speak loudly enough to be heard and the certain knowledge that someone, somewhere, is going to back them up. Staying safe is as much to do with a child's emerging personality as it is to do with vetting, supervision and stay-safe messages. A nurturing family is a jewel beyond price in the life of a child – and so is a good, supportive school.

A safeguarding approach to a personal safety curriculum starts with the ability to think the unthinkable: that those who are expected to love and nurture children sometimes turn on and harm them. This chapter suggests some examples of the way the school curriculum should reflect and enhance the safeguarding environment in school by delivering good quality personal safety information and helping pupils build the skills they need to keep themselves safe. The strategies outlined here are easy, inexpensive and have been used countless times as part of Cambridgeshire's personal safety programme, *Staying Safe*, which has been working successfully in schools for over 20 years. This programme is explored in more detail later in the chapter.

The best personal safety work does not give children a notion of the world as a frightening place with scary people waiting to prey on them. It does not mention abuse: it has no need to, since the message we need to give children about abuse are exactly the same as the messages that will help them deal with fears of the dark, being lost or having no friends. The skills that they need to stay safe from abusers are the same skills that will help them become confident, independent thinkers who can deal with bullies, peer pressure, risk and uncertainty. Good personal safety work, in short, equips children to face the world with a bold fearlessness that enables them to explore and stretch their horizons, combined with an understanding that sometimes things go wrong and they need to be able to deal with them.

Harnessing what children know: the school survey

It is important to give children the chance to express a view about what they see around them and to take their views seriously. They are then more likely to seek help and advice from school staff when they are distressed about something sensitive, whether its source is in or outside the school. School staff should walk around their school – inside and out – and try to view it with the eyes of a pupil in each age range. They need to imagine being a child in the school to begin to understand its strengths and weaknesses. Ideally pupils would also be involved in any assessment of the school. Even the youngest children can be involved by asking them to look at areas of the school at different times of the day and to record their feelings by indicating which 'face' best reflects how they are feeling (see Figure 9.1). The older groups are able to score on a range from 1 to 5.

Figure 9.1: Feelings faces

For older children a basic survey can encompass aspects of the curriculum including, among others:

- design and technology (content and layout of survey)
- art (publicity posters)

- maths (using the results)
- English, humanities and citizenship (looking at themes that come up in the survey).

The list of places and times should be a mixture of those about which staff are confident the children will feel positively, and others where it is thought there may be a problem. For example, the school playground may be included just before school opens and again at lunchtime and after school. Classrooms may be looked at for what it feels like when a class teacher is there compared with during break time. Similarly the toilet areas, the far-flung corners of the field, and the nooks and crannies unique to any school should be explored in a way that appreciates how children might feel as they go about the building. But they also need the opportunity to mention any places that make them feel particularly safe or vulnerable.

Children are also quite capable of coming up with suggestions for how 'sad face' places can be made happier. Some of these may need judicious filtering. One child wanted anyone found being horrible at play time to be tied to a tree, another wanted barbed wire on the top of toilet cubicles to stop people peeping over. However, young children can be surprisingly perceptive. One five-year-old suggested that a new supply teacher should come to the class with the head teacher and should be introduced to every child so that the teacher – and pupils – did not feel so shy. Another pupil in the same class agreed this was a good idea, because it would also help the teacher if someone was naughty as she could 'shout at them *properly*'. This led to an interesting discussion about why people shout and how it made them feel and, in turn, what should be done about it.

With older children the survey can, of course, be more detailed and explore other areas. One good example was developed by the Norfolk Educational Psychology Service[1] in relation to bullying. The survey asked pupils to think about the previous week and identify how many times a specific event had occurred. The cue statements were both positive and negative so as not to add to the burden of children who are already struggling with school life and other problems. Figure 9.2 provides examples of the questions used.

Surveys such as this may be devised by the pupils and staff working together to frame questions designed specifically for the individual school environment. They may be completed by the whole school or by one year group. The results can provide the opportunity to deal with specific problems and involve pupils in safeguarding strategies, as well as informing staff about what is working well and what needs to improve in terms of management and supervision.

---

1   This survey was used in Norfolk and Cambridgeshire in the early 1990s but its origin is now untraceable and Norfolk Education Service are unable to provide a full reference for it.

In the last week:

Someone has shared a joke with me

a) not at all

b) at least once

c) a few times

d) lots of times

I have been teased about the way I look:

a) not at all

b) at least once

c) a few times

d) lots of times

Figure 9.2: Examples of questions aimed at older pupils

The circle of safety

The circle of safety is especially useful as an introduction to personal safety work for Key Stages 1 and 2, but can be adapted for use across the school age range. The aim of this activity is to build around each individual child the awareness of a network of people to whom the child can turn for advice and help when in any kind of difficulty. This is not solely to do with abuse, and should be seen as a positive affirmation of the child's place in the family and community, rather than as a frightening message about how unsafe the world is. Ideally, the safety circle activity would be done at the beginning of each academic year, which also provides the opportunity to help children learn the names and roles of the school staff.

The circle of safety is a discussion exercise and there are several ways it can be introduced. Ideally, this work should be done with the class teacher, fitting into an existing *circle time* provision so that children know what to expect when they sit in a circle and take their turn at speaking and listening. A class activity, during circle time, may be a general discussion about people who help us such as police, doctors, nurses, social workers and so on. This then moves on to name those who help in school including teachers, learning support assistants and lunchtime supervisors. Finally, each child is given a large circular piece of paper (or a large sheet with a circle drawn on it). The children draw themselves at the centre (or a small photo of the child could be placed there), and then, with an adult helper if necessary, write down the names of all the people they can think of who would help them if they were worried, unhappy or afraid.

Alternative versions of this that have worked well include where teachers place a photo of themselves at the age of their pupils in the centre of the circle and talk briefly about who was in their own circle of trust when they were children. The teacher could also build a composite child as an example, perhaps one boy and one girl, including a few suggestions for people who could go on the circle and asking for more ideas. Finally, for very young children a picture of a persona doll could be used (see Figure 9.3).

Figure 9.3: Example of a circle of safety

The essential ingredient of every circle of safety, however it is done, is free choice. It is acceptable to suggest people that the child may have forgotten, but adults should never insist that parents, carers or anyone else goes on the child's circle if the child does not want to put them there. However, it is important to ensure that each child's circle includes the different environments of home, school and the community, to give the child the greatest chance of finding someone who will help.

Bullying: a way in

Dealing with, and countering, bullying is part of both the Department for Children, Schools and Families' guidance on Social and Emotional Aspects of Learning (SEAL) (see www.teachernet.gov.uk/teachingandlearning/socialandpastoral/sebs1/seal/) and the Primary National Strategy. It is also an essential part of the safeguarding curriculum. The subject can be looked at through many curriculum subjects including history, psychology, literature, citizenship, creative writing, statistical analysis, art, design and information technology. Many children have experienced bullying by the end of their first school year, whether as a bully, a target or a bystander. The messages that are designed to help keep children safe from abuse are exactly the same as those used in the context of bullying.

Bullying and abuse: key messages

Whatever curriculum is planned around personal safety, a number of central messages need to be included across the school age range. The messages that children need to hear, in an age-appropriate form, are described below.

My body, and some space around it, belongs to me and I am in control of it

Bullies and abusers alike invade personal space and make their victims feel uncomfortable. Therefore, if someone comes into that space and does something that makes the child feel uncomfortable or afraid, the child has a right to say 'No, stop that!' If that does not work, they have the right to tell someone in their circle of safety. Similarly, of course, they should not go into someone else's space in a way that makes that person feel uncomfortable or afraid.

Secrets can be happy or sad. You should always tell someone you trust a sad secret, whatever anyone else says

It is possible to talk about the difference between happy and sad secrets with young children. Surprises for Mummy's birthday, for example, might be a happy secret. Children will provide examples of sad secrets that must then be explored. Bullying will probably come up in some form or can be introduced. Secrecy, like invasion of personal space, is common to bullying and to abuse. Trickery may be examined with older children and, with secondary pupils, the boundaries of confidentiality: what would they do if they were asked to keep a friend's secret, when that secret was dangerous or causing their friend harm?

There is always someone who can help me, but I may need to ask more than one person before I get help

Children who take on board the message about sharing sad secrets may well come unstuck when they tell someone, even someone identified in their circle of safety exercise. Children may have to tell several times, particularly about sexual abuse, before they find someone who listens, believes and takes protective action. They need to understand that telling once about bullying or abuse may not be enough, without giving the idea that people around them are unreliable. It is possible to return to the circle of safety with the youngest children and ask them who they would go to first if they were worried or afraid about something that might happen at school, or at home or in the park. Who would they tell? Let each child identify one individual from their circle. It will usually be a parent, but each child must be allowed to nominate for themselves. The teacher can then ask whom they would go to if that person was not listening, or told you it was fine yet the child did not think it was fine. Who else could you tell? It is important to try to steer children in the direction of a progression from one environment into another. So if a child initially names someone from home the teacher can then explore if there is anyone at school and then in the neighbourhood.

With older pupils, who are beginning to get to grips with concepts such as abuse as well as bullying, they can be guided to sites on the Internet that help children who are in trouble, such as Kidscape, Childline and NSPCC (details are in the resource list at the end of the chapter).

Don't go anywhere, with anyone...

- (Younger children) – unless the person looking after you knows where you are going.

- (Older children) – unless someone you trust knows where you are, who you are with, and how to contact you.

Traditionally, this is where 'stranger-danger' education has been widely used, but we now know that most sexual abuse comes from someone the child knows well and trusts. Research into children's perceptions of strangers (Mayes, Gillies and Warden 1990) has shown that the very concept of a 'stranger' is difficult for children to grasp. Fifty-five per cent of six-year-olds, 54% of eight-year-olds and 38% of ten-year-olds would comply with an approach from a stranger. Nevertheless, the core message is relevant, especially when, instead of the word 'stranger' the word 'anyone' is substituted and includes the neighbour, the distressed passer-by with the lost puppy, your best friend's mum or dad, the older child who lives down the street. 'What if?' scenarios that use familiar people as well as strangers are useful.

Box 9.1 Example of 'what if?' scenario for young children

'What if you were playing in the garden and your next door neighbour told you her cat's kittens had just been born and asked you to come in and see them? Do you need to tell whoever is looking after you, or can you just quickly pop in to her house?'

(You need to tell, because that person will be worried if they look out of the window and find you gone.)

'What if your neighbour said she was in a hurry and you had to go now? What could you say?'

(You might have to look at the kittens later, then. But you still have to tell someone where you are.)

This sort of exercise is usually associated with young children, but actually it has relevance for young people.

Box 9.2 Example of 'what if?' scenario for older children

'What if you were outside the night club on your own and there were no taxis? What if someone you'd met that evening offered you a lift home?'

(Call or text someone – in front of the driver – to tell them who you are with, giving the registration number of the car, and when you expect to be back.)

In an ideal world, clubbers do not get separated from friends, do not get drunk, and do not accept lifts from people they barely know. A series of 'what if?' situations such as this can help teenagers think through the risks and the options when something goes wrong, and share strategies. But good safeguarding, while it points out the need for caution, has to deal with what is likely to happen, not the ideal. A study of 11- to 14-year-olds by the Child Accident Prevention Trust (2002) found that 40% said they spent their leisure time in dangerous places, and half those questioned said they took risks and dares when out with their friends. This leads naturally into the next key message.

When you're in a difficult situation, you should always assess the risk and the consequences of what you want to do

For younger children, this involves talking about situations such as being lost. Stories and picture books about lost toys and about children being separated from carers while shopping or on a day out provide a helpful introduction to the more abstract concept of risk assessment. Most children can understand and empathize with the fear of being lost.

Box 9.3 Example of what to do if lost

'What can you do if you look around the crowded supermarket and realize the grown-up you came with is out of sight?'

Children should be encouraged to talk about the strategies they may already have been told. It is important to reinforce the good ones and build their skills in being able to look at situations from several angles. Staying still, for example, is a good thing to tell them to do in a supermarket as they will probably be found quite quickly once a carer realizes the child is no longer with them. But it is not such a good response in a big shopping mall where it might be better to find a grown-up who has children with them, or someone who is working in a shop, to tell them they are lost.

With older children, assessing risk must also consider the influences of drugs, alcohol and peer pressure on their behaviour. The core message – consider the options, assess and minimize the risk – remains the same.

Say no, and show that you mean it

Whatever the age of the child, the ability to say 'no' clearly and effectively is an important skill for life. Assertiveness is a very different thing from aggressiveness, although adults often confuse the definitions themselves and mislabel the children in their care. Through drama and music children can explore the range of the human voice, and the art of body language. They can hear the difference between a squeaky, timid voice, an assertive 'I mean it' voice and an angry roar. They can also learn how to get the 'I mean it' voice and the 'I mean it' body language giving the same message.

The ability to say no assertively and stand your ground is not just an abuse prevention strategy as it also works when dealing with bullies, resisting peer pressure and, later on, dealing with partners, families and work.

The following exercise, *Excuses excuses* (Box 9.4), adapted to suit the age and mix of the children, is one way to help them practise the useful art of thinking on their feet. It is not always enough to simply say 'no'. It can provoke a question in return – 'why not?' If a child is stumped for an answer, it leaves them vulnerable to persuasion. A child needs to be able to cope with a 'why not?' conversation – and also needs to know that it is all right to tell lies, in order to stay safe.

Box 9.4 Excuses, excuses

The pupils work in pairs. Each pair lays a coloured piece of wool or string between them. Pupil A is the adult or peer trying to get pupil B to cross the line. Pupil B has to say no and give a reason why they will not do it.

A: Cross the line and I'll let you see my new puppies.

B: Actually, I'm allergic to dogs.

A: Cross the line and I'll share my chocolate.

B: No, thank you. I'm still full from lunch.

A: Cross the line, and you can have a go on my motorbike.

B: Thanks for offering, but I have been on a motorbike and didn't like it.

A: Cross the line, and we can go swimming together.

B: Not today, I've got a cold and I'm too tired.

With older pupils, see how far the conversation can go before one side or the other gives up – this can be used in feedback to generate discussion about other ways to handle a persistent request that you don't want to grant. How assertive should you get, and at what point do you call for help?

Cambridgeshire approach to personal safety; a case study

In Cambridgeshire in the late 1980s a pilot project in child sexual abuse prevention work began in a selection of primary schools across the county. The *Personal Safety Programme* (Cambridge Health Authority and Cambridgeshire Local Education Authority 1987, revised in 1998), later gave way to the currently used *Staying Safe* (Education Child Protection Service 2001) which sought to get schools and parents working together to give children the skills they needed in order to stay safe from abuse – or at least to know what to do if they encountered it. After the introduction of the 1989 Children Act, the authority expanded to become the Education Child Protection Service, a training and advisory service helping schools with all child protection issues. Today, the majority of primary schools in Cambridgeshire and Peterborough[2] successfully integrate *Staying Safe* into their schemes of work for personal, social and health education. The *Staying Safe* materials have undergone several major revisions over the years in order to keep them fresh and relevant.

Staying Safe materials for Key Stages 1 and 2 comprise two ring binders of lesson plans, activity ideas and supporting resources, endorsed by the National Society for the Prevention of Cruelty to Children (NSPCC). The materials can be used as a stand-alone resource or integrated into a wider programme of citizenship, personal, social and health education. For Key Stages 3 and 4 a *staying safe* strand has been written into the local framework for personal, social and health education and citizenship.

The Education Child Protection Service, located in Cambridgeshire's children's services, has prime responsibility for offering and monitoring child protection training within educational establishments in the county. All staff working with children in schools should, in accordance with government guidelines (DfES 2006a), undergo basic or refresher child protection training every three years, so a basic half-day or day training is designed for all teaching and non-teaching staff. More in-depth two-day courses are on offer for designated teachers and other key workers in child protection, and a range of training options are available in related areas such as childhood bereavement, domestic violence, dealing with chronic anger in children, and so on. A database is kept of those who have received training and when, so that the team can access the level of training a school has received and when it is due for an update.

The basic safeguarding training covers recognition and reporting of abuse and procedures; it also looks at how to deal with the situation of a distressed child sharing information about abuse, and how to keep effective records. This is important for all staff because one of the effects of implementing personal

---

2   Peterborough split from the county of Cambridgeshire to become a unitary authority in 1998.

safety work is that children may decide to confide what is happening to them. While it would be convenient if the person chosen for this confidence was the designated, trained teacher for child protection, it is as likely to be the class-room assistant or the lunchtime supervisor so they too need to know what to do.

Schools are encouraged to involve parents in the personal safety messages that are given to children during the curriculum work. Reinforcement of central messages by family and friends brings home to the children most effectively what they have learned in school. Leaflets designed by the Education Child Protection Service are available for schools to send home at intervals, as the work in school progresses. A twice-yearly newsletter for staff is sent to all schools in Peterborough and Cambridgeshire, to every purchaser of the *Staying Safe* resource, to various officers in the Office for Children and Young People's Service and to representatives of partner agencies on the local children safe-guarding board, keeping them in touch with the pack's development and the key messages being used.

In Cambridgeshire, this provision of a team of professionals has become a valued part of the children's services provision for schools. The team of workers, all with a background in education and/or social work, have an intimate knowledge of how schools work. They are available for advice on a whole range of child protection and personal safety issues, either by telephone or in person and they work within an inter-agency structure but with a prime focus on education. Where disputes occur between the school and another agency, the team is often called on to be involved in negotiating a solution, being trusted by both sides to understand the issues at stake. It is this underpin-ning that provides the bedrock for personal safety work and makes *Staying Safe* such a successful contribution to the safeguarding curriculum.

Resources

There are many good resources available for safeguarding work. Some of these are listed below, with a brief note of their target audience. For a wider view, PSHE advisors in the local children's service department are usually able to provide further information. It is possible to spend a fortune on glamorous-looking resources that do not achieve very much so it is important to examine carefully what is offered and to take advice from those experienced in the field. Over time, it will be possible to build up a useful range of resources that are flexible enough to keep up with the changing situations pupils are dealing with day by day.

Acknowledgments

Thanks to Christine Welburn of the Education Child Protection Service, Cambridgeshire's Office for Children and Young People, for advice and permission to use the material created for the *Staying Safe* programme, especially the 'circle of safety'.

Thanks to the educational psychology service in Norfolk County Council for permission to refer to the anti-bullying school survey developed by the service.

Resources available

Books to use with children

Coppard, Y. (2006) *Abuse: Sometimes, Families Hurt.* Blackburn: Educational Printing Services Ltd.

Education Child Protection Service (2001) *Staying Safe – a Personal Safety Programme for Schools: Foundation and Key Stage One; Key Stage Two.* Cambridge: Cambs County Council.

Fine, A. (1992) *The Angel of Nitshill Road.* London: Methuen.

Oxenbury, H. (1987) *Tickle Tickle.* London: Walker Books.

Petty, K. and Firmin, C. (1992) *Being Bullied; Feeling Left Out; Playing the Game.* London: Bracken.

Pielichaty, H. (2003) *Getting Rid of Karenna.* Oxford: Oxford University Press.

Wilson, J. (2007) *Secrets.* London: Corgi Yearling.

Videos/resource packs

BBC Television (date unknown): *Bullying* (a video exploring the topic for 5–7-year-olds).

BBC Television (date unknown): *Go For It! Relationships* (video for 12- to 16-year-olds with learning difficulty).

Carlton UK Television (date unknown): *No Bullying Here* (Carlton TV4Schools video aimed at KS2).

Websites

ChildLine – www.childline.org.uk

Kidscape – www.kidscape.org.uk

NSPCC – www.nspcc.org.uk

Part 3

Safeguarding
and Schools: Training

Chapter Ten

Training School Staff to Safeguard Children and Young People

Enid Hendry and William Baginsky

Introduction

It has been estimated that one in six children will at some time in their lives experience serious maltreatment by parents.[1] While the family is the arena in which children are most likely to experience abuse, the fact that they also face risk of violence within schools cannot be ignored. 'Bullying and discrimination by young people, especially at school, is the most common form of harmful aggression experienced by children and young people in the United Kingdom' (Cawson *et al.* 2000). The risks of abuse by school staff have been highlighted by recent inquiries, both of which have implications for training. The Clywch inquiry in Wales (Children's Commissioner for Wales 2004) looked into extensive bullying and abuse by a drama teacher, and the Bichard inquiry (Bichard 2004) examined events leading up to the murder of Jessica Wells and Holly Chapman by Ian Huntley, a school caretaker.

Other authors in this book have written about the consequences of abuse and its impact on children's ability to learn and achieve. We also know that children and young people find it difficult to tell anyone that they are being harmed. School-based staff in various roles see children for a significant part of the day and are particularly well placed – provided they have the necessary skills, confidence and support – to recognize when children are anxious or distressed and to see worrying changes in behaviour that may indicate they are being abused or bullied. They can and should be someone to whom children can turn for help. But recognizing possible maltreatment is not easy or straightforward. Taking appropriate and timely action requires knowledge, confidence

---

1   Cawson, P. (2002) *Child Maltreatment in the Family: The Experience of a National Sample of Young People.* London: NSPCC.

and a degree of courage. Research (for example, Baginsky 2000; Birchall 1992; Campbell and Wigglesworth 1993) indicates that many school staff lack such confidence to act on concerns and feel the need for additional training.

For schools to play their full part in safeguarding and promoting the welfare of children and young people in schools there is a need for a whole-school approach and a comprehensive safeguarding-training and development strategy that identifies who needs what level of training and how this can best be delivered. This chapter will help in the development of such a strategy by clarifying statutory requirements; outlining their implications for the different contexts within which education takes place and for different roles; and proposing a framework for identifying who needs what level of training and what the key areas of content should be. It also examines some development solutions and indicates sources of help and support.

Developing a comprehensive approach to training on safeguarding children and young people

Local safeguarding children's boards (LSCBs) have a role in ensuring that single-agency and inter-agency training on safeguarding is provided to meet local needs. However, it is not necessarily the responsibility of the LSCB to organize or deliver this training. No co-ordinated plan currently exists for safeguarding training in all educational settings across the UK or in the different nations. There are statutory requirements[2] in all four nations relating to schools' duties to safeguard and promote the welfare of children, and each nation has published guidance specifically for the education sector.[3] However, there is considerable variation in the extent to which they describe what school staff should know and almost nothing about the practicalities of training them. The guidance to schools in Scotland is the most comprehensive, practical and user-friendly. But, for the most part, the development of training strategies and plans and the commissioning, development and delivery of training programmes is left to the discretion of individual local authorities, training organizations, individual schools and colleges. This inevitably results in considerable variation and duplication of effort.

A comprehensive approach to safeguarding training has to recognize the many different contexts in which education takes place. This includes the maintained and independent sector; schools such as academies and city technology colleges that operate independently of the local authority; and residential and

---

2   England – Education Act 2002; Northern Ireland – Welfare and Protection of Pupils Education and Libraries (Northern Ireland) Order 2003; Scotland – The Children (Scotland) Act 1995; Wales – The Education Act 2002 (Commencement No.8) (Wales) Order 2006.

3   England – DfES (2006a); Northern Ireland – Department of Education Northern Ireland (DENI) (1999); Scottish Executive (2005); Wales – Welsh Office (1995).

non-residential schools. It has to cover those in early-years settings as well as young people up to the age of 18, who may be in further- or higher-education settings. An inclusive approach would also take account of those young people educated outside schools, for instance in pupil referral units and in hospitals, and by peripatetic services. Training strategies should also take account of those extended services which increasingly operate on school premises both before and after school and involve people coming onto the school premises who will not have been through the school's normal screening procedures. In developing comprehensive training strategies relevant to each of these different contexts, consideration has to be given to the particular needs of the children and young people and the demographics of the community served by the educational establishment. So, for example, a school serving children from black and minority ethnic families may need to build in time to understand the particular safeguarding issues faced by these children. Depending on their particular backgrounds and beliefs it may be necessary to include training on female genital mutilation or forced marriage and, in some areas, even on ritual killings.

If we accept that safeguarding children is everyone's responsibility then this has significant training implications. An unpublished survey of training needs in relation to safeguarding children was carried out by the NSPCC in 2005 in which 19,000 individuals responded to a questionnaire. Of the educational staff that responded 70% had had concerns about a child's welfare. This compares to the findings of Baginsky's research (2003) into newly qualified teachers, which found that 52% had been involved in a child protection case in the first 12 to 18 months of teaching after qualifying. Concerns can come to the attention of anyone within an educational setting who has contact with children, no matter what their role. Each has the opportunity to make a difference. A young person who is being abused is just as likely to turn for help to a learning mentor or lunchtime supervisor as to a class teacher. A caretaker or classroom assistant is just as likely to notice a child who is being bullied or to recognize a worrying change in a young person's behaviour.

While all those in contact with children are in a position to recognize cause for concern, their responsibilities for action vary. Some will be expected to inform someone within the school or college of their concerns, but will not usually be responsible for taking further action. Others will be expected to make a judgement about whether concerns are such that an assessment and referral are required. Some staff will primarily be involved in identifying child-welfare concerns, while others have a role at different stages of the child protection system in contributing to assessments and planned interventions to help a child.

It follows, therefore, that a whole-school approach is needed to safeguarding training, which recognizes different roles and responsibilities. This should include not only those working directly with children and young people but

also those with strategic and managerial accountability – for example, designated teachers, head teachers and governors. Lord Laming made strong recommendations in *The Victoria Climbié Inquiry* (Laming 2003) on the need for clear
lines of accountability and for those with accountability to be able to satisfy
themselves that the necessary safeguarding arrangements are in place and
working effectively. In England, for example, the Children Act 2004, and the
related guidance and inspection arrangements, strengthen and reinforce that
accountability. Training plans must include access to safeguarding training and
development for those with this weighty responsibility.

Working Together to Safeguard Children (HM Government 2006) provides a
model for grouping different roles together for the purposes of determining
their safeguarding-training needs. This is based on the frequency and nature of
contact with children and young people and with their families or carers and on
the nature of accountability they carry. The groups are as follows:

- A: those in regular contact with children and young people and with
  adults who are parents/carers

- B: those who work regularly with children and young people and
  with adults who are parents/carers

- C: those with particular responsibility for safeguarding children,
  such as designated educational professionals

- D: operational managers who supervise practitioners and volunteers

- E: those with strategic responsibility for commissioning and
  providing educational services to children, young people and adults
  who are parents/carers.

The first of the above groups of people needs a general awareness of safeguarding and where to get further information and help. The second needs a greater
depth of understanding and skills, while the third group has to be sufficiently
expert to guide and direct others. Those with strategic responsibilities need to
know enough to question and challenge and to ensure the necessary resources
and support are in place. All will need to refresh knowledge, particularly as legislation and practice change and as they may have limited direct contact with
safeguarding issues. In the next part of this chapter we consider each of these
groups in turn and what level of competence they need to develop in order to
play their role in safeguarding children. We then look in more detail at the
content of training and options for delivery.

Group A: Those in regular contact with children and young people and with adults who are parents/carers

This group will include lunchtime supervisors, caretakers, school secretaries, those transporting children and volunteers. They need a *general awareness* of safeguarding and where to get further information and help. They should be:

- able to describe what is meant by safeguarding and promoting the welfare of children

- alert to potential indicators of abuse, neglect and bullying

- alert to the risks that abusers may pose to children

- able to report and record concerns in line with procedures

- able to describe their own role and responsibilities for safeguarding children.

Inter-agency training is not essential for this group, but an awareness of the roles of others and the importance of working together would be valuable.

Group B: Those who work regularly with children and young people and with adults who are parents/carers

This will include, for example, teachers, classroom support staff, learning mentors, teaching staff in further education and school nurses. They need *introductory training* that is in more depth than the basic awareness described above and that equips them with the skills and knowledge to:

- describe the different ways in which children and young people can be harmed

- describe what is meant by safeguarding and promoting the welfare of children

- be alert to potential indicators of abuse, neglect and bullying

- be alert to the risks that abusers may pose to children

- know how to communicate effectively and develop working relationships with other staff, volunteers, children and parents to safeguard and promote children's welfare

- describe the roles of other practitioners and agencies in supporting and advising families and safeguarding and promoting children's welfare

- understand and contribute to multi-agency processes to promote and safeguard children, assess their needs and protect children from abuse

- demonstrate knowledge of legislation and guidance relevant to their role
- demonstrate knowledge of organizational policies and procedures and know how to apply these in practice.

Opportunities to participate in inter-agency training would be valuable for this group.

Group C: Those with particular responsibility for safeguarding children

This includes those with designated responsibility within schools and colleges and within the local authority. These staff act as a source of expertise and advice in the school and have responsibility for ensuring others are trained. These are senior staff nominated by the school and it is the duty of the local authority to ensure they are effectively trained. There are no specified training programmes for designated teachers. This means in practice that the level and availability of training for designated educational professionals varies widely. To fulfil their responsibilities they should have the competencies described above for group B and additionally be able to:

- advise others working with children on implementation of organizational policies and procedures to safeguard and promote children's welfare
- support others working with children to respond appropriately to concerns about children's welfare and safety and to contribute to multi-agency safeguarding processes
- maintain, develop and implement policies and procedures to safeguard children and young people
- co-ordinate action within the school to safeguard children, including the provision of training
- create and/or maintain relevant records in line with procedures
- communicate effectively internally and with other organizations regarding specific concerns about a child or children.

Participation in inter-agency training is vital for this group as they need to develop effective working relationships and a full appreciation of the roles and constraints under which others operate, so they can provide appropriate advice, support, mediation and, when necessary, challenge.

*Groups D and E: Operational managers who supervise
practitioners and volunteers and those with strategic responsibility
for commissioning and providing educational services to children,
young people and adults who are parents/carers*

We have grouped together groups D and E and this includes middle and senior managers in schools and colleges, and governors. This group needs the same level of understanding of safeguarding as group B and in addition should be able to:

- contribute to the development, review and implementation of policies, procedures and systems for safeguarding and promoting children's welfare, including safer recruitment and vetting

- contribute to internal and inter-agency plans to protect individual children

- make judgements about the way staff are discharging their safeguarding responsibilities and understand their support and development needs

- represent the school/college's approach to safeguarding at internal and external meetings

- work collaboratively with external agencies on cases of serious poor practice, allegations of abuse against staff and child deaths

- ensure the school/college's safeguarding arrangements are robust and compliant with legislation and guidance.

The content of training

We have described above what different groups of staff should be able to do in relation to safeguarding children with the support of training and development. We now consider what training should cover in order to equip staff with the necessary knowledge, skills and confidence to fulfil their responsibilities. While there are no specified training programmes for different groups of staff in schools, there are various sources of guidance on what should be covered and on learning outcomes. The following are particularly relevant:

- the *Common Core of Skills and Knowledge for the Children's Workforce* (HM Government 2005)

- the framework for suggested learning outcomes for inter-agency safeguarding training referred to in *Working Together to Safeguard Children* (HM Government 2006)

- the Children's Workforce Development Council *Induction Standards* for the children's workforce (CWDC 2006).

The national *Induction Standards* include a unit on safeguarding children and spell out what should be covered in the induction of all professionals new to their role, and include:

- laws, policies and procedures
- providing safe environments
- recognizing and responding to abuse
- working with other agencies
- whistle-blowing.

Whistle-blowing refers to the duty to report unsafe practice of others and knowing what to do if on reporting concerns there is an unsatisfactory response – two very challenging areas that benefit from inclusion in training programmes.

The *Common Core of Skills and Knowledge for the Children's Workforce* (HM Government 2005) has been developed by the Department for Children, Schools and Families (DCSF) and is intended for use in the design of induction, in-service and inter-agency training, and as a tool for training-needs analysis and workforce planning. It sets out six key areas of knowledge and skills for everyone working with children, young people and their families. These are intended to support more effective inter-agency working, through the creation of shared language and understanding. They form part of the integrated qualifications framework under development in England. While specifically developed for England, the content is likely to be more widely relevant.

The six areas are:

- effective communication and engagement with children, young people, their family and carers
- child and young-person development
- safeguarding and promoting the welfare of the child
- supporting transitions
- multi-agency working
- information-sharing.

While one of these areas focuses specifically on the knowledge and skills required for safeguarding, most of the other areas are also essential to this. For example, an understanding of normal child development is essential to recognizing when a child's health and development are being significantly delayed through neglect. Knowing when and what information to share and the limits of confidentiality are critical to safeguarding.

The content of training – values and principles, attitudes and emotions

> All training on safeguarding and promoting the welfare of children should create an ethos which values working collaboratively with others, respects diversity (including culture, race and disability), promotes equality, is child centred and promotes the participation of children and families in the safeguarding processes. (HM Government 2006, 4.15)

Training on safeguarding will never be effective if it does not address emotions, values and attitudes. There is a danger with limited time available for training that the focus is on procedures and what to do. Training that focuses purely on these will not enable staff to fulfil their statutory responsibilities or to meet the needs of children. It must also address the strong feelings evoked by this subject, and attitudes that can get in the way of an appropriate response.

Child abuse is a subject that many prefer not to think about, and participants in training can experience both shock and distress when faced with powerful case material. This can be even more difficult for those with direct personal experience of abuse. Training can trigger painful memories and emotions. It is vital that trainers create an environment where it is possible to explore the emotions evoked safely and with support. Training on child abuse should, as a matter of course, be delivered by two facilitators so the necessary support is always available, and information should be made available on sources of advice and counselling. Children may try to tell someone they are being abused but find they are unwilling or unable to hear. By dealing with the emotional impact of abuse in a training setting participants are more likely to be able to listen and respond to children's abusive experiences.

Training should also provide opportunities for participants to consider their attitudes and values. There are few absolutes in relation to child protection and, therefore, there is a risk of judgements and actions being skewed by unexamined prejudices and personal views. The following areas are particularly important to address in training.

- *Beliefs about what is abusive.* In any group there are likely to be a wide range of views influenced, for example, by an individual's upbringing, religion or culture. This may affect how someone responds to hearing that a child has been beaten by a parent for misbehaving. Exercises asking participants to rank in order of seriousness different scenarios and then to discus the factors informing the judgements made can prove illuminating but require careful handling.

- *Attitudes in relation to equality and diversity.* Children will not be afforded equal protection unless people are aware of how their beliefs, assumptions and prejudices about gender, ethnicity, sexuality, religion, culture and disability could affect their actions. Numerous child death inquiries have highlighted, for example, how cultural relativism and a fear of being thought racist have led to inaction and a failure of protection. Exploration of these issues in a training setting requires skill, sensitivity and sufficient time.

- *Views about other agencies and professions.* No one agency or profession can protect a child on their own, and a lack of trust or confidence in other agencies can inhibit information-sharing and working together. Training should promote better appreciation of the roles of others and create opportunities to look frankly at some of the barriers to working together.

Additional areas of development

It is important that teaching staff are able to contribute to *assessments of children thought to be in need.* The Common Assessment Framework (CAF) (www.everychildmatters.gov.uk/deliveringservices/caf) introduced in England and Wales, the Integrated Assessment Framework in Scotland and the Understanding the Needs of Children in Northern Ireland (UNOCINI) framework in Northern Ireland each emphasize the importance of multi-disciplinary contributions to holistic assessments of children's developmental needs, including their educational development. Teaching staff have a unique contribution to make to these assessments and training should ensure they are familiar with the relevant framework, dimensions and assessment processes.

The Bichard Inquiry (2004) followed the murder of Jessica Chapman and Holly Wells by Ian Huntley, a school caretaker with a history of abusive sexual relationships with underage girls. Those who appointed him were unaware of his history. Legislation and guidance on vetting and barring have been introduced as a result and all those involved in recruitment and selection in schools and colleges need training on the legislation and on *safer recruitment practice.* This should not focus solely on vetting checks, important as they are, but also on the attitudes and behaviours of applicants who seek to work with children.

Those *working with disabled children* and those with special educational needs require training on 'good practice in intimate care, working with children of the opposite sex, handling difficult behaviour, consent to treatment, anti-bullying strategies, sexuality and sexual behaviour among young people' (HM Government 2006, 11.29). They need to understand the additional vulnerability to abuse of disabled children; what may make it harder for them to disclose and the barriers to recognizing abuse in disabled children.

Understanding peer abuse – both physical and sexual – is important given the evidence of the extent of this problem. A number of resources exist to help staff in tackling bullying. What is perhaps less well developed is training to support staff in recognizing what is normal sexual development and exploration and when young people's sexual behaviour is harmful to others.

Training should also include an understanding of the potential risks to children in their use of *information communication technology* (ICT). In recent years there has been an enormous growth in children and young people's access to the Internet from home and from school – via computers, mobile phones, games machines and television. At the same time, there is evidence of children lacking key skills in evaluating content, a skills gap between adults and children in using the technology and a lack of awareness by adults of how ICT use has an impact on their children's lives (see, for example, Brennan 2006 and Livingstone and Bober 2005). Though the benefits to children – social and educational – are considerable and the risks should not be over-estimated, there is a need for those who work with children to have an awareness of the safe use of ICT (see HM Government 2006, paragraphs 11.58–11.62). Training would need to include:

- the ways, and changing ways, such as social networking, in which children and young people use ICT

- the characteristics of the technology that can make children vulnerable – such as opportunities to pretend to be someone else on the part of those who seek to harm children

- the means by which those with a sexual interest in children may use ICT to make contact with them both online and offline

- the possible effects on children of exposure to unsuitable images and text

- the effects on children of online bullying by peers and ways of supporting them

- recognizing signs that a child may be a victim of cyber bullying or abuse

- the ways in which children can use ICT more safely.

Delivering training and development solutions

We begin by clarifying *where responsibility rests for safeguarding training*, as this can be a source of some confusion. The local safeguarding children board (LSCB) is responsible for ensuring single-agency and inter-agency training are provided to meet local needs. They have a monitoring role and are required to check whether training is reaching staff in individual agencies. They can also be a provider or commissioner of inter-agency training. In most areas a co-ordinated programme of inter-agency training is offered to those working with children and families, which schools can access.

The local education authority is responsible for ensuring workforce strategies are developed and training needs identified. They must also ensure those with designated child protection responsibilities in schools have access to training. Schools and colleges are responsible for ensuring their employees are competent and confident to fulfil their safeguarding roles, 'ensuring that members of staff receive relevant single-agency training' (HM Government 2006, 4.6). They are also expected to identify adequate resources, including time, for staff to take part in inter-agency training courses. Teacher training providers are expected to cover a basic introduction to child protection and safeguarding in their qualifying programmes. Finally, individual members of staff working with children have a professional responsibility to keep up to date and to continue their professional development in this area.

There are a number of different ways of meeting the safeguarding training needs of staff in education, and key considerations are outlined below.

Box 10.1 Key consideration 1: Who is trained with whom?

Options
- Whole staff in-service training
- Selected/targeted staff training
- Inter-agency training

Comment

It is particularly important for designated staff to take part in inter-agency training. Whole-school training needs to take account of differences of power and status in the group.

Box 10.2 Key consideration 2: What method of learning will be most effective?

Options
- Self-directed learning and study
- Facilitated group learning
- Distance learning

- Online learning
- Shadowing
- A combination of these

Comment

It is important to build on the experience of adult learners and recognize different learning styles. Training that is wholly didactic is unlikely to be effective. Training that draws on participants' day-to-day experiences and dilemmas is more likely to prove useful.

Box 10.3 Key consideration 3: Who should deliver training?

Options
- Designated lead for child protection
- External trainers

Comment

Trainers should be knowledgeable about safeguarding in an education setting and have good facilitation skills. It should not be assumed that every designated senior person will have the necessary skills to provide this training and that appropriate training for trainers should be available for those who wish to undertake this responsibility.

Box 10.4 Key consideration 4: How will the learning be evaluated and reviewed?

Options
- Will training be evaluated at reaction level? If so, how?
- Will there be a follow-up to determine what has been learnt and whether learning has been retained?

- Will there be an evaluation of the impact of training on practice – for example, by measuring changes in referral rates or in contributions to assessments?
- How will training take account of evaluations and changes in legislation, guidance and research?

Comment

Training should be subject to continuous review and revision, taking account of the learners' experiences and the changing state of evidence and understanding.

Conclusion

Many children who are being abused do not tell anyone at the time. It is far from easy to recognize signs of abuse and neglect and to have the courage and confidence to take action. At times this requires persistence, assertiveness and a willingness to challenge others. All those working in education settings need to have opportunities to learn about how to recognize, respond to and act on concerns about abuse and bullying. As no one agency or discipline can keep children safe on their own, an ability to work effectively across agency boundaries is vital, knowing when and how to share information.

Guidance from government sets clear expectations that employers ensure staff have the necessary knowledge and skills to fulfil their safeguarding responsibilities. However, relatively limited time is made available in qualifying training or continuing professional development to enable staff working with children in schools to feel confident to play their role in safeguarding and promoting their welfare. This chapter has outlined learning outcomes for different groups of staff and what should be covered in training. We have also explored some of the particular challenges faced by schools in providing training and have offered some different delivery solutions.

Sources of information
England

- Teachernet
  Information and resources for education staff –
  www.teachernet.gov.uk/wholeschool/familyandcommunity/childprotection

- Every Child Matters
  Access to legislation and guidance on all aspects of the Every Child Matters
  agenda – www.everychildmatters.gov.uk

Northern Ireland

- **Department of Health, Social Services and Public Safety**
  Links to legislation and guidance – www.dhsspsni.gov.uk/
  Go to Health and social services; Child care; Child protection

Scotland

- **Scottish Executive**
  Details of the child protection reform programme and implementation of the Protection of Children (Scotland) Act 2003 as well as guidance documents –
  www.scotland.gov.uk/Home
  Go to People and society; Young people; Support for children and families

Wales

- **Social Services Improvement Agency**
  Access to information, legislation and guidance documents –
  www.allwalesunit.gov.uk
  Go to Children's Services; Key documents, legislation and guidance.

- **Children in Wales**
  National umbrella organisation for those working with children and young people in Wales. Includes access to details of news and events as well as policy information, forums, networks and related websites.

UK

- **NAPAC (The National Association for People Abused in Childhood)**
  A registered charity that provides support and information for people abused in childhood – www.napac.org.uk
  NAPAC support line: 0800 085 3330

- **NSPCC Helpline**
  Confidential and free service open 24 hours a day, seven days a week: 0808 800 5000

- **NSPCC inform**
  Free, online child protection resource for professionals working to protect children with access to current information on child abuse, child protection and safeguarding – www.nspcc.org.uk/inform
  Includes – at www.nspcc.org.uk/learningresources – details of child protection learning resources for face-to-face training and distance/online learning, some specifically for schools.

- **Office of Public Sector Information**
  Access to all UK legislation from 1987 – www.opsi.gov.uk

Chapter Eleven

Training to Safeguard: The Australian Experience

Louise Laskey

Introduction

Schools and teachers have a critical role in protecting children, not least because, as other contributors have pointed out in their chapters, apart from a child's family, teachers spend more time with children than any other professional or adult (Briggs and Hawkins 1997). Their close daily contact uniquely situates them to observe changes in children's behaviour, appearance and characteristics that might signal the possibility of abuse or neglect occurring. In addition, a teacher may well be the only trusted adult to whom a child can turn for assistance (Watts 1997). Unfortunately, the ability of Australian educators to assist in the maintenance of children's safety is sometimes constrained by a limited appreciation of the potential for schools to contribute to child protection. Consequently while some teachers and schools commit themselves wholeheartedly to this issue, many lack not only the requisite knowledge and skill, but also the confidence to fully embrace this responsibility.

The principal aim of this chapter is to explore issues related to the participation in, and preparation of, Australian teachers for safeguarding children. Recent research on teachers' involvement in child protection suggests that the emphasis on a legislative policy framework together with a lack of resources in the child protection system undermines their enthusiasm and commitment to ongoing participation.

Gaining an understanding of the nature of the contribution of Australian teachers requires at least a passing familiarity with the geographical, legislative and systemic variations that characterize the Australian system of child protection. Hence, this chapter commences with a brief delineation of the context, before considering major themes such as the predominance of legislation in shaping policy and practice, its ramifications in the narrowly interpreted role of teachers and schools and the challenge of providing educators with adequate training to fulfil child protection roles confidently.

Child protection in Australia

Australia has not one system of child protection, but several: the six states (Queensland, New South Wales, Victoria, Tasmania, South Australia and Western Australia) and two territories (Australian Capital Territory and Northern Territory) each have individual systems arising from varied histories. This has produced differences in the scope and emphases of child protection legislation, policies and practices (Australian Institute of Health and Welfare (AIHW) 2006; Bromfield and Higgins 2005). In particular there are differences in definitions of maltreatment, the specific types of harm to be notified, the ages of children to whom the legislation applies and the nature of obligations to notify for specified professional groups. However, as Bromfield and Higgins (2005) indicate, the processes used to safeguard Australian children across the nation are generally comparable. Apart from Queensland, which has a separate, specialized department of child safety, all other jurisdictions locate child protection within a broader department of human services, community development or family services. A recent trend sees the appointment of commissioners for *children*, thereby signalling an attempt by some state governments to integrate functions such as health, safety, out of home care and screening of employees in children's services while simultaneously emphasizing their increased focus on their commitment to services for children. (Referrals to an ombudsman in the case of complaints against professional staff are also used.)

Children at risk come to the attention of child protection services in a variety of ways. These include reports of concerns about a child by a community member, by a professional mandated to report suspected maltreatment, by an organization that has contact with the child or family, or even by the child, parents or a relative (AIHW 2006). Child protection departments then assess reports to establish whether further action is required by departmental officers (that is via investigation) or whether referral to an external child and family support agency is appropriate. All such departments operate under broadly similar procedures for receiving and processing notifications of suspected child abuse: intake, investigation, substantiation (that is establishing that the child has been or is at risk of harm) and referral to other services. Readers interested in detailed overviews of this system should consult Bromfield and Higgins (2005) and AIHW (2007).

In recent years, systemic changes in policies and practices, together with increased public awareness, are thought to have contributed to an increased rate of growth in child protection notifications across the nation. According to AIHW (2007) there has been a doubling of the volume of child protection notifications over the past five years (from 137,938 in 2001–2 to 266,745 in

2005–6, with substantiation rates across most jurisdictions of between 5 and 11 per 1000 children).

The role of legislation

All Australian states and territories utilize legislation that specifies who is compelled by law to notify concerns, suspicions or reasonable grounds for a belief in relation to suspected cases of child abuse and neglect to a statutory child protection authority (AIHW 2006). This is known as *mandatory reporting*. The groups of people and the grounds for notification under this legislation vary across the nation. For example, in Western Australia and Queensland, this applies to only a limited number of specified persons, whereas in Northern Territory and Tasmania it extends to every adult (Bromfield and Higgins 2005). In other states, particular occupation groups who come into contact with children are nominated. These range from a small cluster, as in Victoria where presently medical doctors, nurses, police and teachers are included, through to very extensive lists as in South Australia and Australian Capital Territory. Table 11.1 indicates state and territory variations.

Table 11.1 Australian mandatory reporting requirements*

Jurisdiction	Who is mandated to notify	What is to be notified
Australian Capital Territory	Doctors, dentists, nurses teachers, police, school counsellors, childcare providers, government health/well-being services providers to children, youth or families; the community advocate or official visitor	A reasonable suspicion that a child or young person has suffered or is suffering sexual abuse or non-accidental physical injury
New South Wales	Persons who deliver health, welfare, educational and children's services, residential services or law enforcement to children	Current concerns that a child aged under 16 is at risk of harm.
Northern Territory	Police and all other people with reasonable grounds	Reasonable grounds to believe that a child has suffered or is suffering maltreatment
Queensland	Doctors and nurses	Aware of or reasonably suspects that a child has, is or is likely to suffer harm
	Officers employed to implement the Child Safety Act, 1999; all staff of residential care services	Reasonable suspicion of abuse or neglect to a child in residential care

Jurisdiction	Who is mandated to notify	What is to be notified
	Education personnel (teaching and non-teaching staff in government and non-government schools)	Aware of or reasonably suspects sexual abuse of a child under 18 by an employee of the school
South Australia	Doctors, pharmacists, police, dentists, nurses, teachers, psychologists, social workers, family day care providers, employees or volunteers (government department, agency or instrumentality) or agency providing health, welfare, education, children's sporting or recreational services, child care or residential services (local government or non-government wholly or partly to children; ministers of religion, staff of religious or spiritual organizations	Reasonable grounds to believe that a child has been or is being abused or neglected
Tasmania	Professionals working with children and employees or volunteers working in government or government-funded organizations	Suspicion or knowledge of abuse or neglect
	Any adult	Reasonable grounds to believe or suspect that a child is suffering, has suffered or is likely to suffer abuse or neglect or is being exposed to domestic violence
Victoria	Police, doctors, nurses and teachers	Reasonable grounds that physical or sexual abuse is occurring
Western Australia	Court personnel, counsellors and mediators	Allegations or suspicions of child abuse in Family Court cases
	Licensed providers of child care or outside school hours care services	Allegations or suspicions of child abuse in a childcare service

* Adapted from Child Abuse Prevention Resource Sheet, National Child Protection Clearinghouse, Australian Institute of Family Studies, No.3, September 2005 and AIHW 2007.

The impact of mandatory reporting legislation

As Tomison (2002) noted, while there were many challenges presented by the implementation of mandatory reporting legislation, one of the unforeseen benefits of its introduction was that some form of child protection training for mandated professionals was necessitated. Although there have been changes to the resources made available to teacher preparation over time and in response to political concerns, regional/state variations are once again the norm with programmes on offer for teachers ranging from a few hours to half and full days. *Train-the-Trainer* models where selected staff (usually those in guidance or welfare roles) attend more in-depth child protection training, for example, two-day programmes, and then deliver components of that programme to staff in their base schools, are widely employed.

At one end of the spectrum, South Australian teachers are required to obtain certification based on a full-day programme (approximately six hours) in *Mandatory Notification Training* as a condition of being offered employment. At the other extreme, most teachers in Victoria received only two hours of compulsory training subsequent to the legislation being introduced in 1994. Since that time, responsibilities for mandatory reporting have been devolved to the regional offices of education and, while new graduates are 'encouraged' to attend, anecdotal evidence suggests that coverage does not extend to all Victorian teachers. For instance, many who have returned following breaks in service have not participated in any form of preparation on this subject. At the pre-service level, it appears that the demands of teacher education curricula are such that core units in professional studies are generally limited to devoting no more than one to three hours to child protection content (Watts and Laskey 1997). This is consistent with reports from the UK (Baginsky and Hodgkinson 1999) and the USA (Bluestone 2005).

In terms of content, it seems that programmes at both pre-service and in-service levels have a common (but restricted) focus, given their tendencies to concentrate attention on meeting the legislative provisions for making notifications. Hence, the identification of suspected child maltreatment and the protocols for reporting suspicions to statutory child protection authorities receive maximum consideration in the limited time available. This tends to concentrate learners' attention on *intervention* rather than *prevention* as the primary focus of the teacher's role. As is argued below, such a narrow, legalistic focus overlooks many possibilities for teachers to contribute to combating child abuse both as educators and as members of the community. In addition, the need for school structures, policies and practices supportive of teachers' child protection roles are often overlooked.

Australian research on teachers and child protection

Australian research has examined teacher responses to mandatory notification legislation, the nature of training programmes and the teaching of personal safety. The results of these enquiries highlight the need for a more integrated model in relation to schools, curriculum, teacher support, training and policy. Generally, the pattern of findings suggests that school staff have difficulty in accepting and fulfilling their child protection obligations and that there is considerable confusion about their roles. Indeed, the intensity of their reactions is captured in the following observation by a teacher union representative: 'Teachers are extremely worried about this issue. They feel unconfident about identifying or reporting anything but the most obvious physical abuse... The stress of making a report is huge' (quoted in Davies 2002).

Notifier behaviour

The manner in which teachers responded to legislation requiring them to report suspicions of child abuse has been the subject of a number of research enquiries highlighting professional and personal ambivalence, the need for structural and collegial support and expanded preparation. Teachers and principals interviewed 12 months after the legislation on mandatory reporting was introduced for Victorian teachers reported feeling insufficiently prepared for their new roles and many were overwhelmed with anxiety. Of those who had already made notifications, many reported disappointment in the outcomes for the child and with the limited feedback from child protection services (CPS). Reflecting on their training experience, many expressed dismay at the inadequacy of the preparation offered: for most teachers this consisted of a two-hour after-school session focused predominantly on notification procedures and basic information on the detection of child abuse. What teachers preferred was the opportunity to have comprehensive coverage of child maltreatment issues, the functioning of the child protection system and ways in which they might become active participants in prevention (Laskey 1995).

Factors influencing community professionals' decisions about whether to report suspected child abuse or neglect to statutory child protection services as required under the law appear to be multi-faceted. Three-quarters of the participants in a study of Victorian frontline staff (including psychologists, social workers, medical practitioners, nurses, childcare workers and teachers) found it complex or difficult to determine whether child abuse had occurred and when they should notify the child protection authority, the Department of Human Services (DHS). Significantly, almost 90% of respondents based their decision to proceed on their *view of the anticipated outcomes for the child* (as opposed to following the requirement of the law to notify on the basis of 'having formed a belief based on reasonable grounds that child abuse may have occurred').

Moreover, more than half of the respondents believed the outcome would *not* be positive for the child or for the child's family. Notification behaviour was influenced by the source of information about the abusive event, some informants being judged as less than credible (Goddard *et al.* 2002).

The most important influences on the decision to report, however, 'were the perpetrator's access to the child, the functioning of the primary caregiver, the nature of parent/child interaction and the type and severity of abuse and neglect' (Goddard *et al.* 2002, p.89). The authors noted that while community professionals view their responsibility to protect children from maltreatment seriously, they do require *support* in their decision-making about suspected abuse. Goddard *et al.* assert that 'information about what they should consider to be abuse is imperative' and, they suggest, 'knowledge about the way the child protection system works will also assist in raising their confidence about identifying and reporting cases of child abuse' (p.89).

The results of this study indicate that considerable confusion exists among professionals as to whether or not they are mandated to report child abuse, 29% of those surveyed being either inaccurate or uncertain about their obligations under Victorian law. According to Goddard *et al.*, 'this represents a major impediment to the effective protection of children from abuse and neglect' (p.3). Consequently, the authors advocated a major education campaign to ensure that all community professionals understand what constitutes child abuse, are aware of their notification obligations and fully understand the procedures to follow in making a report to DHS (p.4). Such findings confirm the challenges posed by mandatory reporting, given that many professionals regard notification as *discretionary* in the absence of skills, professional support and feedback from the child protection authority.

The issue of greater support for teachers involved in decisions about notification also emerges in a South Australian investigation (McCallum 2001). Lack of supportive school structures, too little experience in teaching, personal concerns (for example, fear of retaliation from parents) and increased workload were all identified as impediments to reporting suspected child abuse. For the more experienced teachers in the study, personal isolation within schools posed particular difficulties for notifiers. Furthermore, teachers' feelings of doubt and negative self-efficacy seemed to characterize the process. Under such conditions, McCallum concluded, 'current models of training are ineffective in preparing educators to report suspicions of child abuse and neglect' (p.5). Overcoming the inhibiting factors in notification thus requires a preparation that takes into account the local contexts of schools, teacher needs and concerns (including post-notification consequences for the victim and family), support structures for the notifier and conditions of educator learning. In addition, and in line with the work conducted by Baginsky (2000) on scaffolding practice during training, McCallum recommended careful support via mentoring for beginning teachers.

Further confirmation of the tendency for professionals to seek support from colleagues regarding the decision to notify suspected child maltreatment is provided in a Victorian investigation with education, health and welfare professionals. Blaskett and Taylor (2003) examined the extent to which such workers comply with legislative requirements and the manner in which they influence one another in their notification behaviours. Resonating with results reported above, the study's conclusions indicate that professionals often influence one another when forming a belief or reporting that a child is subject to abuse, contrary to legislative provisions largely requiring *confidentiality*. There are variations in reporting behaviours across the professional groups, with 10% of the sample admitting to non-reporting. It is perhaps surprising then that there were generally positive attitudes towards mandatory reporting. However, most participants harboured some fear of recriminations resulting from notifications (see also Kenny 2001; McCallum 2001). Low levels of confidence were expressed in the child protection system as a whole. Inadequate preparation for, and lack of awareness of, reporting responsibilities were common to the group, although teachers had one of the highest rates of training in the sample. Conversely, teacher participants reflected a trend to discretionary reporting: the greater the frequency of their contact with DHS, the less inclined were they to utilize this avenue in future. However, in Victoria, the access to, and the nature and quality of such training, appears problematic, with more than 40% of survey respondents requesting further opportunities.

One teacher commented:

> I'm a little sorry for those people who have been teaching in the short time since the first lot of training came out to the second – there is a big group of people that really didn't know the legislation applied to them other than what their Principal might have told them and that would have been the Principal's interpretation of it anyway, so I think the training should be offered much more regularly than every nine years. (Blaskett and Taylor 2003, p.155)

Thus, despite a high level of concern to protect children from abuse, professionals responsible for the care of children expressed reservations about reporting for a variety of reasons. These included lack of confidence in the child protection system, concern to protect confidentiality, fear of reprisal and concern at loss of trusted clients. Several of those who are most experienced in dealing with cases of child abuse and with child protection services are those who are now most reluctant to invoke assistance from child protection authorities (Blaskett and Taylor 2003).

Similar trends are apparent in a Queensland study in which teachers were found to be committed to reporting, but unsure of their abilities to recognize abuse (Walsh *et al.* 2005). In keeping with McCallum's findings, Walsh *et al.* established that where the culture of the school encouraged discussion of these matters, teachers were more confident about identifying physical abuse and neglect. Sexual abuse however, was the most difficult to identify in any circumstance. Teachers invoked discretion in their decision-making where they judged that notification would not serve the child's best interest. There was often a lack of feedback on the outcomes of notifications, even when reports had been made via their own principal. Walsh *et al.* assert that situations such as this undermine confidence in the child protection system, further discouraging participation. Informal discussions with colleagues and personal factors (parental status, for example) appeared to be more influential than the impact of training in child protection. However, given that half the number of teachers involved had fewer than five hours of child protection training (the average being 2.8 hours), this is perhaps unsurprising.

In the light of such evidence, it is difficult to argue with Walsh *et al.*'s recommendation for enhanced training, with compulsory study in initial teacher training. This would consist of both embedded content across units (for example, in professional studies or child development) combined with focused study in dedicated units. At the in-service level, annual updating is suggested. In accord with the South Australian 'precedent', these authors recommend compulsory child protection training as a prerequisite to employment (see also Laskey 1995; McCallum 2001; Watts and Laskey 2002).

The nature of training programmes

As might be surmised on the basis of the above discussion, the nature and quality of information required for notification appear to be difficult for many practitioners to grasp. In an empirical assessment of the one-day South Australian mandatory notification programmes, training was found to increase participants' confidence in their ability to recognize the indicators of abuse, their awareness of reporting responsibilities, their knowledge of what constitutes reasonable grounds for reporting and how to respond appropriately to a child's disclosure of abuse (Hawkins and McCallum 2001). However, in spite of these quantitative gains in knowledge and skill, it is interesting to examine those areas where teacher attitudes proved to be resistant to change. For example, although participants are advised that they are not required by law to investigate or prove that abuse has occurred, 20% of recently trained teachers believed they should investigate further if unsure of their suspicion.

Similarly, despite being instructed to respond to a child's disclosure by listening supportively, allowing the child to talk without pushing for investigative details, 20% of the recently trained teachers indicated they would persuade the child to give more details. In the words of one respondent, 'I believe it is sometimes better to do some investigation first or checking up before notifying the authorities' (Hawkins and McCallum 2001, p.1618). Hawkins and McCallum observe that for some teachers, 'there is clearly a mismatch between the level of evidence required by law for reporting to occur and the level teachers expect to satisfy their own personal need for confidence in initiating the serious step of a child abuse report' (2001, p.1618).

Pre-service teachers' approaches to hypothetical cases eligible for notification have also been demonstrated to be less than objective. Their participation in training courses notwithstanding, participants' decisions were found to be consistent with other results reported above, such as those of Goddard *et al.* (2002), above. Queensland student teachers were thus:

> ...more likely to be influenced by some personal experience – such as previous relationship with a person in a similar position, a child of a similar age, or identifying with one of the people involved in a case, such as the mother, child or father – than by the definitions, evidence and procedures they are aware of...beliefs [such as] 'a mother wouldn't do that,' despite the fact that abuse is also perpetrated by women. (Watts 1997, p.113)

Specific instances have led to calls for deeper levels of teacher knowledge and understanding. For example, Taylor and Lloyd (2001) have argued that in rural areas concerns about the possibility of disclosures being rejected may have explained the reluctance of adolescents and children in a Victorian rural area to disclose sexual abuse, and of non-offending parents failing to access services. Consequently, Taylor and Lloyd argue, 'teacher training programmes need to develop greater understanding of abuse within the family unit, especially as the majority of sexual and physical violence against children and adolescents occurs within the family' (2001, p.3).

Before leaving this section, it is worth noting that an emphasis on legal obligations (in contrast to ethical responsibility) as the core of training programmes only serves to reinforce the notion that the teacher's role in child protection is a *reactive* (rather than a *proactive*) one. Thus, a further challenge is to develop a conceptualization of the teacher's role that shifts the focus to *prevention* as opposed to *intervention*. The need to broaden our understanding of the teacher's role in safeguarding children is all the more apparent in the face of the anomalies in reporting behaviour described above. Providing teachers with positive opportunities to combat child abuse through child advocacy and the teaching of personal safety skills for example (in addition to their legal obligation to report suspected maltreatment) allows the profession a more balanced and empowered contribution to child safety (Briggs and Hawkins 1997; Watts 1997; Watts and Laskey 2002).

Personal safety

The teaching of personal safety skills to children has been seen as an important strategy in the primary prevention of child abuse. The US-developed 'Protective behaviours' programme has been used in various locations since the mid-1980s. However, problematic features of this framework have been identified. These include an over-reliance on uncomfortable feelings as the basis for confiding in a trusted person (Briggs and Hawkins 1997) and pedagogical barriers to implementation with many teachers selectively omitting content that they found 'too personal and controversial' (Johnson 1995). These issues notwithstanding, the Protective behaviours programme continues to be offered on a voluntary basis by some schools, for example, in Victoria and the ACT.

By contrast, the inclusion of personal safety education as a *core curriculum component* embedded at every level of schooling extends and amplifies its capacity to develop children and young people's ability to resist abuse. Such is the situation in New South Wales where the Department of Education and Training has produced an impressive six-volume set of personal safety curriculum materials. *Child Protection Education* is thus an integral component of the personal development, health and physical education curriculum in that state. A parallel exercise is currently under way in South Australia with promising results being reported by Johnson (2005).

School factors

Endorsement of personal safety teaching as core curriculum is just one of many ways in which schools can demonstrate a commitment to this issue. As we have seen, a school culture that positively embraces child protection responsibilities, and actively develops child protection policy and procedures, can encourage staff to deepen their involvement (Crenshaw, Crenshaw and Lichtenberg 1995; McCallum 2001; Skinner 1999). Providing connections between families in need of service and community agencies in partnership would further heighten the schools' contribution to child abuse prevention (McInnes 2002; Walsh *et al.* 2005).

Implications for training

Addressing attitudes and beliefs about child abuse, as we have seen, might well hold the key to overcoming barriers to reporting. However, as previously argued, the kind of values clarification and experiential work required cannot be accommodated in the few hours generally allocated in the majority of programmes discussed. Thus the length of time to be devoted to such training is of crucial importance. It is now clear that a more comprehensive and substantial pre-service course in child protection is warranted in the interests of allowing students to develop in-depth knowledge of, and practical skills in child protection issues (Taylor and Lloyd 2001; Walsh *et al.* 2005). There is evidence that longer programmes are more effective in changing teachers' behaviour (MacIntyre and Carr 2000). And as Baginsky (2003) contends, such a course should be seen as a starting point to be followed by opportunities for regular updating during the in-service phase.

Based on the preceding analyses, it is clear that it is predominantly the attitudes and values of teachers that initially influence their response to suspected child maltreatment. With Skinner (1999) and Taylor and Lloyd (2001), I would argue that the design of training programmes must be capable of surmounting negative community attitudes and values, and the extent to which these permeate school environments and local agencies involved in protecting children from abuse. Furthermore, training programmes will have increased efficacy if they take into account teachers' pre-training knowledge, attitudes and child protection beliefs (Bluestone 2005; Watts 1997). There is a strong case for teachers and academic teacher educators to develop a compulsory core child protection course that could be conducted both as a single unit (Walsh *et al.* 2005), and embedded as a course that is interwoven across the span of the education curriculum (Taylor and Lloyd 2001).

Thus, Australian research on notifier behaviour has produced results typical of those conducted elsewhere (see for instance, Abrahams, Casey and Daro 1992; Kenny 2001; Reiniger, Robison and McHugh 1995). A pattern of discretionary reporting is evident, often with subjective impressions influencing whether notifications are made. While training, usually of short duration, has occasionally been found to be effective, some attitudes are extremely resistant to change. Many teachers continue to lack confidence in their decision-making and seek reassurance from colleagues, in spite of admonitions to report directly to CPS. Consequently, they seem unable to be dissuaded from feeling the need to collect 'evidence' from children, contrary to guidelines. In addition, concern about family disruption and/or retaliation by parents weighs heavily on teachers in deciding whether to proceed with notifications, especially in rural communities (see also O'Toole *et al.* 1999).

Lessons from the Australian experience of safeguarding children

A number of patterns in teachers' responses to statutory notification have been identified. In particular, there was evidence of discretion or 'under-reporting' of child maltreatment (Blaskett and Taylor 2003; Goddard *et al.* 2002; Walsh *et al.* 2005). An exploration of the factors involved in decision-making about suspected child abuse reveals the process to be heavily influenced by subjective appraisals about the situation or people involved (Walsh *et al.* 2005; Watts 1997). There is concern for the teacher's own safety, with fear of parental retaliation being a common rationale for failing to report. Moreover, many teachers have developed a distrust of the child protection system's capacity to secure an improved outcome for child victims (Goddard *et al.* 2002; Hawkins and McCallum 2001). This is aggravated if CPS fail to liaise with notifiers in the post-notification phase (Blaskett and Taylor 2003; Goddard *et al.* 2002).

Overall, there are clear implications for training. 'One-off' sessions of limited duration are ineffective, as are programmes that focus on procedural aspects rather than personal/emotional perspectives on child maltreatment (Trudell and Whatley 1988; Kenny 2001). An extended time frame is preferable, one that allows for revisiting of difficult topics and time to reflect on personal values, attitudes and beliefs (Webb and Vulliamy 2001b). A multi-agency approach needs to be taken, given the realities of present circumstances and the desire of some teachers to find community-based solutions (Baginsky 2003; Walsh *et al.* 2005). At the systems level, consistency of response (including feedback) from CPS is needed to restore confidence in the notification process as well as strengthening the inter-agency collaboration essential to securing children's safety (Goddard *et al.* 2002).

Finally, a whole-school approach to child protection (McInnes 2002) is required to capitalize on the moral commitment teachers bring to their work with children. As we have seen, the potential for teachers to contribute to the prevention of and response to suspected child abuse is strongest when facilitated by the provision of in-depth training, supportive school culture and structures, and the opportunity to make use of well-designed curriculum materials in personal safety. Thus empowered, all teachers can become partners in proactively protecting and safeguarding children.

Chapter Twelve

Conclusion

Every School Matters

Mary Baginsky

Laming (2003) viewed strong universal services as the most effective way of both safeguarding children and meeting their needs, as did those speaking at a conference entitled *Society and the schools: Communication challenges to education and social work* that was held in Chicago in 1964 (see Bronstein and Abramson 2003 and Popper 1965). The debate was pursued in relation to the role of social work and social action – one participant likened individual case work to the application of a plaster to a severed artery. The discussion widened and took on board the possibility of schools working together with other agencies in relation to families with multiple problems. The debates focused on the respective roles of the social worker working in a school and the teacher. As far as social workers were concerned were they there as an outside expert called in to rescue a teacher or as a member of the school staff, to link school and community *and* link school and other agencies? Much seemed to depend on the stance taken by the school. While a social worker may want to be seen as a member of the school's professional team, contributing to the central work of the school, this would be challenged by some teachers who placed themselves as the *superordinates* pursuing, in their opinion, the most important task, which was to teach. But it was the alternative perspective – where teachers saw the progress of students as dependent on their input alongside that of others who were needed to secure their welfare – that was the one judged most likely to lead to the more productive collaboration. There will still be schools that fit in those extremes and all points between; and, as well as the institutional response, there is also the individual's response. Within schools there are those who see the dissemination of knowledge and skills as being the focus and at the other end of the spectrum are those who see this imperative as married to an obligation to secure the well-being of students. In 1960s America they came to the conclusion that while teachers and social workers might be in agreement about values at a very high level of abstraction, when this was transmitted to professional practice the range of views held across education as compared to the more unified approach of social workers made inter-professional dialogue and collaboration more difficult.

Maguire and Ball's vision of 'the good society' is one where education might be expected to support children who experience disadvantage or injustice (Gipps 1993, quoted in Maguire and Ball 1994). This would seem to require all those involved to be reflective practitioners, able to engage in partnership working. At the 1964 Chicago conference it was widely recognized that teachers and social workers had different perspectives, which impacted on the way in which they looked at the issues that brought them together and which arose out of the differences in their training and the nature of their work. This still continues to be the case. It is very different to be responsible for curriculum and pastoral care in a school, where welfare responsibilities are a part of a job, than to be a social worker where it is a major section of the work. In a recent study (Baginsky 2007) there were reports of teachers being suspicious of social workers' motives and of social workers believing schools had failed to support parents. There were teachers and social workers who had images of the other that must have impacted on their relationship: the social workers who saw teachers as having the child at the centre and ignoring the family and the teachers who thought children's needs took second place to those of the family unit. Reaching an understanding of what schools were like was not easy in view of the level of variation that occurred between schools. In some cases one team would be dealing with over 100 schools, and struggled to understand and respond to the differences between them. There were also misconceptions about the relationship between the authority and schools, with social workers often expressing opinions that appeared to be based on a belief that a local authority would be able to direct the school to do anything, whereas schools had a great deal of autonomy. Perhaps one of the major difficulties in the past has been a failure to engage professionals in a conversation about the context, process and intention of multi-agency or integrated working. The partial vision of child protection that teachers were given is described in Chapter 1. They were expected to report concerns and sometimes to handle those judged not to be so serious without often being told what to do. This was one consequence of the fact that in the past too much work with children and families had focused on an assessment of risk rather than on need.

All authorities have struggled to deal with the fact that resources have not been available to provide the required level of support or to meet the real level of poverty. The hope is that the improvement of universal services and an emphasis on prevention will prevent the emergence of serious problems. Universal services, such as schools, play a key role in identifying need and vulnerability, and well as in dealing with a level of risk where appropriate and working with other services to access more targeted support when specialist help is needed. As was explored in Chapter 1, while services have been remodelled the messages that have informed radical reorganization have been around for a long time and have underpinned previous legislation and guidance. The lessons learnt in relation to collaboration and policy implementation will continue to be needed in the future. The planned reforms are based on service reconfiguration to support universal services, supplemented by targeted support to prevent problems arising, and to act early and effectively if they do.

It is clear that schools also have a role in addressing the lack of capacity in Tier 2 services, which are the ones that straddle universal and specialist service and form the next, and important, layer of preventative activity. They provide a response to indications of higher level of difficulty with the aim of preventing escalation into less manageable problems. In the past the universal services have not always dealt with problems of this sort themselves, even when they have identified them, usually because there has been the expectation that another service was more equipped to do so. Unfortunately these other services were not always able to apply their expertise because demand for it too often outstripped supply. But if Tier 1 agencies are to be expected to operate in this way, staff will need appropriate training to be able to identify risk more effectively and will require additional support to deliver appropriate targeted interventions. Despite the rhetoric that schools are being placed at the centre of services for children this will probably be a 'restricted' centre. Schools are being encouraged to become 'extended' schools but in reality for most this will mean possibly longer opening hours and the provision of child care. There will be some full service schools along a similar model to the one developed in the USA. But there is not a single model of an extended school and there is no target for all schools to become 'full service'. The Department of Children, Schools and Families makes it clear that schools will develop those services that reflect the needs of the community, which may or may not include the core services of the full service model. But schools will be expected to have established networks and partnerships to make sure that other support is in place. If schools are to be society's 'child safeguarding' gatekeepers they need the tools with which to work. This means they need to be able to access agencies that are able to provide appropriate support. These are the same agencies that were often unable to respond in the past because they did not have the level of resources with which to do so. Plans to improve services for vulnerable children will once again fall short of expectations on their implementation unless there are well-trained and well-resourced workforces across children's services.

In a study conducted in three English local authorities (Baginsky 2007) teachers believed that the *Every Child Matters* agenda should lead to improvements in multi-agency working because it provided a policy framework that would go alongside structural changes to support collaboration. In this respect the existence of structures such as children's service departments, which bring education and children's social care together, should make the linkages more robust, but they will not guarantee improvements unless other challenges are addressed. Despite the repeated calls for better co-ordination the fracturing of the education system has made this more difficult. Schools faced challenges in the past in engaging with other agencies but there are new challenges. These include the competing agendas of achievement and inclusion; the sometimes diffuse notion of extended schools and limited plans for full service schools; and the uncertain status of the 'new' institutions such as city academies.

But now that all schools have been directed to co-operate by mandate, it is imperative to find a balance between fragmentation *and* integration and co-operation. The coming together of education and other services will only make a difference if bridges are built at an operational as well as a strategic level, which underscores the importance of developing a skilled workforce. Gibbs and Bennett (1990) found that partnerships were possible once the different agencies believed that they could not succeed alone. The argument has been won with schools. Most schools are clearly anxious to work with other services in relation to children's welfare, but they are not necessarily aware of how best to do this. Teachers are key to identifying students who may need services, sharing information with service providers, and even ensuring delivery of services (Fletcher-Campbell *et al.* 2003). According to recent research (Baginsky 2007) teachers believed they had become very good identifiers of problems, but they did not have the time or the expertise to meet the complex needs of an increasing number of pupils.

It will require a change in practice and philosophy to make this happen (Parton 2006) because the focus has shifted to the needs and different vulnerabilities of children and families. It is a huge task as it involves ensuring attention is given to addressing the factors that exclude children from the five outcome areas. This requires the identification of those children and young people with problems, the establishment of appropriate and effective preventative interventions and targeted services for those where problems persist or are more serious. The evidence makes clear that there is no universal model of intervention that will help all children or young people. Support needs to be tailored to the needs of the individual; resources and opportunities are lost if an intervention is not appropriate to needs. At present too many interventions are crisis-driven rather than providing lower level, ongoing support. The thresholds for accessing social care services for both adults and children are very high, so families asking for help are often refused but when a crisis arises the intervention that then follows may lead to the removal of the child from the family. Parents and professionals often give examples of having asked for help only to be turned away because their needs were not at sufficiently high a level. Some years down the line when their children had been in prison, excluded from school or on hard drugs they put some of the blame at the door of those who had not given them the help they had needed at that early stage. Given the complexity of many of their needs, the level of impact is likely to be low when the problems have escalated.

Delivering improved services depends on how policies are *implemented* rather than just how they are *structured*. Integrated services require shared vision, a commitment to learn from each other, a willingness to compromise and a clear focus on what those using the service need. A rush to restructure without really addressing some of the underlying issues will not work. Improvements in services depend more than anything else on professionals and agencies working together. There have been less ambitious plans in the past to bring these together. Some have been successful but many have faltered. The reasons for failure have been explored but not often addressed. The work examined in the preceding chapters provides examples of how schools can engage with other agencies to make sure that this next attempt will be successful.

Talking to Teachers
about Every Child Matters[1]

Emma Westcott

Background

The General Teaching Council (GTC) hosted a series of meetings on the *Every Child Matters* (ECM) theme in late 2006 to early 2007. The Council chose this theme as part of its commitment to the agenda set by *Every Child Matters*, and to helping to support GTC registrants to make a difference to children's well-being and development, as well as to their learning and achievement. Teachers have told the GTC that these aspirations for children are inextricable, and this belief is embodied in the Council's statement of values and practice.

The GTC also has a particular interest in learning more about the workforce development implications of ECM, because of its duty to advise the secretary of state on teachers' initial and continuing education and development, and in order to inform its work as a member of the children's workforce network, established by the DfES.

In contrast to many other ECM-related events, this series was not targeted at any particular sub-set of teachers, such as school leaders or specific post-holders, and it was not identified with any particular initiative, such as extended services, or aspect of ECM, such as child protection. Although the participants were self-selecting and the processes for eliciting and recording responses were not conducted under research conditions, the geographical range and volume of participants allows the GTC to feel confident in presenting the outcomes as a fairly representative snapshot of teachers' understanding and perceptions of ECM, and capacity to contribute effectively to its goals for children and young people. For example, at each event it was apparent that participants included those who were only vaguely aware of ECM, to those from schools that had reviewed and reoriented everything they did in the light of the ECM agenda. Bringing this range of teachers together for peer learning was one of the strengths of the series, as reflected in the feedback form responses.

---

1   *Talking to Teachers about* Every Child Matters is an edited version of a paper first considered by the Policy and Research Committee of the General Teaching Council for England held on 5 June 2007.

In total, just under 500 teachers attended events in Colchester, Coventry, Darlington, Ealing, Hull, Nottingham, Plymouth, Stoke. At each event there were school leaders at different levels, and classroom teachers; teachers from different phases and settings, and from the maintained and independent sectors.

There was an unprecedented interest in this series, and at the events there was also a great appetite for more opportunities to think and learn about the implications and possibilities of ECM.

Structure of the report

The outcomes of the events are set out in three sections: *Key findings* presents the most commonly expressed views across the series of events; *Other findings* includes other relevant outcomes, all of which were raised more than once during the series; and *Workforce development* sets out the findings related to learning and development needs and opportunities associated with ECM.

Inevitably, the bulk of the report details concerns and shortcomings around *Every Child Matters*, but these should be set in the context of overwhelming support for and commitment to the ECM goals, and a strong desire to be equipped to realize them.

Key findings

Attitudes

Most teachers are positive about *Every Child Matters* as a principled framework setting learning and achievement in the context of wider outcomes for children and young people. This finding supports evidence from the GTC's 2005 Survey of Teachers, in which ECM was one of the two national initiatives teachers thought most likely to make a positive difference for children and young people. (The other was assessment for learning.) Many teachers expressed the view that ECM legitimized the approach to work with children that they believe in – a commitment to the development of the child in the fullest sense. 'ECM is what I came into teaching for' (Secondary teacher, Darlington).

Within this general support for the ECM goals, there were particular aspects that teachers frequently highlighted as positive, including:

- a boost to pupil voice/democratic schooling

- improved emphasis on 'learning for life'

- better interaction with parents and carers about what matters to them regarding their child's development and progress – more genuine partnership with parents

- greater responsiveness to early signs of difficulty or disengagement

- more opportunities for collaborative approaches to meeting the needs of particular children

- greater opportunities for inter-professional work – in particular this was cited as something that would make headship more attractive to some potential leaders.

There were a small number of dissenting voices across the series of meetings. Outright cynicism was rare; more common was scepticism about aspects of implementation – particularly whether resources such as time, money and capacity would enable delivery against the ECM goals.

There is still some concern about the fit between the standards and ECM agendas. This does not mean that teachers necessarily believe they are mutually exclusive. A few head teachers used the DfES formulation ('No standards without ECM; no ECM without standards'), usually voicing agreement. Teachers by and large perceive themselves to be sharply accountable for educational outcomes and hazily accountable for other outcomes. Although many participants noted the seriousness with which ECM is now treated in school and related this to prominence in inspection and the self-evaluation form (SEF), other teachers reported that inspection focused on academic outcomes to the exclusion of other good work towards broader ECM outcomes and demoralized staff. Some participants were sceptical about the weight placed on wider outcomes for children by school inspection teams.

Awareness

At each event there were participants across the awareness spectrum from 'What is it?' to 'We're doing it all already.' Both ends of the spectrum might be cause for concern! Many teachers described a journey from finding ECM daunting to believing they are 'doing it already' via mapping their school activity against the five goals. This suggests that some of the tick-box mentality that has developed in response to prevalent forms of external accountability has spread from educational outcomes to wider objectives for children and young people. Practitioners from more reflective, effectively self-evaluative environments were not complacent about what they were doing, even where there appeared to be a lot of good and relevant work under way.

Communication about ECM to schools and within schools is still variable. There are still many teachers who aren't sure if they understand what 'it' is. In some schools consideration of the ECM agenda has had a fundamental impact on all planning, delivery and evaluation; in others, 'it' is perceived as someone's job. 'As an ordinary classroom teacher my SMT has not shared information about ECM so I don't really know what it means for me' (Secondary teacher, Portsmouth).

It was common to find teachers who had not heard of the Common Assessment Framework, or the Information Sharing Index (now known as ContactPoint) – they were not aware that such tools were in the system, let alone what they were called.

There was a strong emphasis on the need to communicate the ECM agenda to parents and governors – teachers thought schools could contribute to this but it would be helpful if national government was also clear that it expects schools to attend to the five outcomes. Governor involvement was described variously as a challenge, and an opportunity – the latter with particular reference to strengthening community links.

Implementation: capacity, sustainability

There is frustration about the failure to join up a lot of apparently linked initiatives, such as healthy schools, extended schools, personalization, targeted youth support.

There was a perception at all events that getting ECM right meant time to invest in the quality of relationships, between school staff and other practitioners, between professionals and with children and young people, parents and families. Many teachers, especially school leaders, referred to the structural challenges associated with teachers being available to contribute to integrated working.

Information for schools on where to refer children/seek specific expertise was often said to be sparse. School leaders and relevant post-holders experienced particular difficulties in navigating the resources and processes of the health sector, especially in the context, for many, of financial crises in primary care trusts (PCTs) contributing to staff turnover. Information on voluntary sector provision was often out of date. Many teachers felt they needed to know more about the roles and processes of other children's services in order to signpost and refer effectively. This was often expressed as a training need on the part of school staff, but also as an aspect of other services' communication that could be enhanced. 'I understand why colleagues in health and social work can't always share the reasons for their decisions but I don't understand why there can't be transparency about processes for arriving at decisions, thresholds for intervention, and so on' (School leader, Ealing).

Sustainability of children's centre and extended school developments was a concern, as was speed of roll-out – particularly in settings (e.g. rural areas, or areas of affluence) where practitioners believed there was a template for provision that did not suit their contexts.

There were questions about the capacity of other services to respond to that part of the extended school portfolio known as 'swift and easy referral'. Some of the factors cited included PCT efficiency savings, staff shortages and turnover, staff who should be involved in preventative work tied up in hard cases. There was a lot of concern about Tier 2 capacity, although at the Ealing event a number of teachers reported more positive recent experiences of referral. Some school leaders felt burdened by managing expectations on the part of children and families, and of teachers about meeting additional needs through external provision.

Anxieties were expressed, in different ways, around targeting preventative/early intervention work. Teachers feel ill-informed/qualified to make the judgements about risk and those with the appropriate expertise are often tied up with case work and not available for more strategic, or preventative work.

Other findings

These outcomes are notably more diffuse, and more positive, than the most frequently cited views set out above.

There was a suggestion that greater opportunities for inter-professional learning were available to teachers working with younger children – teachers attributed this to an assumption that whole-child approaches were still associated with younger children, but it is as likely to be because the local authority plays a different role in relation to the development of the wider children's workforce than it does in teacher development, in which the school has a strong role. This was a helpful reminder to guard against the scenario in which teachers and other school staff are left out of children's workforce development opportunities.

The GTC is aware from its annual survey that assessment for learning is held in high regard by teachers. Participants in this series of events suggested the need to develop a similar approach to the pursuit of the wider ECM goals.

One or two schools working across local authority and primary care trust boundaries highlighted the particular complexity of navigating different provision and processes.

More than one teacher wanted to know more about how ContactPoint would work for newly arrived children and young people.

A number of teachers in children's centres reported a negative response to their presence from other non-teaching early-years colleagues. Some children's centres also reported mistrust or negativity on the part of local schools about their role, resources, and so on.

There were a number of positive accounts of school workforce remodelling contributing effectively to the ECM agenda – such as support staff working on parent liaison, attendance, and so on. Also, there were a number of positive references to the synergy in self-assessment and peer assessment, between 'skills for learning' and 'skills for life'.

It was suggested that the 14–19 agenda necessitated a greater emphasis on thinking about the ECM agenda post-16 – 'Every Young Person Matters'. (The consultation on raising the school leaving age had not been announced at the time of the events but makes this point even more apposite.)

Teachers' effective involvement in inter-professional work was said to be predicated on their own effectiveness in their own role/area of expertise.

Some teachers wanted to see improvements in systems support for effective inter-agency working – such as tracking systems and protocols about response times.

Participants suggested the need to review, variously, the role of the special educational needs co-ordinator (SENCO), the special school, and the pupil referral unit (PRU) in the light of ECM.

Independent sector colleagues appreciated the opportunity to participate in peer learning about ECM. They suggested there was a misconception that ECM did not concern independent schools.

More than one supply teacher made a plea for greater consideration to be given to updating and developing supply teachers to make a contribution to ECM goals.

One or two participants commented on the gender imbalance among participants and wondered if this reflected an imbalance in the allocation of ECM-focused roles in schools, and/or in the interest in ECM objectives among teachers.

Workforce development

Comments on learning and development needs were mostly concerned with continuing professional development (CPD) opportunities and processes, although there were a few mentions of initial teacher training (ITT). Participants focused mainly on teachers' needs but often suggested wider children's workforce development needs in doing so, and frequently referred to the desirability of inter-professional learning. The overwhelming message was that participants reported a great appetite for learning opportunities associated with ECM, and the GTC used these events to begin to build a more detailed understanding of these.

Teachers identified the following needs:

- A greater focus on helping classroom teachers bring ECM to bear on their teaching practice – curriculum, pedagogy, assessment, (a) to make manifest the relevance of ECM to their teaching professionalism; and (b) to ensure that ECM is not something that goes on around teaching without influencing it. 'Is ECM about teaching and learning?' (Classroom teacher, Darlington).

- A greater understanding of the roles, expertise and processes of other professionals who work with children, with particular reference to local frameworks, procedures, resources, and so on.

- Grounding in the difference between, and means of moving between, universal, targeted and specialist services.

- Better focus on ECM in ITT and induction – some participants raised concerns about awareness of trainees/newly qualified teachers (NQTs), and some higher education institution (HEI) participants commented that they had not been adequately supported to prepare new entrants for an ECM environment.

- Inter-professional training in using inter-agency frameworks and protocols such as the CAF and ContactPoint.

- Time and space for illumination and debate of key concepts between agencies – such as 'user voice'.

- Skills associated with quasi-therapeutic interventions, like circle time – but with caveats about not wanting to cross professional boundaries.

- A greater awareness of risk predictors, manifestations of risk, and interventions.

- Interpersonal skills (it was suggested that not all teachers were well placed to model the aspirational visions of citizenship, and human fellowship, implicit in ECM).

- Opportunities to collaborate with colleagues from other services to develop an analysis of local needs which might also be addressed collaboratively – such as issues like raising aspirations, on the part of pupils or parents; engaging parents, and so on.

- Exposure to ideas about the contribution schools can make across the five goals. Repeated reference was made to the difficulty schools had in considering their contribution to the economic well-being goal.

- Access to good exemplification – how did other schools work on 'hard to reach' parents, allocate management responsibilities for ECM, secure funding for particular interventions, and so on? Some teachers suggested local authority children's services were well placed to meet this need if resourced to do so, building on their traditional detailed knowledge of schools' teaching and learning strengths; they could also develop intelligence on schools' strengths in ECM areas to facilitate networked learning as has been developed around teaching and learning.

- A clear inter-professional framework for generalist and specialist training and education, coupled with better access to 'in time' CPD that could be accessible to diverse practitioners on topics such as bereavement, compulsive disorders, and so on.

- More support for the development of multi-agency teams, particularly around planning, identification and sharing resources, joint commissioning, measuring impact, self-evaluation.

- Opportunities for middle managers who have gained greater responsibility in their own sectors to develop into wider roles.

- More support for leadership and management of multi-agency settings – in particular:

  - performance management beyond one's own specialism/service
  - managing complex accountabilities; setting and pursuing inter-service targets
  - commissioning as a new skill set
  - staffing structures and development for ECM.

Next steps

The GTC reported these outcomes to the Minister for Children, Young People and Families, at her request. It used the outcomes in its own collaborative work with ECM partners, and to shape its own work programme. For example, the views teachers expressed about CPD led to a project to help CPD leaders within and beyond schools to identify ECM-related CPD needs effectively, and to secure appropriate development opportunities for colleagues.

The GTC welcomes views on this report and on the implications for teaching of *Every Child Matters*. These can be addressed to: emma.westcott@ gtce.org.uk

The Contributors

Mary Baginsky is Head of Research at the Children's Workforce Development Council. She was previously a senior research officer for the NSPCC and a senior consultant at GHK Consulting. She has many years' experience as an educational researcher, and, at NSPCC, developed a programme of research on the role of education and child protection and safeguarding and evaluated many educational /social care initiatives, contributing to the development of policy within the Department for Children, Schools and Families (DCSF).

William Baginsky is Head of Child Protection Learning Resources at the NSPCC, developing and producing training, informational and other materials for all those whose work or voluntary activities bring them into contact with children and young people. Before joining the NSPCC, he ran his own business, providing editorial services and research. This was after many years working in secondary schools, as an English teacher, a head of English, a director of sixth form and a deputy head teacher with responsibilities including pupil welfare and child protection.

Yvonne Coppard was the manager of Cambridgeshire's Education Child Protection Service for some years. She is currently the Bishop of Ely's Child Protection Adviser and a freelance child protection trainer, working mostly with education staff.

Felicity Fletcher-Campbell is Programme Director: Professional Studies in Education in the Faculty of Education and Language Studies at the Open University. In addition to this, she has a particular brief for inclusive education. Previously, she was Principal Research Officer at the National Foundation for Educational Research, where she undertook a series of research and evaluation projects relating to the education of children in care.

John Guest is Head of Education Welfare and Safeguarding for the London Borough of Southwark, where he has responsibility for school attendance, exclusions, child employment and the education of school-age parents. He is the lead officer for safeguarding within education services and advises and trains school staff and governors on their child protection responsibilities. John also chairs the multi-agency Practice Sub-committee of the Southwark Safeguarding Children Board.

Simon Hackett is Head of the School of Applied Social Sciences at Durham University, UK. His work in relation to sexual abuse and sexual aggression by children and young people is internationally known. He was previously a programme director of G-MAP, a leading UK community-based specialist service for young people. Simon is the author of two books and a variety of other book chapters and journal articles relating to intervention with children and young people with sexually abusive behaviours, including the (2004) Barnardo's publication *What Works for Children and Young People with Harmful Sexual Behaviours?* Simon is editor of the *Journal of Sexual Aggression.*

Enid Hendry is Director of Training and Consultancy for the National Society for the Prevention of Cruelty to Children (NSPCC), where she heads a service working with professionals and organizations throughout the UK and internationally to improve safeguards for children and young people. Her professional background is in social work. She has a particular interest in promoting effective inter-agency working to safeguard children through training, standards and learning resources.

Louise Laskey is a lecturer in the School of Education at Deakin University in Melbourne, Australia. She has previously worked as a teacher and psychologist and has experience in working with families and professionals involved in the child protection system. Louise is presently conducting doctoral research on professional education in child protection with the Australian Centre for Child Protection at the University of South Australia.

Ken McCulloch is a senior lecturer in community education at the University of Edinburgh. From a professional practice background in youth work and community education he has developed teaching and research work on young people and non-formal education, including youth work, aspects of outdoor and adventure education, and young people's citizenship and participation in decision making. Alongside these main interests he has also undertaken work on community schools and on the evaluation of various kinds of educational provision and practice.

Susan McGinnis is Manager of the Glasgow Counselling in Schools Project for the University of Strathclyde. As a counsellor and a long-term advocate of counselling provision for children and young people in Scotland, Susan has an interest in policy-making and is a member of the Counselling and Psychotherapy in Scotland (COSCA) Working Group for Counselling Children and Young People. She has been editor of the British Association for Counselling and Psychotherapy (BACP) journal *Counselling Children and Young People* as well as contributing a chapter to *How We Feel: An Insight Into the Emotional World of Teenagers* (Jessica Kingsley 1997).

David Miller qualified as a social worker in 1983 and has worked with disabled children and their families both as a practitioner and manager. He has contributed to the development of services and managed child protection work. He moved to the NSPCC in 2000 where his role is to promote the safeguarding of disabled children. He co-chairs the National Working Group on Child Protection and Disability.

Graham Music is a consultant child and adolescent psychotherapist at the Tavistock Clinic in London and an adult psychotherapist in private practice. He has a particular interest in service provision for 'hard to reach' groups, and has developed therapeutic services in over 30 schools in four London Boroughs. Other clinical specialties include fostering and adoption and infant mental health. He teaches, supervises and lectures on various child psychotherapy and other trainings in Britain and abroad.

Ann Raymond is an independent consultant and trainer, specializing in the promotion of effective safeguarding for disabled and special needs children in education settings. Ann spent many years as a teacher and manager in special education and was also the NSPCC Education Adviser for South West England. She is a member of the National Working Group on Child Protection and Disability.

Abi Taylor has recently completed a PhD in the School for Applied Social Science at the University of Durham. Her thesis explores the ways in which child care social workers make decisions and the role that the 'Framework for the Assessment of Children in Need and their Families' plays in this process. Prior to this Abi gained an MA with distinction in Research Methods and she has also completed the MA/DipSW.

Lyn Tett is Professor of Community Education and Lifelong Learning in the Moray House School of Education at the University of Edinburgh. Her research interests lie within community education and lifelong learning and have involved an investigation of the factors such as class, gender, disability that lead to the exclusion of adults from post-compulsory education and of the action that might be taken to promote social inclusion. Her most recent books include Community Education, Lifelong Learning and Social Inclusion (2006) and Adult Literacy, Numeracy and Language: Policy, Practice and Research (2006), edited with Mary Hamilton and Yvonne Hillier.

Emma Westcott is a senior policy adviser to the General Teaching Council for England, and a member of the Children's Workforce Network. She has previously held education policy posts with the Local Government Association and the Association of University Teachers.

References

Abrahams, N., Casey, K. and Daro, D. (1992) 'Teachers' knowledge, attitudes, and beliefs about child abuse and its prevention.' *Child Abuse and Neglect 16*, 2, 229–238.

Aldgate, J., Colton, M., Ghate, D. and Heath, A. (1992) 'Educational attainment and stability in long-term foster care.' *Children and Society 2*, 6, 91–103.

Araji, S. (1997) *Sexually Aggressive Children: Coming to Understand Them.* Thousand Oaks: Sage.

Atkinson, M. and Hornby, G. (2002) *Mental Health Handbook for Schools.* London: Routledge.

Atkinson, M., Wilkin, A., Stott, A. and Kinder, K. (2001) *Multi-Agency Working: An Audit of Activity.* Slough: National Foundation for Educational Research.

Audit Commission (1994) *Seen But Not Heard. Co-ordinating Community Child Health and Social Services for Children in Need.* London: HMSO.

Australian Institute of Health and Welfare (AIHW) (2006) *Child Protection Australia 2004–2005.* AIHW Cat No. CWS 26, Child Welfare Series, No. 37. Canberra: Australian Institute of Health and Welfare.

Australian Institute of Health and Welfare (AIHW) (2007) *Child Protection Australia 2005–2006.* AIHW, Cat No. CWS 28, Child Welfare Series, No. 38, Canberra: Australian Institute of Health and Welfare.

Baginsky, M. (2000) *Child Protection and Education.* London: NSPCC.

Baginsky, M. (2003) 'Newly qualified teachers and child protection: a survey of their views, training and experiences.' *Child Abuse Review 12*, 2, 119–127.

Baginsky, M. (2004) *Evaluation of the NSPCC's School Teams Service.* Unpublished report for NSPCC.

Baginsky, M. (2007) *Schools, Social Services and Safeguarding Children: Past Practice and Future Challenges.* London: NSPCC.

Baginsky, M. and Hodgkinson, K. (1999) 'Child protection training in initial training: a survey of provision in institutions of higher education.' *Educational Research 41*, 2, 173–181.

Baginsky, M. with Davies, S. (2000) *Report on the Evaluation of the Piloting of 'Child Protection in Initial Teacher Training' 1999–2000.* Internal report for the National Society for the Prevention of Cruelty to Children.

Ball, M. (1998) *School Inclusion: The School, Family and the Community.* York: Joseph Rowntree Foundation.

Berridge, D. (1985) *Children's Homes.* Oxford: Blackwell.

Berridge, D., Brodie, I., Ayre, P., Barrett, D., Henderson, B. and Wenman, H. (1996) *Is Anybody Listening? The Education of Young People in Residential Care.* Luton: University of Luton.

Bichard, M. (2004) *The Bichard Inquiry Report (HC653).* London: The Stationery Office. www.bichardinquiry.org.uk/report

Birchall, E. (1992) *Report to the Department of Health: Working Together in Child Protection; Report of Phase Two: A Survey of the Experience and Perceptions of Six Key Professionals.* Stirling: University of Stirling.

Blake, S. and Muttock, S. (2004) *PSHE and Citizenship for Children and Young People with Special Needs: An Agenda for Action.* London: National Children's Bureau.

Blaskett, B. and Taylor, S.C. (2003) *Facilitators and Inhibitors of Mandatory Reporting of Suspected Child Abuse.* Canberra: Report for the Criminology Research Council.

Bluestone, C. (2005) 'Personal disciplinary history and views of physical punishment: implications for training mandated reporters.' *Child Abuse Review 14*, 4, 240–258.

Booker, R. and Sargeant, A. (2004) *Achievement through Partnership.* Surrey Child and Adolescent Mental Health Service. Paper presented at Twelfth European Social Services Conference, Dublin, 16–18 June.

Bonner, B.L., Walker, C.E. and Berliner, L. (1999) *Children with Sexual Behavior Problems: Assessment and Treatment. Final report.* Washington, DC: Department of Health and Human Services.

Bor, R., Ebner-Landy, J., Gill, S. and Brace, C. (2002) *Counselling in Schools.* London: Sage.

Brennan, M. (2006) *Understanding Online Social Network Services and Risks to Youth.* London: CEOP. www.ceop.gov.uk/mediacentre/pressreleases/2006/ceop_04122006.asp

Briggs, F. and Hawkins, R. (1997) *Child Protection: A Guide for Teachers and Child Care Professionals.* St Leonards: Allen and Unwin.

Bromfield, L. and Higgins, D. (2005) 'National comparison of child protection systems.' *National Child Protection Clearinghouse 22.*, Autumn.

Bronstein, L. and Abramson, J. (2003) 'Understanding socialization of teachers and social workers: groundwork for collaboration in the schools.' *Families in Society 84*, 3, 323–330.

Burton, D.L., Rasmussen, L.A., Bradshaw, J., Christopherson, B.J. and Huke, S.C. (1998) *Treating Children with Sexually Abusive Behaviour Problems: Guidelines for Child and Parent Intervention.* New York: Haworth Press.

Butler Sloss, E. (1988) *Report of the Inquiry into Child Abuse in Cleveland 1987 (Cleveland Inquiry).* London: HMSO.

Calder, M.C. (2001) *Juveniles and Children who Sexually Abuse: Frameworks for Assessment,* 2nd edn. Lyme Regis: Russell House.

Cambridge Health Authority and Cambridgeshire Local Education Authority (1987) *Personal Safety Programme.* Cambridge: Cambs County Council.

Campbell, C. (ed.) (2002) *Developing Inclusive Schooling: Perspectives, Policies and Practices.* London: Institute of Education, University of London.

Campbell, H. and Wigglesworth, A. (1993) 'Child protection in schools: a survey of the training needs of Fife schoolteachers.' *Public Health 107*, 413–419.

Cawson, P., Wattam, C., Brooker, S. and Kelly, G. (2000) *Child Maltreatment in the United Kingdom: A Study of the Prevalence of Child Abuse and Neglect.* London: NSPCC.

Central Advisory Council for Education (1967) *Children and their Primary Schools (The Plowden Report).* London: HMSO.

Chaffin, M., Letourneau, E. and Silovsky, J.F. (2002) 'Adults, adolescents and children who sexually abuse children: a developmental perspective.' In J. Myers, L. Berliner, J. Briere, C.T. Hendrix, C. Jenny and T. Reid (eds) *The APSAC Handbook on Child Maltreatment,* 2nd edn. Thousand Oaks, CA: Sage.

Challis, L., Fuller, S., Henwood, M., Klein, R., Plowden, W., Webb, A., Whittingham, P. and Wistow, G. (1988) *Joint Approaches to Social Policy: Rationality and Practice.* Cambridge: Cambridge University Press.

Chazan, M. (1994) 'The attitudes of mainstream teachers towards pupils with emotional and behavioural difficulties.' *European Journal of Special Needs Education 9*, 3, 261–274.

Child Accident Prevention Trust (2002) *Taking chances: The Lifestyles and Leisure Risk of Young People.* London: CAPT.

ChildLine (2005) *ChildLine Annual Review.* London: ChildLine. www.childline.org.uk/Annualreview.asp

Children's Commissioner for Wales (2004) *Clywch – Report of the Examination of the Children's Commissioner for Wales into Allegations of Child Sexual Abuse in a School Setting.* Swansea: Children's Commissioner for Wales. www.childcomwales.org.uk

Children's Workforce Development Council (CWDC) (2006) *CWDC Induction Standards.* Leeds: CWDC. www.cwdcouncil.org.uk

Clarke, M. and Stewart, J. (1997) *Handling the Wicked Issues – A Challenge for Government.* Discussion Paper, University of Birmingham.

Cm 6932 (2006) *Care Matters: Transforming the Lives of Children and Young People in Care.* Cm 6932. Norwich: The Stationery Office.

Cole, T., Visser, J. and Upton, G. (1998) *Effective Schools for Pupils with Emotional and Behavioural Difficulties.* London: David Fulton.

Collishaw, S., Maughan, B., Goodman, R. and Pickles, A. (2004) 'Time trends in adolescent mental health.' *Journal of Child Psychology and Psychiatry 45*, 8, 1350–1362.

Commission for Social Care Inspection (CSCI) (2007) *About Education: A Children's Views Report.* London: CSCI.

Commission for Social Care Inspection (CSCI), HM Inspectorate of Court Administration, The Healthcare Commission, HM Inspectorate of Constabulary, HM Inspectorate of Probation, HM Inspectorate of Prisons, HM Crown Prosecution Service Inspectorate, and The Office for Standards in Education (2005) *Safeguarding Children: The Second Joint Chief Inspectors' Report on Arrangements to Safeguard Children.* www.safeguardingchildren.org.uk

Committee on Local Authority and Allied Personal Social Services (1968) *Report of the Committee on Local Authority and Allied Personal Social Services (Seebohm Report)* (Cmnd 3703). London: HMSO.

Continyou (2005) *Taking Part: Making Out-of-School-Hours Learning Happen for Children in Care.* London: ContinYou.

Cooper, M. (2006) *Counselling in Schools Project: Phase 2.* Glasgow: University of Strathclyde.

Cooper, P., Drummond, M., Hart, S., Lovey, J. and McLaughlin, C. (2000) *Positive Alternatives to Exclusion.* London: Routledge.

Crenshaw, W.B., Crenshaw, L.M. and Lichtenberg, J.W. (1995) 'When educators confront child abuse: an analysis of the decision to report.' *Child Abuse and Neglect 19,* 9, 1095–1113.

Cunningham, C. and MacFarlane, K. (1991) *When Children Molest Children.* Orwell: Safer Society Press.

Dagley, V., Howe, A., Salter, C., Brandon, M., Warren, C. and Black, J. (2007) 'Implications of the new common assessment framework and lead professional working for pastoral care staff in schools.' *Pastoral Care,* March.

Daniels, H., Visser, J., Cole, T. and De Reybekill, N. (1999) *Emotional and Behavioural Difficulties in Mainstream Schools.* London: DfEE.

Davies, J. (2002) 'Frustration at child abuse reports.' *The Age,* Friday 8 February, p.7.

Deakin, G. and Kelly, G. (2006) *Children's Workforce Research.* London: DfES.

Department for Education and Employment (DfEE) (1995) *Protecting Children from Abuse: The Role of the Educational Service (Circular 10/95).* London: Department of Education and Employment.

Department for Education and Employment (1998) *Section 550A of the Education Act 1996: The Use of Force to Control and Restrain Pupils.* London: DfEE.

Department for Education and Employment (2000) *Sex and Relationship Education Guidance.* London: DfEE.

Department for Education and Skills (2001) *Special Educational Needs Code of Practice.* London: DfES.

Department for Education and Skills (2002) *Guidance on the Use of Physical Interventions for Pupils with Severe Behavioural Difficulties.* London: DfES.

Department for Education and Skills (Cm5860) (DfES) (2003) *Every Child Matters* (Cmnd 5860). London: The Stationery Office.

Department for Education and Skills (2004a) *Safeguarding Children in Education.* London: DfES.

Department for Education and Skills (2004b) *Every Child Matters: Change for Children.* London: DfES.

Department for Education and Skills (2004c) *Removing Barriers to Achievement.* London: DfES.

Department for Education and Skills (2004d) *Working Together: Giving Children and Young People a Say.* London: DfES.

Department for Education and Skills (2006a) *Safeguarding Children and Safer Recruitment in Education.* London: DfES.

Department for Education and Skills (2006b) *National School Attendance Codes.* London: DfES.

Department for Education and Skills (2006c) *What to Do if you're Worried a Child is Being Abused.* London: DfES. www.everychildmatters.gov.uk/safeguarding

Department for Education and Skills (2007) *Care Matters: Transforming the Lives of Children and Young People in Care.* London: DfES

Department for Education and Skills and Department of Health (2002) *Guidance on the Use of Physical Interventions for Staff Working with Children and Adults who Display Extreme Behaviour in Association with Learning Disability and/or Autistic Spectrum Disorders.* London: DfES.

Department of Education and Science (DES) (1988) *Working Together for the Protection of Children from Abuse: Procedures within the Education Service (Circular 4/88).* London: Department of Education and Science.

Department of Education and Training (2000) *Child Protection Education: Curriculum Materials to Support Teaching and Learning in Personal Development, Health and Physical Education.* New South Wales: Department of Education and Training.

Department of Education Northern Ireland (DENI) (1999) *Pastoral Care in Schools: Child Protection.* Bangor Co Down: DENI. www.deni.gov.uk/dc1999–10–5.pdf.

Department of Education Northern Ireland (2001) *Pastoral Care in Schools: Promoting Positive Behaviour.* Bangor Co Down: DENI. www.deni.gov.uk/ppbehaviour-4.pdf.

Department of Health (DoH) (1995) *Child Protection: Messages from Research.* London: HMSO.

Department of Health (2001) *Education Protects: Guidance on the Education of Children and Young People in Public Care – Summary for Foster Carers.* London: DoH.

Department of Health (2004) *National Service Framework for Children, Young People and Maternity Services.* London: DH. www.dh.gov.uk

Department of Health and Department for Education and Employment (2000) *Guidance on the Education of Children and Young People in Public Care.* London: DfEE.

Department of Health, Home Office and Department for Education and Employment (1999) *Working Together to Safeguard Children: A Guide to Interagency Working to Safeguard and Promote the Welfare of Children.* London: Stationery Office.

Department of Health and Social Security (DHSS) (1974a) *Report of the Committee of Inquiry into the Care and Supervision Provided in Relation to Maria Colwell.* London: Department of Health and Social Security.

Department of Health and Social Security (DHSS) (1974b) *Memorandum On Non-Accidental Injury To Children.* London: Department of Health and Social Security.

Department of Health, Social Services and Public Safety (2003) *Co-operating to Safeguard Children.* www.dhsspsni.gov.uk/show_publications?txtid=14022

Dicker, R. and Gilbert, J. (1988) 'The role of the telephone in educational research.' *British Educational Research Journal 14,* 1, 65–72.

Dolan, M., Holloway, J., Bailey, S. and Kroll, L. (1996) 'The psychosocial characteristics of juvenile sexual offenders referred to an adolescent forensic service in the UK.' *Medical Science Law 36,* 4, 342–352.

Dowling, E. and Osborne, E. (1985) *The Family and the School.* London: Routledge.

Dryfoos, J. (1996) 'Full service schools.' *Educational Leadership 53,* 7, 18–23.

Dyson, A., Lin, M. and Millward, A. (1998) *Effective Communication between Schools, LEAs and Health and Social Services in the Field of Special Educational Needs.* Research Report RR60. London: DfEE.

Dyson, A. and Robson, E. (1999) *School Inclusion: The Evidence.* Newcastle: Department of Education, University of Newcastle.

Education Child Protection Service (2001) *Staying Safe – a Personal Safety Programme for Schools: Foundation and Key Stage One; Key Stage Two.* Cambridge: Cambs County Council.

Erooga, M. and Masson, H. (2006) 'Children and young people with sexually harmful or abusive behaviours: underpinning knowledge, principles, approaches and service provision.' In M. Erooga and H. Masson (eds) *Children and Young People who Sexually Abuse Others: Current Developments and Practice Responses.* London: Routledge.

Evans, J., Harden, A. and Thomas, J. (2003) *Support for Pupils with Emotional and Behavioural Difficulties (EBD) in Mainstream Primary Classrooms: A Review of the Effectiveness of Interventions. EPPI-Centre Review.* London: Social Science Research Unit, Institute of Education.

Featherstone, B. and Evans, H. (2004) *Children Experiencing Maltreatment: Who Do They Turn To?* London: NSPCC. www.nspcc.org.uk/inform

Fife Council (2000) *New Community School Policy Plan.* Glenrothes: Fife Council.

Finkelhor, D. (1984) *Child Sexual Abuse: New Theory and Research.* New York: Free Press.

Fletcher, C. (1983) *The Challenges of Community Education. A Biography of the Sutton Centre 1970 to 1982.* Nottingham: University of Nottingham.

Fletcher-Campbell, F. (1997) *The Education of Children who are Looked-After.* Slough: NfER.

Fletcher-Campbell, F., Archer, T. and Tomlinson, K. (2004) *The Role of the School in Supporting the Education of Children in Public Care.* Research Report 49. London: DfES.

Fletcher-Campbell, F., Pijl, S.J., Meijer, C., Dyson, A. and Parrish, T. (2003) 'The distribution of funds for special needs education.' *The International Journal of Educational Management 17,* 5, 220–233.

Fox, C. and Butler, I. (2003) *Evaluation of the NSPCC Schools Teams.* Unpublished study for NSPCC.

Gibbs, J. and Bennett, S. (1990) *Together We Can.* Seattle, WA: Comprehensive Health Education Foundation.

Gilligan, R. (2000) 'Adversity, resilience and young people: the protective value of positive school and spare time experiences.' *Children and Society 14,* 37–47.

Gipps, C. (1993) 'The profession of educational research' (Presidential address). *British Educational Research Journal 19,* 1, 3–17.

Goddard, C., Saunders, B., Stanley, J. and Tucci, J. (2002) *A Study in Confusion: Factors which Affect the Decisions of Community Professionals when Reporting Child Abuse and Neglect.* Melbourne: Australians Against Child Abuse.

Gray, A., Pithers, W.D., Busconi, A. and Houchens, P. (1999) 'Developmental and etiological characteristics of children with sexual behavior problems: treatment implications.' *Child Abuse and Neglect 23,* 6, 601–621.

Gray, P. and Noakes, J. (1998) 'Current legislation for pupils with emotional and behavioural difficulties: a clear way forward?' *Support for Learning 13,* 4, 184–187.

Green, L. and Masson, H. (2002) 'Adolescents who sexually abuse and residential accommodation: issues of risk and vulnerability.' *British Journal of Social Work 32,* 149–168.

Griffin, S., Williams, M., Hawkes, C. and Vizard, E. (1997) 'The professional carers' group: supporting group work for young sexual abusers.' *Child Abuse and Neglect 21,* 7, 681–690.

Hackett, S. (2004) *What Works for Children and Young People with Harmful Sexual Behaviours?* Barkingside: Barnado's.

Hackett, S. and Masson, H. (2006) 'Young people who have sexually abused: what do they (and their parents) want from professionals?' *Children and Society 20,* 3, 183–195.

Halsey, A.H. (1972) *Educational Priority Areas,* Vol. 1. London: HMSO.

Harker, R., Dobel-Ober, D., Berridge, D. and Sinclair, R. (2003) 'Who takes care of education? Looked-after children's perceptions of support for educational progress.' *Child and Family Social Work 8,* 2, 89–100.

Hatcher, R. and Leblond, D. (2001) 'Education action zones and zones d'éducation prioritaires.' (2001) In S. Ridell and T. Tett (eds) *Education, Social Justice and Inter-agency Working: Joined Up or Fractured Policy?* London: Routledge.

Hawkins, R. and McCallum, C. (2001) 'Mandatory notification training for suspected child abuse and neglect in South Australian schools.' *Child Abuse and Neglect 25,* 12, 1603–1625.

HM Government (2005) *Common Core of Skills and Knowledge for the Children's Workforce.* London: Department for Education and Skills. www.everychildmatters.gov.uk/commoncore

HM Government (2006) *Working Together to Safeguard Children: A Guide to Inter-agency Working to Safeguard and Promote the Welfare of Children.* London: The Stationery Office. www.everychildmatters.gov.uk/safeguarding

HM Inspectorate of Education (2004) *The Sum of its Parts? The Development of Integrated Community Schools in Scotland.* Edinburgh: HM Inspectorate of Education.

Home Office, Department of Health, Department of Education and Science and Welsh Office (1991) *Working Together Under the Children Act 1989: A Guide to Arrangements for Interagency Co-operation for the Protection of Children from Abuse.* London: HMSO.

Huxham, C. (ed.) (1996) *Creating Collaborative Advantage.* London: Sage Publications.

Huxham, C. and Vangen, S. (1996) 'Working together: key themes in the management of relationships between public and non-profit organizations.' *International Journal of Public Sector Management 9,* 7, 5–17.

Jackson, E. (2002) 'Mental health in schools: what about the staff?' *Journal of Child Psychotherapy 28,* 2.

Jackson, S. (1987) *The Education of Children in Care.* Bristol: School for Advanced Urban Studies.

Johnson, B. (1995) *Teaching and Learning about Personal Safety: Report of the Review of Protective Behaviours in South Australia.* Adelaide: Painters Prints.

Johnson, B. (2005) *Identifying and Resolving Dilemmas and Tensions Associated with Teaching Child Protection Curricula in Schools: A South Australian Case Study.* Paper presented at the Annual Conference of the British Educational Research Association, University of Glamorgan, Wales, September 2005.

Johnson, T.C. and Doonan, R. (2005) 'Children with sexual behaviour problems: what we have learned in the last two decades.' In M.C. Calder (ed) *Children and Young People who Sexually Abuse: New Theory, Research and Practice Developments.* Lyme Regis: Russell House Publishing.

Jones, J. (2007) *What Really Matters in Integrated Working. Report of a Qualitative Evaluation of Telford and Wrekin and Shropshire ISA Trailblazer 2004–2006.* Leicester: Mindful Practice Ltd, Shropshire County Council and Telford and Wrekin Council.

Kazdin, A. (1987) 'Treatment of antisocial behavior in children: current status and future directions.' *Psychological Bulletin 102,* 187–203.

Kendrick, A. (1995) 'Supporting families through inter-agency work: youth strategies.' In M. Hill, R. Kirk and D. Part (eds) *Supporting Families.* Edinburgh: HMSO.

Kennedy, E. (2004) *Child and Adolescent Psychotherapy: A Systematic Review of Psychoanalytic Approaches.* London: North Central London Strategic Health Authority.

Kenny, M.L. (2001) 'Child abuse reporting: teachers' perceived deterrents.' *Child Abuse and Neglect 25*, 1, 81–92.

Kent, R. (1997) *Children's Safeguards Review.* Edinburgh: Scottish Office.

Kettunen, P. (1994) *Implementation in a Multi-Organizational Setting: Local Networks in Environmental Health Policy.* Annales Universitatis Turkuensis. Turku: Turun Yliopisto.

Klinefelter, P. (1994) A school counselling service. *Counselling,* August, 215–217.

Kovic, Y., Lucas-Hancock, J. and Miller, D. (forthcoming) *Safe: A Safety and Awareness Group Work Programme for Deaf Children.* London: NSPCC.

Kvam, M.H. (2004) 'Sexual abuse of deaf children. A retrospective analysis of the prevalence and characteristics of childhood sexual abuse among deaf adults in Norway.' *Child Abuse and Neglect 28*, 3, 241–251.

Laming, H. (Cm 5730) (2003) *The Victoria Climbié Inquiry: Report of an Inquiry by Lord Laming.* Norwich: The Stationery Office. www.victoria-climbie-inquiry.org.uk

Laskey, L. (1995) *Mandatory Reporting: Teacher Responses to Implementation.* Paper presented at the Fifth Australasian Conference on Child Abuse and Neglect, Melbourne.

Leathard, A. (ed.) (2003) *Interprofessional Collaboration: From Policy to Practice in Health and Social Care.* Hove: Brunner/Routledge.

Levy, A. and Kahan, B. (1991) *The Pindown Experience and the Protection of Children.* Stafford: Staffordshire County Council.

Lipson, J. (ed.) (2001) *Hostile Hallways: Bullying, Teasing and Sexual Harassment in School.* Washington, DC: American Association of University Women Educational Foundation.

Little, M., Axford, N. and Morpeth, L. (2004) 'Research review: risk and protection in the context of services for children in need.' *Child and Family Social Work 9*, 105–117.

Livingstone, S. and Bober, M. (2005) *UK Children Go Online: Final Report of Project Findings.* London: LSE. www.children-go-online.net

Lloyd, G., Stead, J. and Kendrick, A. (2001) *Hanging On In There: A Study of Inter-agency Work to Prevent Social Exclusion in Three Local Authorities.* London: National Children's Bureau and The Joseph Rowntree Foundation.

Lloyd, G., Stead, J. and Kendrick, A. (2003) 'Joined-up approaches to prevent social exclusion.' *Emotional and Behavioural Difficulties 8*, 1, 77–91.

Lovell, E. (2002) '*I Think I Might Need Some More Help With This Problem...' Responding to Children and Young People who Display Sexually Harmful Behaviour.* London: NSPCC.

MacIntyre, D. and Carr, A. (2000) 'Prevention of child sexual abuse: implications of program evaluation research.' *Child Abuse Review 9*, 3, 183–199.

Maguire, M. and Ball, S. (1994) 'Discourse in educational reform in the United Kingdom and the USA and the work of teachers.' *British Journal of In-Service Education 20*, 1, 5–16.

Manocha, K.F. and Mezey, G. (1998) 'British adolescents who sexually abuse: a descriptive study.' *Journal of Forensic Psychiatry 9*, 3, 588–608.

Martin, P.Y. and Jackson, S. (2002) 'Educational success for children in public care: advice from a group of high achievers.' *Child and Family Social Work 7*, 121–130.

Masson, H. (2001) *Children and Young People who Sexually Abuse Others: A Report to Inform the Initial Work of NOTA's National Committee on Sexual Abuse by Young People.* Unpublished Report.

Masson, H. and Hackett, S. (2003) 'A decade on from the NCH Report (1992): Adolescent sexual aggression policy, practice and service delivery across the UK and Republic of Ireland.' *Journal of Sexual Aggression 9*, 2, 109–124.

Mayes, G., Gillies, J. and Warden, D. (1990) 'Stranger danger: what do children know?' *Child Abuse Review 6*, 1, 11–23.

McCallum, F. (2001) *Cracks in the Concrete: The Demise of the Teacher's Role in Reporting Child Abuse and Neglect.* Paper presented at the Australian Association for Research in Education (AARE), 2–6 December 2001 in Fremantle, Australia. www.aare.edu.au/01pap/mcc01550.htm

McInnes, E. (2002) *Supporting mandatory reporting in schools.* Paper presented at the Role of Schools in Crime Prevention Conference, Melbourne, 30 September – 1 October 2002. http://aic.gov.au/conferences/schools/mcinnes.html

Mencap (2005) *They Won't Believe Me: Bullying of Children with a Learning Disability.* London: Mencap.

Milbourne, L. (2005) 'Children, families and inter-agency work: experiences of partnership work in primary education settings.' *British Educational Research Journal 31*, 6, 675–695.

Miner, M.H. and Crimmins, C.L.S. (1995) 'Adolescent sex offenders: issues of etiology and risk factors.' In B.K. Schwartz and H.R. Cellini (eds) *The Sex Offender.* Kingston NJ: Civic Research Institute.

Morgan, R. (2004) *Children's Views on Restraint: The Views of Children and Young People in Residential Homes and Residential Special Schools.* Newcastle-upon-Tyne: Commission for Social Care Inspection.

Morris, J. (2006) *Safeguarding Disabled Children: A Resource for Local Safeguarding Children Boards.* London: DfES. www.everychildmatters.gov.uk/resources-and-practice/search/IG00048

National Child Protection Clearinghouse (2005) *Child Abuse Prevention Resource Sheet No. 3.* Melbourne: Australian Institute of Family Studies.

National Committee on Adolescents Who Sexually Harm (NOTA) (2003) *Response to Protecting the Public – Strengthening Protection Against Sex Offenders and Reforming the Law on Sexual Offences* (2002, Cm 5668, TSO). Available from www.nota.co.uk

National Working Group on Child Protection and Disability (NWGCPD) (2003) *It Doesn't Happen to Disabled Children: Child Protection and Disabled Children.* London: NSPCC.

Newman, T. (2002) *Promoting Resilience: A Review of Effective Strategies for Child Care Services.* Exeter: Barnardos.

Nisbet, J., Hendry, L., Stewart, C. and Watt, J. (1980) *Towards Community Education: An Evaluation of Community Schools.* Aberdeen: Aberdeen University Press.

Norfolk Health Authority (2002) *Summary Report of the Independent Health Review.* www.nscsha.nhs.uk/resources/pdf/review_inquiry/lauren_wright/lauren_wright_indep_report_0 302.pdf

Norwich, B. and Poulou, M. (2000) 'Teachers' perceptions of students with emotional and behavioural difficulties.' *European Journal of Special Needs Education 15*, 2, 171–187.

Nuffield Foundation (2004) *Time Trends in Adolescent Well-being.* London: Nuffield Foundation.

O'Callaghan, D. (1998) 'Practice issues in working with young abusers who have learning difficulties.' *Child Abuse Review 7*, 435–448.

Office for National Statistics (ONS) (2005) *Mental Health in Children and Young People in Great Britain.* London: ONS.

Office of the First Minister and Deputy First Minister (2006) *Our Children and Young People – Our Pledge: A Ten Year Strategy for Children and Young People in Northern Ireland 2006–2016.* www.allchildrenni.gov.uk/ten-year-strategy.pdf

O'Toole, R., Webster, S.W., O'Toole, A.W. and Lucal, B. (1999) 'Teachers' recognition and reporting of child abuse: A factorial survey.' *Child Abuse and Neglect 23*, 11, 1083–1101.

Parsons, C. (1999) *Education, Exclusion and Citizenship.* London: Routledge.

Parton, N. (2006) *Safeguarding Childhood: Early Intervention and Surveillance in a Late Modern Society.* Hampshire: Palgrave Macmillan.

Paul, A., Cawson, P. and Paton, J. (2004) *Safeguarding Disabled Children in Residential Schools.* London: NSPCC.

Pickles, T. (1992) 'Youth Strategies in Scotland.' In G. Lloyd, (ed.) *Chosen with Care? Responses to Disturbing and Disruptive Behaviour.* Edinburgh: Moray House Publications Scotland.

Pierre, J. and Peters, B.G. (2000) *Governance, Politics and the State.* London: Macmillan.

Pithers, W.D. and Gray, A. (1993) *Pre-adolescent Sexual Abuse Research Project.* Washington, DC: National Center on Child Abuse and Neglect.

Popper, S.H. (1965) 'The challenge to the two professions.' In R.H. Beck (ed.) *Society and the Schools: Communication Challenge to Education and Social Work.* New York: NASW Press.

Power, S. (2001) 'Joined up thinking? Inter-agency partnerships in educational action zones.' In S. Riddell and L. Tett (eds) *Education, Social Justice and Inter-agency Working: Joined Up or Fractured Policy?* London: Routledge.

Prentky, R., Harris, B., Frizzell, K. and Righthand, S. (2000) 'An actuarial procedure for assessing risk with juvenile sex offenders.' *Sexual Abuse 12*, 4, 71–89.

Print, B., Morrison, T. and Henniker, J. (2001) 'An inter-agency assessment framework for young people who sexually abuse: principles, processes and practicalities.' In M.C. Calder (ed.) *Juveniles and Children who Sexually Abuse: Frameworks for Assessment,* 2nd edn. Lyme Regis: Russell House Publishing.

Pugh, K. and Meier, R. (2006) *Stressed Out and Struggling Project Report 1: Service-Mapping.* London: Young Minds.

Rassmussen, L. (1999) 'Factors related to recidivism among juvenile sexual offenders.' *Sexual Abuse: A Journal of Research and Treatment 11*, 1, 69–85.

Rée, H. (1973) *Educator Extraordinary: The Life and Achievements of Henry Morris.* London: Longmans.

Reid, S. (1999) 'The group as a healing whole: group psychotherapy with children and adolescents.' In A. Horne and M. Ianyado (eds) *The Handbook of Child and Adolescent Psychotherapy.* London: Routledge.

Reiniger, A., Robison, E. and McHugh, M. (1995) 'Mandated training of professionals: a means for improving reporting of suspected child abuse.' *Child Abuse and Neglect 19*, 1, 63–69.

Riddell, S. and Tett, L. (2001) *Education, Social Justice and Inter-agency Working: Joined Up or Fractured Policy?* London: Routledge.

Righthand, S. and Welch, C. (2001) *Juveniles Who Have Sexually Offended. A Review of the Professional Literature.* Washington, DC: Office of Juvenile Justice and Delinquency Prevention.

Ryan, G. (2000) 'Childhood sexuality: a decade of study. Part 1 – Research and curriculum development.' *Child Abuse and Neglect 24*, 1, 33–48.

Ryan, G., Blum, J., Sandau-Christopher, D., Law, S., Weher, F., Sundine, C. *et al.* (1993) *Understanding and Responding to the Sexual Behaviour of Children: Trainer's Manual.* Denver, CO: Kempe Children's Center.

Ryan, G., Miyoshi, T.J., Metzner, J.L., Krugman, R.D. and Fryer, R.G. (1996) 'Trends in a national sample of sexually abusive youths.' *Journal of the American Academy of Child and Adolescent Psychiatry 33*, 17–25.

Salzberger-Wittenberg, I., Williams, G. and Osborne, E. (1999) *The Emotional Experience of Learning and Teaching.* London: Karnac.

Schaffer, M. (1992) 'Children's hearings and school problems.' In G. Lloyd (ed.) *Chosen with Care? Responses to Disturbing and Disruptive Behaviour.* Edinburgh: Moray House Publications.

Scottish Executive (2000a) *Social Justice Annual Report.* Edinburgh: Stationery Office.

Scottish Executive (2000b) *Making It Happen. Report of the Strategy Action Team.* Edinburgh: Scottish Executive.

Scottish Executive (2001) *For Scotland's Children Report.* Edinburgh: Stationery Office.

Scottish Executive (2002) *Everyone Matters: Delivering Social Justice in Scotland.* Edinburgh: Stationery Office.

Scottish Executive (2005) *Safe and Well: A Handbook for Schools and Education Authorities Describing Good Practice in Child Protection in Education and When a Child Goes Missing from Education.* Edinburgh: Scottish Executive. www.scotland.gov.uk/Publications/2005/08/0191408/14132

Scottish Executive (2006) *Getting it Right for Every Child. Proposals for Action.* Edinburgh: Scottish Executive. www.scotland.gov.uk/Publications/2005/06/20135608/56098

Scottish Office (1964) *The Kilbrandon Report.* Edinburgh: HMSO.

Scottish Office (1999) *Social Inclusion Strategy for Scotland.* Edinburgh: Scottish Office.

Semmens, R. (2001) 'Full-service schooling: from "at risk" students to full-status citizens in Australia.' In S. Riddell and L. Tett (eds) *Education, Social Justice and Inter-agency Working: Joined-up or Fractured Policy?* London: Routledge.

Shoop, R.J. and Edwards, D.L. (1994) *How to Stop Sexual Harassment in our Schools: A Handbook and Curriculum Guide for Administrators and Teachers.* Boston, MA: Allyn and Bacon.

Silovsky, J.F. and Niec, L. (2002) 'Characteristics of young children with sexual behavior problems: a pilot study.' *Child Maltreatment 7*, 3, 187–197.

Skinner, J. (1999) 'Teachers coping with sexual abuse issues.' *Educational Research 41*, 3, 329–339.

Smith, M. and Tett, L. (2003) 'New community schools and pupils with social, emotional and behavioural difficulties.' *Scottish Educational Review 34*, 2, 151–162.

Social Exclusion Unit (1998) *Bringing Britain Together: A National Strategy for Neighbourhood Renewal.* London: Stationery Office.

Social Work Inspection Agency (2006) *Extraordinary Lives: Creating a Positive Future for Looked After Children and Young People in Scotland.* Edinburgh: Social Work Inspection Agency. www.scotland.gov.uk/Publications/2006/09/08145438/1

Stead, J., Lloyd, G. and Kendrick, A. (2004) 'Participation or practice innovation: tensions in inter-agency working to address disciplinary exclusion from school.' *Children and Society 18*, 42–52.

Stein, M. and Carey, K. (1986) *Leaving Care.* Oxford: Blackwell.

Steineger, M. (2001) *Preventing and Countering School-based Harassment. A Resource Guide for K-12 Educators,* revised edn. Portland, OR: Northwest Regional Educational Laboratory.

Sullivan, P.M. and Knutson, J.F. (2000) 'Maltreatment and disabilities: a population based epidemiological study.' *Child Abuse and Neglect 24,* 10, 1257–1273.

Taylor, J.F. (2003) 'Children and young people accused of child sexual abuse: a study within a community.' *Journal of Sexual Aggression 9,* 1, 57–70.

Taylor, S.C. and Lloyd, D. (2001) 'Mandatory reporting and child sexual abuse: contextualising beliefs and attitudes.' *Australian Association for Research in Education, National Conference Proceedings.* Perth.

Tett, L., Crowther, J. and O'Hara, P. (2003) 'Collaborative partnerships in community education.' *Journal of Education Policy 18,* 1, 37–51.

Timms, S. and Goreczny, A.J. (2002) 'Adolescent sex offenders with mental retardation. Literature review and assessment considerations.' *Aggression and Violent Behavior 7,* 1–9.

Tomison, A. (2002) 'Mandatory reporting: a question of theory versus practice.' *Developing Practice: The Child, Youth and Family Work Journal 4,* 13–17.

Trowell, J. and Bower, M. (1995) *The Emotional Needs of Young Children and Their Families.* London: Routledge.

Trudell, B. and Whatley, M.H. (1988) 'School sexual abuse prevention: unintended consequences and dilemmas.' *Child Abuse and Neglect 12,* 1, 103–113.

Utting, W. (1991) *Children in the Public Care: A Review of Residential Child Care.* London: HMSO.

Utting, W. (1997) *People Like Us: The Report of the Review of the Safeguards for Children Living Away from Home.* London: The Stationery Office.

Vizard, E. (2002) 'The assessment of young sexual abusers.' In M.C. Calder (ed.) *Young People Who Sexually Abuse. Building the Evidence Base for Your Practice.* Lyme Regis: Russell House Publishing.

Walsh, K., Farrell, A., Schweitzer, R. and Bridgstock, R. (2005) *Critical Factors in Teachers Detecting and Reporting Child Abuse: Implications for Practice.* Brisbane: The Abused Child Trust.

Warnock Report (1978) *Special Educational Needs* (Report by the Committee of Enquiry into the Education of Handicapped Children and Young People). London: HMSO.

Watts, V. (1997) *Responding to Child Abuse: A Handbook for Teachers.* Rockhampton: Central Queensland University Press.

Watts, V. and Laskey, L. (1997) 'Where have all the flowers gone? Child Protection education for preservice teachers in Australian universities.' *Asia Pacific Journal of Teacher Education 25,* 2 171–177.

Watts, V. and Laskey, L. (2002) 'Including teachers as real partners in child protection.' *Nuance: International Journal of Family Policy and Related Issues 4,* 1–11.

Webb, R. and Vulliamy, G. (2001a) 'Joining up the solutions: the rhetoric and practice of inter-agency co-operation.' *Childhood and Society 15,* 315–332.

Webb, R. and Vulliamy, G. (2001b) 'The primary teacher's role in child protection.' *British Educational Research Journal 27,* 1, 59–77.

Webb, R. and Vulliamy, G. (2004) *A Multi-agency Approach to Reducing Disaffection and Exclusions from School. University of York Research Report 568.* Nottingham: DfES Publications.

Weissberg, G.R.P. and O'Brien, M.U. (2004) 'What works in school-based social and emotional learning programs for positive youth development.' *Annals AAPSS 591,* 86–97.

Welsh Assembly Government (2002) *Children and Young People: Rights to Action.* Cardiff: Welsh Assembly Government.

Welsh Assembly Government (2005) *Framework for Restrictive Physical Intervention Policy and Practice.* Cardiff: Welsh Assembly Government.

Welsh Assembly Government (2006) *Guidance for Governing Bodies on the Establishment and Operation of Schools Councils.* Cardiff: Welsh Assembly Government.

Welsh Assembly Government (2007a) *Safeguarding Children in Education: The Role of Local Authorities and Governing Bodies Under the Education Act 2002.* Consultation Document. Cardiff: Welsh Assembly Government.

Welsh Assembly Government (2007b) *Safeguarding Children: Working Together Under the Children Act 2004.* Cardiff: Welsh Assembly Government.

Welsh Office (1995) *Protecting Children from Abuse: the Role of the Education Service.* Circular 52/95.

Whittle, N., Bailey, S. and Kurtz, Z. (2006) *The Needs and Effective Treatment of Young People Who Sexually Abuse: Current Evidence.* London: Department of Health.

Worling, J. and Curwen, T. (2000) 'Adolescent sexual offender recidivism: success of specialized treatment and implications for risk prediction.' *Child Abuse and Neglect 24,* 965–982.

Subject Index

Author Index

Abrahams, N. 177
Abramson, J. 179
Aldgate, J. 14
Araji, S. 86, 93
Archer, T. 61
Atkinson, M. 19, 45
Audit Commission 13
Australian Institute of Health and
    Welfare (AIHW) 167, 168
Axford, N. 98

Baginsky, M. 14, 20, 152, 153, 170,
    172, 176, 178, 180, 181, 182
Bailey, S. 82
Ball, M. 45
Ball, S. 180
Bennett, S. 182
Berliner, L. 93
Berridge, D. 14
Bichard, M. 31, 151, 160
Birchall, E. 152
Blake, S. 81, 82
Blaskett, B. 173, 177
Bluestone, C. 170, 175
Bober, M. 161
Bonner, B. L. 93
Booker, R. 19
Bor, R. 21
Bower, M. 113
Brennan, M. 161
Briggs, F. 166, 175, 176
British Association for Counselling
    and Psychotherapy 127
Bromfield, L. 167, 168
Bronstein, L. 179
Burton, D. L. 87
Butler-Sloss, E. 12
Butler, I. 20

Calder, M. C. 98, 99
Cambridge Health Authority and
    Cambridgeshire Local Education
    Authority 146
Campbell, C. 45
Campbell, H. 152
Carey, K. 14
Carr, A. 176
Casey, K. 177
Cawson, P. 2002 151
Cawson, P. 83
Chaffin, M. 97
Challis, L. 16
Chazan, M. 102
Child Accident Prevention Trust 144
ChildLine 75
Children's Commissioner for Wales
    151

Children's Workforce Development
    Council (CWDC) 157–8
Clarke, M. 16
Cm 6392 63
Cole, T. 102
Collishaw, S. 104
Commission for Social Care
    Inspection (CSCI) 29, 64, 71,
    72
ContinYou 64
Cooper, M. 20, 121
Crenshaw, L. M. 176
Crenshaw, W. B. 176
Crimmins, C. L. S. 98
Crowther, J. 45
Cunningham, C. 87
Curwen, T. 97

Dagley, V. 18
Daniels, H. 19
Daro, D. 177
Davies, J. 171
Davies, S. 14
Deakin, G. 18
Department for Education and
    Employment (DfEE) 13
Department for Education and Skills
    (DfES 2001) 101, 122
Department for Education and Skills
    (DfES 2003) 23
Department for Education and Skills
    (DfES 2004a) 123
Department for Education and Skills
    (DfES 2004b) 15, 106
Department for Education and Skills
    (DfES 2004c) 102
Department for Education and Skills
    (DfES 2004d) 71
Department for Education and Skills
    (DfES 2006a) 24, 26, 31, 68,
    77, 78, 79, 80, 99, 101, 146,
    152
Department for Education and Skills
    (DfES 2006b) 32
Department for Education and Skills
    (DfES 2006c) 134
Department for Education and Skills
    (DfES 2007) 15
Department of Education and Science
    (DES) 13
Department of Education Northern
    Ireland (DENI) 68, 74, 152
Department of Health 12, 13, 15,
    106
Department of Health and
    Department for Education and
    Employment 15
Department of Health and Social
    Security (DHSS) 11, 12
Department of Health, Home Office
    and Department for Education
    and Employment 27

Department of Health, Social Services
    and Public Safety 69
Dicker, R. 46
Dolan, M. 95, 96
Doonan, R. 92, 94
Dowling, E. 116, 120
Dryfoos, J. 45
Dyson, A. 45, 53

Education Child Protection Service
    146
Edwards, D. L. 88
Erooga, M. 86
Evans, H. 74
Evans, J. 21

Featherstone, B. 74
Fife Council 46
Finkelhor, D. 1984 136
Fletcher, C. 43
Fletcher-Campbell, F. 14, 59, 61, 63,
    65, 182
Fox, C. 20

Gibbs, J. 182
Gilbert, J. 46
Gillies, J. 142
Gilligan, R. 98
Gipps, C. 180
Goddard, C. 172, 175, 177, 178
Goreczny, A. J. 96
Gray, A. 92, 93
Gray, P. 102
Green, L. 101
Griffin, S. 101

Hackett, S. 86, 95, 97, 98, 102
Halsey, A. H. 45
Harden, A. 21
Harker, R. 59
Hatcher, R. 52
Hawkins, R. 166, 174–5, 175, 176,
    177
Henniker, J. 99, 100
Higgins, D. 167, 168
HM Government 26, 69, 154, 157,
    158, 159, 160, 161, 162
HM Inspectorate of Education 44
Hodgkinson, K. 170
Home Office, Department of Health,
    Department of Education and
    Science and Welsh Office 12,
    16
Hornby, G. 19
Huxham, C. 16

Jackson, E. 114, 116
Jackson, S. 14, 63
Johnson, B. 176
Johnson, T. C. 92, 94
Jones, J. 18